Protecting Civil Rights:

A Leadership Guide for State, Local, and Tribal Law Enforcement

This project was supported by Grant Number 2003-HS-WX-K309 awarded by the U.S. Department of Justice Office of Community Oriented Policing Services (the COPS Office). Views expressed in this document are those of the International Association of Chiefs of Police and do not necessarily represent the official position or policies of the COPS Office or the U.S. Department of Justice.

September 2006

Dear Colleague:

The International Association of Chiefs of Police (IACP) is pleased to present the new publication, *Protecting Civil Rights: A Leadership Guide for State, Local, and Tribal Law Enforcement*. Funded by the Office of Community Oriented Policing Services, the guide examines the experiences of a wide cross section of agencies proactively engaged in protecting civil rights as well as those that have come under federally mandated monitoring resulting from investigations of patterns or practices of civil rights violations. The guide references the exemplary policies and practices of departments promoting civil rights as well as the content of the consent decrees and memorandums of agreement that individual police agencies have signed with the U.S. Department of Justice. The guide relies on information obtained from focus groups, as well as key advisors in the law enforcement community and the IACP standing committees on civil rights and professional standards. Finally, the guide is informed by the activities and staff of two distinct, yet complementary, agencies within the U.S. Department of Justice: the Special Litigation Section of the Civil Rights Division and the Community Relations Service.

By bringing these sources together, the guide provides a comprehensive overview of the civil rights issues and challenges that today's law enforcement leaders face. It offers practical recommendations for addressing these challenges, but more important, it includes recommendations that encourage leaders to engage in full community partnerships in ways that both protect and promote civil rights.

In short, this effort expresses the conviction that law enforcement leaders can and must learn as much as possible from the perspectives and direct experiences of their professional peers. Through such exchanges, chief executives can gain insights into the best ways to serve their communities using promising strategies and practices that are respectful, ethical, and effective. We hope that all law enforcement leaders will recognize the need for visionary leadership in these areas and will look to this guide as a valuable tool in their ongoing efforts to protect and promote civil rights.

Sincerely,

Chief Mary Ann Viverette
President, IACP
Gaithersburg (Maryland) Police Department

Chief John Finnegan
Barnstable (Massachusetts) Police Department
Chair, IACP Civil Rights Committee

Chief Charles A. Gruber
South Barrington (Illinois) Police Department
Chair, IACP Professional Standards Committee

Acknowledgments

ACKNOWLEDGMENTS

Many individuals representing different organizations and professional vantage points on the issue of civil rights in law enforcement made this publication possible. The scope of their direct contributions, advice, counsel, and editorial comments extends well beyond what can be acknowledged here. Contributors and advisors are discussed below under groupings based on their primary affiliation. This format is a matter of convenience and organization; it should in no way detract from the collaborative nature of this endeavor. Indeed, a tremendous amount of overlap and cross-fertilization occurred among these groups as this project unfolded.

International Association of Chiefs of Police: Standing Committees

Two standing committees of the International Association of Chiefs of Police (IACP), the *Civil Rights* and *Professional Standards*, played pivotal roles in this project from inception to completion. Members of these committees are listed in Appendix A and Appendix B, respectively, of this guide. Individual members contributed their unique insights and perspectives. Several are singled out below.

Fittingly, we start with expressing deep appreciation to Barbara "Bobi" Wallace, whose professional commitment to civil rights and personal drive served as an inspiration for this project. Chief Wallace's enthusiasm was contagious. As the chairperson, she was the driving force behind the Civil Rights Committee and its collective embrace of this project. Ms. Wallace was chief of the Community Relations Unit of the FBI at the onset of the project. Although Bobi has since retired from the FBI and stepped down from the committee's chair, her enthusiasm and vision remained driving forces in this effort.

Charles A. Gruber, chief of the South Barrington (Illinois) Police Department and current chair of IACP's Professional Standards Committee, played a role parallel and complementary to Ms. Wallace. Throughout the course of the project his steadfast guidance, insights, and support were vital. The Leadership Guide has benefited immensely from his long-standing professional commitment to civil rights, his role in initiating IACP's Civil Rights Committee in 1990, and his leadership.

John Finnegan, chief of the Barnstable (Massachusetts) Police Department, assumed the chair of the Civil Rights Committee when Ms. Wallace retired. Chief Finnegan's resolute support and direction helped sharpen the practical focus of the guide and helped to integrate it with the broader work of the Civil Rights Committee. Chief Finnegan was instrumental providing feedback as well as in soliciting valuable input and insights from committee members.

As a whole, the Civil Rights and Professional Standards Committees provided support and guidance. Individual members took on various chapters for review and a debt of gratitude is extended to all. A special debt of gratitude is extended to Leonard Cooke, director of the Virginia Department of Criminal Justice Services, for the detailed review that he and his

Acknowledgments

staff provided across all chapters. Chief Richard Rappoport, Fairfax City (Virginia) Police Department, provided extensive comments and edits on the topic of racial profiling (Chapter 5), a particularly complex and challenging chapter. In the same vein, Chief Charles Reynolds, retired from the Dover (New Hampshire) Police Department, provided keen insights and direction on use-of-force issues (Chapter 4). Chief Susan Riseling, University of Wisconsin—Madison Police Department, contributed perceptive commentary that helped to improve the tone and language of the guide. Chief Patrick Oliver, retired from the Fairborn (Ohio) Police Department, imparted thoughtful insights and edits, particularly on the content related to ethics and community outreach. Chief James Hussey, from the Cohasset (Massachusetts) Police Department, provided commentary and suggestions about the role of personnel management as a means of promoting civil rights.

Project Advisory Group

In April 2004, project staff convened an advisory group in Memphis to discuss the project and the direction it should take. Besides representatives serving on IACP's Civil Rights and Professional Standards Committees, project staff brought together others specializing in civil rights accountability and oversight. Under the umbrella of an advisory group, many individuals representing different perspectives—including academia and persons experienced as monitors for federal consent decree and memorandums of understanding—helped provide direction in the project's early stages. Advisory group members also provided review and direction on substantive content as an annotated outline for the guide was developed and revised. Members of the Project Advisory Group are listed in Appendix C.

Project Focus Group

In April 2005, the IACP convened a group of law enforcement executives from across the nation in Pittsburgh to provide feedback and to help hone a draft of recommendations for law enforcement policies and practices to promote civil rights. This Project Focus Group included representatives from agencies that had successfully navigated federal oversight or were in the process of doing so.

The Pittsburgh Bureau of Police played a key role in helping organize this meeting and provided a wealth of information relevant to its reforms and the successful conclusion of oversight under a federal consent decree. We are particularly indebted to Chief Robert McNeilly (now retired), Deputy Chief Earl Woodyard, and Commander William Valenta (retired), for their assistance, consultation, and their overall contributions to the field, particularly with respect to early intervention strategies. The full list of participants in Project Focus Group is in Appendix D.

Acknowledgments

U.S. Department of Justice

From within the Department of Justice the project relied on the expertise and assistance from three separate offices.

First, we are indebted to the Special Litigation Section (SPL) within Civil Rights Division. As the section responsible for conducting pattern or practice investigations, brokering consent decrees and memorandums of agreement, and overseeing reforms, the SPL played a pivotal and patient role in helping IACP staff understand the complexities and nuances of the process. We are particularly indebted to the direct roles that Shanetta Y. Cutlar, chief of the SPL, and Tammie Gregg, deputy chief, played as advisors and facilitators in this endeavor. Staff from throughout the SPL provided comments on early outlines of the guide and were instrumental in helping ensure that the document was comprehensive and well balanced.

Second, we are also indebted to the Community Relations Service (CRS) within the Department of Justice. Director Sharee Freeman was a loyal advisor throughout the course of this project. George Henderson, general counsel for CRS, and Timothy Johnson, senior conciliation specialist, were instrumental in helping project staff understand the role of CRS in promoting civil rights and distinguishing CRS' role addressing civil rights concerns from that of the Civil Rights Division. Mr. Henderson was also instrumental in convening a group of CRS staff to help underscore and illustrate the scope and variety of assistance.

The third component within the Department of Justice to whom we owe our deepest gratitude is the Office of Community Oriented Policing Services (COPS). We thank the COPS Office not just for funding the project, but also for providing consistent and active support as well as direct contributions. Director Carl Peed was instrumental in helping initiate the project. His participation in and support for the project was invaluable and helped to underscore the important role that community policing, and the COPS Office in particular, have played in promoting policing that is more fair, more responsive to the community, and more effective. Deputy Director Pam Cammarata served as the COPS project manager. Her support, insights, and direct involvement helped to bring us together with other COPS grantees involved in similar work. These contacts and our participation in various workshops and symposia sponsored by COPS were indispensable in helping define the scope of the project and ensuring that our approach was balanced and complementary to the efforts other COPS grantees working on projects focused on civil rights. A final debt of gratitude is extended to two contract employees of COPS: Judith Beres for her editing of this document and Ayonna Johnson for her work on the layout of this document.

Acknowledgments

IACP Leadership and Project Personnel

Many IACP personnel provided guidance, support, and input into this project. Leadership and project staff that had an impact on this work include the following.

Executive Staff

Chief Mary Ann Viverette
President

Dan Rosenblatt
Executive Director

Eugene Cromartie
Deputy Executive Director

John Firman
IACP Research Center Director

Project Staff

John Markovic
Project Director and Principal Author

Christine Allred
Content Editor and Writing Consultant

Colin May
Project Assistant and Contributing Author

Sergeant Steven Brochu
Charlotte-Mecklenburg (North Carolina) Police Department
IACP Visiting Fellow

Lieutenant Ed Dadisho
Suisun City (California) Police Department
(Formerly with Los Angeles Police Department)
IACP Visiting Fellow

Major Keven Gray
Maryland State Police
IACP Fellow

Lieutenant Sharon Malloy
U.S. Capitol Police
IACP Fellow

Darron Mason
IACP Intern

Serena Werner
IACP Intern

Executive Summary

Executive Summary

PROTECTING CIVIL RIGHTS:
A Leadership Guide for State, Local, and Tribal Law Enforcement

BACKGROUND

Protecting Civil Rights: A Leadership Imperative

All law enforcement leaders recognize the ethical and legal imperatives to which they and their officers must adhere to ensure that civil rights of all individuals in their communities are protected. Law enforcement officers, in fact, are the most visible and largest contingent of the nation's guardians of civil rights. Every police officer commits to upholding the nation's prime guarantor of rights, the U.S. Constitution, when sworn into office. To be effective, a police department and its individual officers must be seen primarily as protectors of civil rights, rather than agents of social control whose main purpose is to limit individual freedoms. The effectiveness of police in their varied missions—from law enforcement to community service—depends on the trust and confidence of the community. Public trust and confidence are severely reduced when individuals' civil rights are compromised. And when any community perceives that its civil rights are systematically violated by the police, all sense of trust, cooperation, and partnership between the police and that community will be undermined.

Understanding these ethical imperatives, law enforcement leaders must be continually vigilant to ensure that the actions of their officers do not violate civil rights and do not compromise public support. Officers are granted a tremendous amount of authority and discretion to enforce the law, that is, to protect individual rights from being infringed upon by others in the community. At the same time, officers themselves must act within the confines of the Constitution while executing their tremendous power and wide discretion. They must never consider themselves above the law while executing their responsibility to enforce the law. This commitment is what distinguishes police in constitutionally based, democratic societies like ours from police in nondemocratic countries, where they too often are perceived as oppressive agents of a government whose main purpose is to restrict, rather than protect, the rights of civilians.

Across the United States, law enforcement personnel have an overwhelmingly positive record of accomplishment for respecting and protecting civil rights. Leaders should find it heartening and a source of pride that the vast majority of the countless interactions that officers have with civilians result in actions that are conducted lawfully, professionally, and within constitutional boundaries. The fact that the overwhelming majority of police officers routinely respect civil rights under the most trying and volatile conditions is remarkable. Given the risks inherent in police work and the grave consequences that can occur when civil rights are violated, law enforcement leaders must be unwavering in holding their officers accountable. Their officers are vested with authority and discretion that can be abused. Unlike

Executive Summary

any other profession, the possibility of violating civil rights, or being perceived as violating civil rights, is inherent in many of the duties officers are required to perform on a day-to-day basis. Unfortunately, the notoriety and harm that arise from even isolated instances of civil rights violations can easily overshadow the vast majority of police-civilian encounters that are performed respectfully and professionally.

Law enforcement leaders bear the tremendous responsibility to ensure that individual officers and units within their agencies uphold the law and its most basic guarantees. Realistically, law enforcement leaders recognize that on rare occasions officers will violate a civilian's civil rights, wittingly or unwittingly. On even rarer occasions, groups of officers or small factions within an agency may act without regard for civil rights, perhaps even asserting that effective law enforcement can come only at the expense of civil rights. Leaders must be resolute in their responses to isolated incidents of civil rights violations to minimize damage and set a clear example. In the case of officers who systematically violate civil rights, their behavior must not be tolerated and action must be decisive and uncompromising. Effective leaders, supported by the managers who serve them, must strive to identify and intervene when officers exhibit potentially problematic behavior *before* it escalates to the point of violating civil rights.

Against this backdrop, the seriousness of law enforcement leaders' responsibility to communicate a consistent and far-reaching commitment to civil rights protections cannot be overstated. Although laws, departmental policy directives, and standard operating procedures are critically important, law enforcement executives' leadership and communication skills are the most critical elements for ensuring that officers regularly exercise sound judgment and engage in professional and ethical policing.

Law enforcement leaders can and must demonstrate a fundamental and complete allegiance to civil rights protections in a coordinated manner using multiple approaches. They must clearly convey a simultaneous commitment to effective law enforcement and civil rights protection; they must codify this commitment in their agency's mission statements; they must ensure that their department's polices are clear, sound, and consistent with civil rights guarantees; they must train and supervise officers in manners that are consistent with this commitment; and they must respond to alleged civil rights violations with vigilance and with fair and decisive action. As law enforcement leaders succeed in these regards and make these efforts transparent to the public, they validate the core premise that civil rights protection is not only an ethical and legal imperative but a practical imperative as well. Protecting civil rights is good for police, good for the community, and essential for maintaining the partnerships that must exist between the two.

Federal Investigations: A Response to "Patterns or Practices" of Civil Rights Violations

Despite the ethical, legal, and practical imperatives to protect civil rights, law enforcement officers occasionally abrogate their oaths. When these unwitting or intentional violations of citizens' civil rights go unaddressed, they can escalate into more widespread *patterns or practices* of civil rights violations that can undermine the credibility of an entire law enforcement agency and erode public trust and confidence. Moving beyond isolated instances, pattern or practice violations of civil rights comprise an urgent call to law enforcement executives and the municipal, county, or state governments under which they serve to reassume the ultimate responsibility for ensuring that officers uphold their oaths of office and adherence to constitutional guarantees.

During the last decade, the federal government has responded to such situations in the rare, but urgent circumstances where allegations of pattern or practice civil rights violations have arisen. The passage of the *Violent Crime Control and Law Enforcement Act of 1994* (Public Law No: 103-322) enabled the federal government to take action to remedy any pattern or practice of conduct by state and local law enforcement agencies "that deprives persons of rights, privileges, or immunities secured or protected by the Constitution or laws of the United States." In response to this enabling legislation, the Special Litigation Section of the Civil Rights Division of the U.S. Department of Justice assumed the responsibility for investigating alleged pattern or practice civil rights violations and for establishing remedies to such violations.

During the last decade, the Special Litigation Section has investigated an array of alleged pattern or practice civil rights violations including the following:

- Unlawful or excessive use of force
- Inadequate training on use-of-force techniques
- Racial profiling
- Illegal stops and searches
- Intimidation by police
- Harassment of civilians in retaliation for reported misconduct
- Inadequate supervision
- Failure to investigate alleged officer misconduct.

Investigations by the Special Litigation Section resulting in a determination of actionable civil rights violations generally have been resolved through negotiated agreements in the form of memorandums of agreement (MOA) or consent decrees. Through such agreements, the federal government and law enforcement agencies agree to a course of action to correct the patterns of civil rights violations and to remedy the conditions that allowed the violations to occur. Since 1994, 14 agencies have been or currently are under federal monitoring as a result of civil rights violation investigations. While these 14 agencies represent an infinitesimal fraction of the country's nearly 18,000 state, county, local, tribal, and special jurisdictional law enforcement agencies, the impact of these federal investigations and agreements has been and continues to be profound and far-reaching.

ASSERTING A LEADERSHIP ROLE

The very existence of these investigations reminds us of the critical messages and management strategies that law enforcement leaders must assert—or reassert—in their efforts to protect and promote civil rights. Accordingly, the International Association of Chiefs of Police's (IACP) release of *Protecting Civil Rights: A Leadership Guide for State, Local, and Tribal Law Enforcement* is meant to serve as a compass for law enforcement leaders committed to affirmatively addressing civil rights issues. The guide originated in a series of discussions among representatives from U.S. Department of Justice—specifically the Office of Community Oriented Policing Services and the Special Litigation Section of the Civil Rights Division—and the IACP. It realizes their shared conviction that the accumulated knowledge of law enforcement leaders who have undergone a federal civil rights investigation and resultant monitoring, coupled with that of law enforcement leaders who have proactively demonstrated exemplary records of protecting and promoting civil rights, can and should benefit all other law enforcement leaders. To make this accumulated knowledge available to law enforcement leaders, the IACP took several discrete steps.

First, the IACP engaged in a comprehensive review of federal pattern and practice investigatory processes. This review revealed that these processes are constantly evolving. For instance, the Special Litigation Section has increasingly relied on expert consultants with direct law enforcement experience for providing technical assistance to departments under investigation. The investigations themselves have become increasingly transparent to the departments. The IACP's review also revealed that these processes are highly individualized. They are shaped by the nature of the allegations, by the findings specific to each jurisdiction, and by the tone and comprehensiveness of an agency's response. While these investigations often are viewed as adversarial, new leaders with reform agendas and who were intent on resolving inherited civil rights problems, often made the best of these situations. These leaders were committed to responding positively to the direction and assistance that federal intervention could offer and worked with the Special Litigation Section and its consultants to establish cooperative investigatory processes. In fact, several chief executives were instrumental in requesting that the investigations take place. Leadership responses such as these have enabled the Special Litigation Section to work effectively with these agencies and to build on the agencies' preexisting successes.

Second, the IACP engaged in a comprehensive review of the MOAs and consent decrees resulting from these federal investigations. These agreements are of broad value because they condense the insights of formal and extensive inquiries about civil rights violations into clear and practical mandates for new courses of action. These agreements articulate specific remedies for patterns of civil rights violations including the excessive use of force, racial profiling, and other forms of police misconduct. They also address accountability or management practices, such as early intervention systems and critical incident reviews, that can help address and prevent civil rights violations as well as limit department liability. These agreements provide valuable insight for chief executives who are determined that effective law enforcement and the protection of civil rights will be missions that are complementary to their agencies.

Third, the IACP explored other agencies' internal solutions to protecting and promoting civil rights. During the same decade that 14 agencies underwent federal investigation and resultant monitoring for pattern or practice civil rights violations, other agencies addressed challenging civil rights concerns on their own initiatives. In developing the guide, the IACP recognized that these agencies would be an equally important, if not more important, source of insight. Law enforcement leaders in these agencies worked to protect community members' civil rights by proactively enacting sound policies, comprehensive training, far-reaching and close methods of supervision, and more effective systems of accountability.

Finally, the IACP gathered all of this information into this concise, yet comprehensive guide. In its first chapter, *Protecting Civil Rights: A Leadership Guide for State, Local, and Tribal Law Enforcement Leaders* familiarizes law enforcement leaders with federal pattern or practice investigatory processes as well as general resources and strategies available to all departments committed to protecting and promoting civil rights. In the remaining chapters, the guide offers in-depth discussions of the policies, procedures, and practices that are critical to civil rights protection.

For the benefit of law enforcement leaders, the guide crystallizes these in-depth discussions into concise recommendations. In summary, *Protecting Civil Rights* is designed to enable law enforcement leaders to learn from their peers who have engaged in deliberate strategies, both with and without federal intervention, to protect civil rights.

SELECTED RECOMMENDATIONS

Protecting Civil Rights recognizes that the motivation to safeguard civil rights must emerge out of law enforcement executives' visionary leadership, but then must be continually reinforced by internal, and in some instances external, accountability mechanisms. Accordingly, the guide offers recommendations in six substantive areas including early intervention, the civilian complaint process, use of force, racial profiling, personnel management, and data management. The following is a sampling of key recommendations.

Early Intervention Strategies

- **All agencies, regardless of size, should strive to incorporate the core concepts of early intervention into their personnel management practices.** Early intervention strategies, when properly designed and implemented, allow supervisors to address concerns about officers' behavioral patterns before they escalate to a point where discipline would be needed. Many large agencies have now developed sophisticated early intervention systems that rely on computerized data-driven approaches that automatically alert supervisors to potential problems. Any size department, large, medium, or small, however, can use early intervention strategies in its day-to-day supervisory practices without needing to rely on sophisticated technology solutions.

Executive Summary

- **Agencies seeking to develop early intervention should look to their peers for ideas, but must recognize that they will have to tailor their own system to their department's needs.** Every department's supervisory and information management practices are unique. Because these practices are at the core of early intervention strategies, there is no one-size-fits-all strategy. Nonetheless, agencies should look to their peers for practical and technological advice on how to plan for and build these systems and then carefully tailor the best features of these external systems to meet their own department's structure, data, and needs.

- **Agencies should strive to include as many stakeholders as possible in the planning of early intervention systems.** Many individuals, groups, and associations have a stake in early intervention strategies. When designing these strategies, agencies should seek input from a wide cross section of internal representatives including rank-and-file officers, supervisors, personnel managers, and data management/information technology staff. Many departments have also found it useful to seek external input by involving the police union and the community in the planning process.

- **Agencies should ensure that supervisors have the appropriate experiences, skills, and training to perform their early intervention responsibilities.** An early intervention data management system is not a panacea for resolving personnel problems and officer misconduct issues. The system will only work as well as those who use it. First-line supervisors must be trained specifically in the use of the system and in making sound early intervention judgments for the system to be an optimal management tool that will result in genuine and effective assistance being provided to officers. The success of early intervention strategies relies principally on first-line supervisors who are trained on, skilled in, and motivated to use these systems.

- **Agencies must ensure that the early intervention system remains distinct from the disciplinary system.** Properly designed early intervention systems are preemptive and can reduce reliance on reactive disciplinary measures. Law enforcement leaders must make certain that these systems operate independently to avoid the perception among officers that early intervention is simply another form of discipline.

- **Agencies should develop a discrete policy directive addressing the purpose and functional elements of the department's early intervention system.** Once an early intervention system is developed, the department should also develop a clear and precise policy that addresses the system's purposes and outlines the processes of notification, review, and intervention when potentially problematic behavior is identified.

The Civilian and Internal Complaint Process

- **Every department should have a clear policy and well-defined practices for handling civilian and internally generated complaints against officers or against the department as a whole.** Clear policies and well-defined practices are critical for the effective functioning of an agency's complaint process. These policies and practices for handling civilian and internal complaints may be treated as a stand-alone section of the department's policy manual or may be embedded within other appropriate policy sections (i.e., Internal Affairs Unit Policy). Civilian complaint data must be systematically analyzed and used for personnel management purposes, to refine policy and training, and as a general barometer of citizen satisfaction.

- **Departments should establish an accessible complaint-filing process that allows for the receipt of complaints about officer misconduct from a wide range of sources.** To respond effectively to concerns raised by the community and by personnel within the department, agencies must ensure that the process of filing complaints is open, accessible, and free of unnecessary inconveniences that would inhibit individuals from filing complaints. Because requiring civilians to file complaints in police facilities can be inconvenient or intimidating, many departments are making civilian complaint forms available at other public places, e.g., at libraries or community centers, and more agencies are allowing civilians to file complaints on agency web sites.

- **Departments should establish complaint investigation processes that are comprehensive and fair.** Departments will receive complaints ranging from the relatively minor grievances of community members who felt that they were treated rudely to serious allegations against officers for actions that would constitute criminal behavior if proven true. A department must set up an investigatory process that takes all complaints seriously and that fairly and effectively deals with this broad range of diverse complaints.

- **Departments should specifically select and train personnel responsible for investigating complaints.** While departments may rely on the chain of command or use specific units (e.g., Internal Affairs) to investigate complaints of police misconduct, they should recognize that such investigations are unique and apart from other agency investigative functions and that they may require different aptitudes and skill sets. Departments should select and train their personnel carefully to ensure that the complaint investigation process is taken seriously and that all investigations are comprehensive, fair, and adequately documented.

- **Departments must protect officers against fraudulent complaints. Occasionally, civilians lodge complaints out of frustration, retribution, or to purposely undermine legitimate law enforcement actions.** Departments must ensure that complaint investigators identify and appropriately dismiss fraudulent complaints through thorough investigation. In such instances, cases should be documented as unfounded and officers should be fully exonerated. Departments should never use fraudulent complaints to assess the officer for early intervention or disciplinary processes.

Managing Use of Force

- **All departments should have a clear use-of-force policy that specifically addresses both deadly and nondeadly use of force and is consistent with all legal and professional standards.** Regardless of size or function, all departments should have a use of force policy with directives on deadly and nondeadly force. These policies must be clear and easy to interpret. The policies should not be less restrictive than applicable state laws or professional standards.

- **A department's use-of-force policy must address all available use-of-force options, clearly place these options on a use-of-force continuum, and associate these options with corresponding levels of subject resistance.** A department's use-of-force options—weapons and techniques—will evolve over time. Departments must continually review and update their use-of-force policies to keep pace with these changes.

- **A department's polices and training should specifically address alternatives to use of force and encourage their use in appropriate circumstances.** While policies and training typically and appropriately address the use of force, they should also directly address alternatives to the use of force. Policies should encourage officers to consider alternative techniques such as verbal judo and containment whenever possible, yet never at the expense of compromising the safety of officers and the general public.

- **Every department should have a clear policy and set of standards for determining what level of force requires formal written documentation by involved officers.** Every use-of-force policy must stipulate the level of force at which a formal written use-of-force report is required. While this threshold may vary depending on individual department's use-of-force options, their practices, and their precedents, the consensus recommendation of the advisors to this project is that any instance of force above "soft-hand control" should be considered a reportable use of force.

- **Every department should have a clear policy and set of standards for determining what level of force requires formal review by the chain of command or a specialized review unit (e.g., critical incident review team).** Similarly, while every use-of-force policy should stipulate at what level of force deployments are to be reviewed, the consensus recommendation of the advisors to this project is that any instance of force above soft-hands control should be considered a reviewable use of force. Systematically reviewing all use-of-force reports above a designated threshold, not just those reports that raise general suspicion, is a critical accountability tool, both for maintaining civil rights and for limiting department liability. Larger departments often develop graduated review protocols that are relevant to the level of force used and potential liability involved. This is based on the premise that deployments of deadly force, for instance, should be more thoroughly reviewed than deployments of nondeadly force.

Addressing Racial Profiling

- **All departments should have a clear and unequivocal departmental policy prohibiting racial profiling and promoting bias-free policing.** Such a policy directive should include a clear and unambiguous departmental definition of racial profiling and related terminology. It must also clearly convey that behavior and evidentiary standards—not race or ethnicity—shall guide police stop-and-search decisions. The policy should be sufficiently restrictive so that it prohibits the use of race-motivated pretext stops (stopping a car for a minor traffic violation when the real motive for the stop is the race or ethnicity of the driver). The policy should articulate the limited circumstances in which race or ethnicity can be used in a decision to take police action. Race and ethnicity can be used as a specific descriptor about a suspect or suspects in a crime. In other words, race or ethnicity should be used in the same manner as other physical descriptors—such as hair color, weight, or gender—might be used in identifying specific suspects. Similar limitations are expressed in the U.S. Department of Justice's "Guidance Regarding the Use of Race by Federal Law Enforcement Agencies" (June 2003) as they apply to investigative circumstances.

  > In conducting activities in connection with a specific investigation, Federal law enforcement officers may consider race and ethnicity only to the extent that there is trustworthy information, relevant to the locality or time frame, that links persons of a particular race or ethnicity to an identified criminal incident, scheme, or organization.

- **Departments must embed the ideals of bias-free policing in their mission statements, training, accountability mechanisms, and community outreach.** While a clear policy against racial profiling is the foundation for bias-free policing, law enforcement leaders must reinforce this policy throughout their departmental practices. Clearly demonstrating intolerance for racial profiling at every turn is critical for limiting acts of racial profiling by individual officers, curbing the community's perceptions of racial profiling, and sustaining trust throughout all segments of a diverse community.

- **All departments must consider carefully whether or not to collect racial profiling data, while every department that collects racial profiling data must abide by applicable state laws and mandates.** To assess the presence or prevalence of racial profiling, many departments are collecting data on traffic stops voluntarily or as a result of state mandates or legal rulings. Departments' efforts to collect, analyze, interpret, and respond to racial profiling data are highly complicated and tend to be expensive and resource intensive. Every law enforcement leader must educate himself or herself about these processes and should complete some level of cost-benefit analysis to determine whether racial profiling data collection are advisable for his or her department. Leaders should also weigh the benefits of proactively collecting such data against the potential costs of having to collect such data reactively and according to methods or rules imposed by outside interests. Above all, it should be recognized that departments that signal their willingness to address racial profiling in a forthright and deliberate manner are in a better position to maintain and enhance their communities' level of trust in the department.

Personnel Management

With the current shortage of recruit candidates that many law enforcement agencies are facing, agency executives are struggling to maintain their authorized staffing levels and have expressed that it is increasingly difficult to compete for the ideal candidates who show a high aptitude for service-oriented policing and an unfaltering respect for civil rights. As a result, executives and personnel management staff must be more proactive and more creative in their pursuit of candidates. The guide addresses these challenges with several recommendations, including the following:

- **Agencies must recruit, hire, and promote personnel in a manner that best ensures that officers throughout the ranks reflect the communities that they serve.** Many agencies have worked diligently to recruit and retain personnel from groups who have historically been underrepresented in law enforcement. While improvements have been made in the recruitment of ethnic and racial minorities and women in many departments, police executives must continue to work closely with their local governments and communities to devise specific strategies to diversify their police agencies. Improved community trust and confidence in the agency and better insights into the community from within the agency are among the benefits of such strategies.

- **Agencies should start the recruitment process early.** Many agencies have found that they can bring in quality applicants by fostering familiarity with the agency and identifying young candidates with a predisposition to a career in law enforcement. Many agencies find some of their most promising candidates, for instance, among members of police explorer troops and participants in Police Athletic Leagues. Departments not currently doing so should consider sponsoring such activities for the specific recruitment benefits, as well as the overall benefit gained through enhanced community outreach and building trust with the youthful members of the community.

- **Agencies should consider changing maximum age restrictions.** While agencies must look to our youth for future recruits, many are recognizing the strengths that experienced adults can bring to law enforcement. Numerous agencies, motivated in part by a commitment to community policing and in part by a move away from action-oriented recruitment, have increased their maximum age restrictions or done away with them altogether. Changing the maximum age restriction welcomes persons with more maturity and life experience who may be better prepared to deal effectively with the stress inherent in policing, be less likely to engage in impulsive actions, and who can serve as mentors to younger recruits.

Data Management

Effective law enforcement leaders collect and analyze volumes of data to enhance their management practices. The policing profession has made tremendous progress in information technology and information-driven management during the last decade. Relying increasingly on CompStat models and problem-oriented policing approaches, law enforcement leaders have made real progress in measuring crime and disorder and in tracking traditional policing actions such as citations issued, arrests made, and clearance ratios. Increasingly, agencies' data-management practices are becoming more innovative and are more often addressing community engagement and civil rights protection as outcome measures. As many agencies are now enhancing their reliance on data collection and analysis in these areas, the guide offers the following recommendations:

- **Agencies should publicly share data that reflect community policing efforts and key civil rights issues.** Many agencies have become more open and transparent in their efforts to share data with the public. It is now more common, for instance, for agencies to provide summary data about their use-of-force deployments or about their receiving, processing, and disposing of citizen-generated complaints. While agencies must maintain the privacy and confidentiality of individual officers and civilians involved in the process, sharing such data in aggregated form or in sanitized case synopses builds community trust and can help initiate and inform joint problem-solving strategies. Agencies are increasingly tabulating and publishing data about positive civilian-police interactions, including participation in community policing meetings or citizen police academies. These data are often shared with the public through agency web sites or annual reports and can used to target outreach to particular communities that may not yet be sufficiently engaged in partnership with the police.

- **Agencies must recognize that sharing data with the public carries certain risks and involves certain responsibilities.** Agencies sharing data publicly must make certain to put all data in context and discuss the limitations inherent in the collection of administrative data. Data, taken out of context, can be misleading. Law enforcement agencies must be very deliberate in their data-sharing strategies. An increase or decrease in the number of citizen complaints filed, for instance, may reflect positive or negative changes in officers' behavior. These statistical trends, however, may also reflect changes in department policies or in practices governing the complaint process. When agencies take steps to make the complaint process more open and accessible, e.g., through allowing complaints to be filed on the web, they should expect the number of complaints filed to increase. Management should be prepared to explain the reasons for these policy-driven increases and turn them into opportunities for improving public relations, community outreach, and agency assessment.

A Continuing Effort

To some observers, the era of civil rights ended in the 1960s. To others, the equation for balancing civil rights against public safety and security concerns changed abruptly following the terrorist attacks of September 11, 2001. Clearly, today's law enforcement executives are confronted with challenges that they have never before faced and perhaps never imagined. Technology, tactics, laws, and political policies will continually evolve and have an impact on civil rights. While an understanding of historical and contextual factors is important, what remains constant is the fact that law enforcement leaders must keep abreast of promising practices in the areas where policing and civil rights intersect, all while remaining loyal to

Executive Summary

the constitutional rights guaranteed to the public they are sworn to serve. This guide was designed with these objectives in mind, but also with the recognition that the issue of civil rights in law enforcement is not static.

The IACP is committed to remaining at the forefront of civil rights issues, including efforts to help devise better ways to measure police success. Success must be broadly assessed and recognized as more than just crime reduction. Success must also be recognized as service to the public, adherence to the democratic principles of openness and transparency, and faithfulness to the direct role that law enforcement plays in protecting and promoting civil rights. Law enforcement's use of evolving technology—including the use of conducted energy devices (CED, commonly referenced under the brand name Taser™) and the use of hot-spot mapping to identify areas for concentrated enforcement—are giving rise to new civil rights issues that the IACP is intent on tracking. Changes in funding priorities, shifting paradigms about policing, and new challenges will continue to evolve. Accordingly, the IACP recognizes that *Protecting Civil Rights* is a living document, one that will require periodic updates.

Content

ACKNOWLEDGEMENTS I

EXECUTIVE SUMMARY VII

CHAPTER ONE
PROTECTING CIVIL RIGHTS: A LEADERSHIP GUIDE FOR STATE, LOCAL, AND TRIBAL LAW ENFORCEMENT 1

Introduction 1
The Origins of the Leadership Guide 3
Federal Investigation and Oversight of Pattern or Practice Violations 4
Additional Federal Assistance: The Community Relations Service 13
Proactively Protecting Civil Rights: Creating a Culture Bound by Rules 19
Overview of Chapters 20
Sources of Information 23

CHAPTER TWO
SUSTAINING COMMUNITY OUTREACH AND ENGAGEMENT: THE INTERSECTION OF CIVIL RIGHTS AND COMMUNITY POLICING 27

Introduction 27
Chapter Overview and Objectives 27
A Definition of Community Policing 28
The Evolution of Community Policing in a Post-9/11 Era 29
The Prevalence of Community Policing 31
Promising Practices: Protecting and Promoting Civil Rights through
  Community Policing Strategies 33
Conclusion 44
Suggestions for Further Reading 44

CHAPTER THREE
DEVELOPING AN EARLY INTERVENTION STRATEGY 49

Introduction 49
Chapter Overview and Objectives 49
A Definition of Early Intervention 50
The Evolution of Early Intervention 50
The Prevalence of Early Intervention 52
The Benefits of Early Intervention 52
Basic Components of Early Intervention Systems 55
Indicators: The Foundation of Early Interventions Systems 56
Acting on Indicators: The Workings of Early Intervention Systems 58
Integration of Early Intervention Systems into Comprehensive Personnel
  Assessment Systems 67
Identifying Exemplary Performers 68
Moving Beyond Individual Assessment 68
Unit and Agencywide Assessment 68

Assessment over Time 69
Recommendations 69
Conclusion 76
Suggestions for Further Reading... 76

Chapter Four
Managing the Complaint Process 81

Introduction 81
Chapter Overview and Objectives 81
A Definition of the Civilian Complaint Process 82
The Evolution of the Civilian Complaint Process 82
The Prevalence of the Civilian Complaint Process 85
The Benefits of the Civilian Complaint Process 86
The Core Principles of the Complaint Process 86
Variations in the Civilian Complaint Process 90
Assessing Civilian Involvement in the Complaint Process 90
A Typology of Complaint Processes Based on Citizen 91
Considerations for Civilian Review in Complaint Processing 93
Statistical Snapshot of Civilian Involvement in the Complaint Review
 Processes 93
The Basic Steps in Handling Civilian and Internal Complaints 94
Ensuring Accountability in the Complaint Process 102
Recommendations 106
Conclusion 109
Suggestions for Further Reading 109

Chapter Five
Managing Use of Force 113

Introduction 113
Chapter Overview and Objectives 114
Issues in Defining Use-of-Force 115
Use-of-Force Continuum 119
Near Universal Prevalence of Use-of-Force Policies 126
Evolutions in Use-of-Force Policies 127
Core Components of Effective Management of Use-of-Force 127
Recommendations 145
Conclusion 148
Suggestions for Further Reading 148

Chapter Six
Addressing Racial Profiling: Creating a Comprehensive Commitment to Bias-Free Policing 153

Introduction 153
Chapter Overview and Objectives 154
Differing Definitions of Racial Profiling 155
The Prevalence of Efforts to Address Racial Profiling 159
Multiple Motivations for Addressing Racial Profiling 160
Core Components for Addressing and Preventing Racial Profiling 161

    Beyond the Basic Components: Considering Racial Profiling Data
        Collection and Analysis 168
    Steps in Data Collection and Analysis Process 173
    Recommendations 185
    Conclusion 188
    Suggestions for Further Reading 189

Chapter Seven
Personnel Management Issues in the Context of Protecting Civil Rights and Serving the Community 193

    Introduction 193
    Chapter Overview and Objectives 194
    Recommendations 194
    Conclusion 206
    Suggestions for Further Reading 206

Chapter Eight
Data-Management Issues in the Context of Protecting Civil Rights and Serving the Community 209

    Introduction 209
    Chapter Overview and Objectives 210
    Data Management Issues Raised in Preceding Chapters 210
    Rationales for Expanding Data Collection and Analysis by Including
        Nontraditional Data 212
    The Importance of Context in Analyzing Data Trends 213
    Recommendations 216
    Conclusion 230
    Suggestions for Further Reading 231

Appendixes
    Appendix A: IACP Civil Rights Committee 235

    Appendix B: IACP Professional Standards Committee 238

    Appendix C: Project Advisory Group 239

    Appendix D: Project Focus Group 241

    Appendix E: Community Relations Service U.S. Department of
        Justice 242

I. Protecting Civil Rights: A Leadership Guide for State, Local, and Tribal Law Enforcement

Protecting Civil Rights: A Leadership Guide for State, Local, and Tribal Law Enforcement

> We must scrupulously guard the civil rights and civil liberties of all citizens, whatever their background. We must remember that any oppression, any injustice, any hatred is a wedge designed to attack our civilization.[1]
>
> **President Franklin Delano Roosevelt**

Introduction

Civil rights are the rights and freedoms that every person possesses. In the United States, these rights are embodied in the United States Constitution, in numerous amendments, and by acts of Congress. Although these rights are based on the federal constitution, the 14th Amendment makes them applicable to the states. Civil rights are often categorized into rights of due process, equal protection under the law, and freedom from discrimination. Perhaps the most famous and influential civil rights act, the Civil Rights Act of 1964, extended civil rights protection by making discrimination because of race, color, national origin, or religion unlawful in federally funded entities and other enterprises such as employment, education, housing and public accommodations. Under this act, any state or local government or public interest that receives federal funding is required to abide by this law. While civil rights and minority rights have a clear and important historical association, civil rights in the broadest perspective are basic human rights to which all in our society are entitled.

Law enforcement agencies have the ethical and legal imperative to abide by and uphold civil rights. Indeed, when sworn to duty, police officers commit to uphold the foundation of our civil rights—the United States Constitution. This commitment is embodied, for instance, in the model oath of honor adopted by resolution at the 107th Annual Conference of the International Association of Chiefs of Police (IACP) in 2000:

> On my honor, I will never betray my badge, my integrity, my character, or the public trust. I will always have the courage to hold myself and others accountable for our actions. I will always uphold the Constitution, my community, and the agency I serve.[2]

Ideally, all law enforcement officers and agencies uphold their commitment to protect and promote civil rights while enforcing the law. They do this not only because it is an ethical and legal imperative, but because it is a practical imperative as well. From a community outreach perspective, many law enforcement leaders assert that officers who steadfastly protect and promote civil rights succeed where others do not. A fundamental commitment to protecting civil rights is good policy: it is good for the police, good for the community, and good for maintaining the partnerships that exist between the two.

The core principle of this guide is that effective law enforcement and the protection of civil rights are complementary pillars for policing in a democratic society. Law enforcement leaders who understand this principle will not fall into the trap of believing that effective law enforcement has to come at the expense of civil rights protection.

Despite the ethical, legal, and practical imperatives to protect civil rights, officers occasionally abrogate their oaths. When this occurs—when officers unwittingly or intentionally violate citizens' civil rights—law enforcement leaders must take action. Law enforcement leaders must assume the final responsibility for ensuring that officers uphold their oath of office. This responsibility requires clear commitment and constant vigilance. Law enforcement leaders must address every isolated civil rights violation, or these acts may escalate into widespread patterns or practices that will undermine the credibility of the agency and erode public trust and confidence.

This is a challenging responsibility. In fact, during the last decade, 14 law enforcement agencies have been investigated and have subsequently come under federally imposed monitoring for alleged "patterns or practices" of civil rights violations. While these 14 agencies represent but an infinitesimal fraction of the country's nearly 18,000 state, county, local, and tribal law enforcement agencies, the impact of the investigations has been profound and far-reaching. *Protecting Civil Rights: A Leadership Guide for State, Local, and Tribal Law Enforcement* is, in part, about how lessons learned by agencies under this federal oversight process can be used to enhance the learning of other law enforcement agencies.

There is much to learn. The experiences of the agencies that have been investigated and of those that, as a result, now operate under federal consent decrees or memorandums of agreement (MOA) are compelling. Although facing the scrutiny of a federal investigation and possibly a protracted period of monitoring can be daunting, many law enforcement leaders have responded constructively to the realities of federal oversight. These chief executives have revitalized their organizations' commitments to civil rights. Other law enforcement leaders have even recognized the process as a catalyst to bring about positive and necessary change. Indeed, several pattern or practice investigation requests were initiated by police chiefs.

Other agencies are learning lessons about civil rights protection as well. During the same decade that these 14 agencies have been under federal investigation or have been monitored for patterns or practices of civil rights violations, other departments have been addressing challenging civil rights issues on their own. In many of the latter agencies, executives have worked to protect citizens' civil rights by proactively enacting sound policies, comprehensive training, improved methods of supervision, and more effective systems of accountability. Through these means, law enforcement leaders have identified and responded to challenges such as the excessive use of force, racial profiling, and other forms of police misconduct. In part, *Protecting Civil Rights* is also intended to communicate those lessons learned by law enforcement agencies and communities that have benefited from such proactive leadership.

In summary, *Protecting Civil Rights* offers lessons learned from law enforcement leaders and agencies who have taken reactive and/or proactive steps to protect and promote civil rights throughout their communities. This guide recognizes that the motivation to take these steps emerges out of visionary leadership, but must be continually reinforced by internal and external accountability mechanisms.

The Origins of the Leadership Guide

Protecting Civil Rights originated in a series of discussions among representatives from the U.S. Department of Justice Civil Rights Division-Special Litigation Section (SPL), the Office of Community Oriented Policing Services (COPS), and the IACP. These discussions revealed a shared vision—that the accumulated knowledge resulting from pattern and practice investigations and agreements could provide valuable lessons for law enforcement executives who want to take proactive measures to assure that effective law enforcement, public safety, and the protection of civil rights are complementary missions within their agencies. Accordingly, the guide's recommendations are largely the result of analysis of the provisions imbedded in the consent decrees and MOAs themselves. These mandates reflect the insights of intensive and long-term investigations into civil rights violations. Project staff relied heavily on these agreements to help ensure that this guide is comprehensive and responsive to the full range of areas in which civil rights violations can occur.

Simultaneously, however, project advisors and staff recognized that the efforts of agencies proactively and effectively engaged in the protection and promotion of civil rights would be an equally important source of insight. In searching out insights among agencies that were not forced to reform as a result of federal intervention, staff and advisors quickly learned that the distinction between "proactive" and "reactive" reform was an oversimplification. Some agencies that initially reacted to federal investigations undertook reforms that went beyond the demands of their federal requirements. Accordingly, *Protecting Civil Rights* draws on lessons learned by agencies across the spectrum, including agencies that have dealt with civil rights protection either proactively, reactively, or both.

The advisors and staff of *Protecting Civil Rights* encountered dedicated advocates of civil rights protections among the leaders in many agencies, including those under federal civil rights agreements. In some agencies operating under consent decrees and MOAs, new, reform-minded leaders were intent on resolving the problems that they had inherited and that had given rise to the investigations. In other agencies, existing executives responded positively to the direction and assistance that federal intervention made available. The efforts of all agency leaders to protect and promote civil rights are sources of insight.

Accordingly, this introduction to *Protecting Civil Rights* will familiarize the reader with the processes by which agencies protect and promote civil rights. First, it will acquaint the reader with the process by which agencies with alleged pattern or practice civil rights violations are investigated and monitored. Then, it will review the general resources and strategies available to and used by all departments committed to protecting and promoting civil rights. Such information should enable readers to make practical use of subsequent substantive chapters on community policing, early intervention, the complaint process, use of force, racial profiling, and personnel and data management issues. This introduction will conclude with an overview of these individual chapters.

Federal Investigation and Oversight of Pattern or Practice Violations

The following section offers an overview of the federal role in investigation and oversight of pattern or practice civil rights violations. This specialized area of federal intervention focuses on the conduct of law enforcement agencies and is distinct from processes that address civil rights actions against individuals in law enforcement. Federal investigations and oversight in response to allegations of agencies' patterns or practices of violating civil rights are relatively recent phenomena that have evolved rapidly over the last decade.

Origins

Federal intervention on behalf of law enforcement agencies allegedly exhibiting a pattern or practice of civil rights violations began in 1994. The enabling language came from the Violent Crime Control and Law Enforcement Act of 1994, a multifaceted and far-ranging crime bill perhaps best known for its authorization of federal funding to put 100,000 new police officers on the street. Although other facets of the act—including a federal version of the "three-strikes-rule," an expansion of the list of federal crimes eligible for the death penalty, and an increase in funding for services and enhancement of prosecution in the area of violence against women—were relatively well known, Section 14141, one of the lesser known facets of the 1994 act, expanded the role of the United States Attorney General to affect remediation of systematic misconduct by state or local law enforcement agencies, so-called patterns or practices. The relevant sections of the act follow:

> **United State Code**
> Title 42 - The Public Health And Welfare
>   Chapter 136 - Violent Crime Control And Law Enforcement
>   Subchapter Ix - State And Local Law Enforcement
>   Part B - Police Pattern or Practice
>
> **(a) Unlawful conduct**
> It shall be unlawful for any governmental authority, or any agent thereof, or any person acting on behalf of a governmental authority, to engage in a pattern or practice of conduct by law enforcement officers or by officials or employees of any governmental agency with responsibility for the administration of juvenile justice or the incarceration of juveniles that deprives persons of rights, privileges, or immunities secured or protected by the Constitution or laws of the United States.
>
> **(b) Civil action by Attorney General**
> Whenever the Attorney General has reasonable cause to believe that a violation of paragraph [a] has occurred, the Attorney General, for or in the name of the United States, may in a civil action obtain appropriate equitable and declaratory relief to eliminate the pattern or practice.[3]

The Definition of "Pattern or Practice"

Section 14141, which makes government agencies directly responsible for unlawful conduct of their employees if that behavior rises to the level of a pattern or practice, was considered precedent setting. *Individual* actions of law enforcement officers that constitute civil rights violations have long been actionable in federal courts under Title 42, Chapter 21 § 1983. The 1994 act, however, gave the U.S. Department of Justice authority to hold law enforcement agencies responsible when individual actions formed a "pattern of misconduct" or were part of "systematic practices underlying the misconduct."

Federal courts have defined the meaning of "pattern or practice." According to a Supreme Court ruling in an employment discrimination case based on the Civil Rights Act of 1964, the term "pattern or practice" is not to be construed as a "term of art," but rather as "words [that] reflect only their usual meaning."[4] The Court indicated that these words were intended to apply "only where the denial of rights consists of something more than an isolated, sporadic incident, but is repeated, routine, or of a generalized nature."[5]

Based on Section 14141, federal courts can order local or state government agencies to eliminate patterns or practices deemed unlawful. Two criteria must be met for a case to be actionable under Section 14141. First, as discussed, the alleged misconduct must constitute a pattern or practice, not just individual or sporadic acts. Second, that misconduct, if proved true, must constitute a violation of federally protected civil rights.

Federal Investigation and Oversight Responsibility

In response to the 1994 act, the Special Litigation Section (SPL) of the Civil Rights Division (officially abbreviated as CRT)[6] of the Department of Justice was given the responsibility of reviewing and investigating alleged misconduct and enforcing Section 14141. One of 12 sections of the CRT, the SPL is responsible for enforcing federal civil rights pattern or practices in the following four areas:[7]

> (1) Conditions of institutional confinement.
> (2) Law enforcement misconduct.
> (3) Access to reproductive health facilities and places of religious worship.
> (4) Protection of institutionalized persons' religious exercise rights.[8]

For the purposes of this guide, we are concerned with pattern or practice violations as they relate specifically to law enforcement misconduct. The Civil Rights Division's web site describes the SPL's work in this area as follows:

> The Special Litigation Section enforces the police misconduct provision of the Violent Crime Control and Law Enforcement Act of 1994, which authorizes the Attorney General to seek equitable and declaratory relief to redress a pattern or practice of illegal conduct by law enforcement agencies or agencies responsible for the administration of juvenile justice. The Section also enforces the Omnibus Crime Control and Safe Streets Act of 1968, which authorizes the Attorney General to initiate civil litigation to remedy a pattern or practice of discrimination based on race, color national origin, gender or religion involving services by law enforcement agencies receiving financial assistance from the Department of Justice.[9]

The SPL is located in Washington, D.C., but occasionally acts in coordination with regional U.S. Attorneys' offices. All Section 14141 reviews are civil actions, not criminal. This does not preclude the fact that criminal actions, initiated by another component of the Department of Justice or local authorities, may be simultaneously directed at individuals for specific acts.

Patterns or Practices Addressed

On the basis of the 1994 act as well as other such acts, the CRT has addressed an array of alleged pattern or practice violations. The CRT has addressed patterns including, but not limited to, the following:

- Unlawful or excessive force, including unjustified use of deadly and nondeadly force
- Racial profiling or discriminatory enforcement based on race, ethnicity, gender, or other group status
- False arrests
- Harassment of civilians in retaliation for reported misconduct
- Illegal stops or searches
- Intimidation.

On the basis of the 1994 Act, the CRT has also addressed systematic practices—or the absences of practices—including the following:

- Inadequate training on use of force and other law enforcement techniques
- Inadequate supervision
- Failure to adequately investigate allegations of officer misconduct
- Failure to address misconduct through appropriate means (e.g., training, retraining, discipline, or other forms of intervention).

The Stages of Federal Investigation and Oversight

The process that the CRT and, in particular, the SPL use to address alleged pattern or practice violations can be understood as a series of steps that parallel, in many ways, the processes that law enforcement agencies themselves use in the investigations they carry out. Although federal investigatory processes are guided by clear legal standards, they often are quite fluid. In fact, both the investigatory processes and the resolution depend on the nature of the allegations. Investigatory processes may also be affected by the level of cooperation provided by the agency under investigation and may vary as the findings of the investigation unfold. In reality, the investigation and resolution of every pattern or practice case conducted by the CRT have been unique. Not only have they been individually shaped by the nature of allegations, findings, and agency responses, but the CRT's response to investigating and responding to pattern or practice allegations during the last decade has quite naturally evolved. When compared to other legal traditions in the United States, pattern or practice investigations and the resulting oversight of law enforcement agencies are still developing.

As a result, detailing a standard set of circumstances that will suggest definitively when an agency can expect a federal investigation or how that investigation will proceed is not possible. However, common stages and general patterns within the investigatory process have been established. The following discussion outlines five stages in the investigation and resolution of federal pattern or practice complaints, and identifies some of the variations that may occur as such investigations unfold.

Stage 1: Alleged Activities Come to Light
Federal investigations of the past decade reveal that allegations of pattern or practice violations may come to the attention of the SPL in a variety of ways. The SPL may be apprised of police misconduct allegations through complaints brought directly by individuals, advocacy groups, local political officials, police personnel, or local prosecutors. In addition, allegations of civil rights violations may come to the attention of the CRT through the media or through civil or criminal suits filed in local or federal courts. Oftentimes a combination of allegations and events give rise to the CRT's involvement. The following examples demonstrate the variety of ways in which the CRT is alerted of the need for investigation:

- The investigation of the Pittsburgh Bureau of Police stemmed from a 1996 lawsuit filed by the American Civil Liberties Union on behalf of the NAACP, a community group called Parents Against Violence, and 66 individuals alleging various forms of police misconduct.
- The investigation of the Prince George's (Maryland) County Police Department followed a series of incidents, including a number of high-profile shootings, instances in which suspects and bystanders were bitten by canines, and a number of large jury awards. The incidents, dating to 1995, sparked heated media and public attention and resulted in investigation by the FBI and then the CRT.
- In 1999, Washington, D.C. Mayor Anthony Williams and Chief Charles Ramsey of the Metropolitan Police Department requested an investigation of the department to assess potential patterns of excessive use of force.
- In 2002, Mayor Charles Luken of Cincinnati requested that CRT review the police department's use of force. The mayor's request came after several days of civic unrest following a police-involved shooting.

Stage 2: Initial Assessment
During an initial assessment, the CRT determines whether it has authority to pursue the case that has come to its attention. In this stage of the process, the primary objective of CRT attorneys is to determine whether a particular allegation would constitute a federal pattern or practice violation if it were proven true. CRT staff gathers relevant information from a variety of sources. Specifically, CRT staff may attempt to obtain information from the complainant or may access media sources to determine whether patterns of violations are evident. CRT staff may also obtain information about civil suits, criminal proceedings, or legal documents related to the underlying complaint. For instance, if concerns were raised about a pattern of excessive use of force, CRT staff would obtain relevant public documents. CRT staff may also interview persons whose civil rights were allegedly violated as well as advocacy or special interest groups. In accord with various state laws, CRT staff will not interview police personnel at this stage.

When an initial assessment "does not produce evidence tending to support the existence of a pattern or practice violation," the preliminary inquiry is closed.[10] When an initial assessment does discover evidence that tends to support the allegation, internal memoranda, subjected to a thorough, multistage review, are prepared. These memoranda may culminate in a recommendation from the head of SPL within the CRT to the Assistant Attorney General (AAG) seeking to investigate. The AAG makes a final determination about whether to proceed with a formal pattern or practice investigation.

Stage 3: Formal Investigation

The formal investigation begins when CRT notifies the jurisdiction that a pattern or practice investigation will take place. This notification typically takes the form of a letter to the agency's legal counsel, most often preceded by a telephone call. At this stage, CRT investigations become comprehensive and far-reaching. Investigations routinely include the following:

- An inventory and thorough assessments of an agency's relevant policies and procedures
- A review of training documents and practices
- A review of accountability and disciplinary practices
- An assessment of routine police activities, including direct observation of training sessions and participation in patrol ride-alongs
- A request for and a review of relevant forms, such as use-of-force report forms and citizen complaint forms
- During the formal investigation, in-depth interviews are typically conducted with police command staff and all relevant stakeholders, which typically include rank-and-file officers, police union representatives, and parties who believe they were subject to police misconduct. The parties interviewed are not necessarily limited to the complainants.

<u>A Two-Part Process</u>

The formal investigation typically falls into two phases. The first phase focuses on the collection of available documentation in the form of policies and procedures as well as interviews with rank-and-file officers. Once this phase is completed, the second phase begins as CRT staff request relevant documents about police behaviors and actions being investigated. Documents requested could include those such as use-of-force reports, arrest reports, or citizen complaint forms. They may also request documentation of investigatory proceedings related to use-of-force or misconduct investigations.

While awaiting the receipt of the requested forms and internal investigatory reports, CRT staff routinely complete a technical assistance letter. This letter outlines the findings of the first phase of the formal investigation and makes recommendations. This letter, however, does not determine whether a pattern or practice of civil rights violations has occurred.

Technical Assistance Letters

Regardless of whether an investigation results in a finding of a pattern or practice violation, the CRT spends considerable time conducting investigation, particularly in assessing agency policies and practices and in engaging the technical assistance of experienced police practice consultants. The CRT routinely provides technical assistance letters to agencies while they are under investigation. In effect, these letters itemize the deficiencies found during the investigation and make recommendations about remedies. This technical assistance goes beyond a focus on policies and practices to address issues such as supervision and accountability. Since technical assistance letters are offered before the formal investigation is completed and before final determinations are made, they carry no implication as to whether a pattern or practice violation has occurred. In essence, city officials, police chiefs, and city attorneys are being notified of areas of deficiency that do not necessarily reach the threshold of unconstitutionality.

As pattern or practice investigations have evolved over the last 10 years, CRT has relied more heavily on subject matter consultants with direct law enforcement experience, and has provided technical assistance letters and exit interviews throughout the course of the investigation, rather than just at the end. This reflects a conscious shift toward more transparency in the investigation process and has resulted in a greater emphasis on technical assistance as opposed to relying solely on adversarial legal processes.

Tone of Formal Investigations
Although the investigation is formal, at this point the cooperation of the department under investigation is voluntary. Departments are under no legal obligation to cooperate, and the CRT has no subpoena power at this stage.

During the decade that the CRT has been involved in these investigations, the level of cooperation received from departments has varied. Some departments have been highly compliant to requests for information and, in these instances, the tone of the investigation can be described as cooperative. Other departments have been resistant to the CRT's requests. Although, over the decade, the tone of the investigations has generally reflected a greater spirit of cooperation, the balance of power in the relationship between the CRT and the law enforcement agency clearly rests with the CRT. For its part, the CRT has increasingly relied on consultants in various areas of expertise with direct law enforcement experience to provide technical assistance.[11] The CRT has also consciously shifted toward a more transparent investigatory process.

It is important to note that an agency's failure to cooperate will not terminate the CRT's investigation. Instead, the investigation will continue and CRT's findings will be based on sources from outside the department who are willing to cooperate.

It is also important to note that while agencies usually are not required to participate voluntarily in investigations, The Omnibus Crime Control and Safe Streets Act of 1968[12] stipulates that agencies must cooperate if the allegation of pattern and practice is based on race. Agencies with federal funding risk losing their funding, depending on the outcome of a hearing.

A Time-Relevant Process
While past patterns or practices that formed the basis of the complaint are relevant for screening purposes, CRT's main objective in the investigation is to determine how the department is operating at the time of the investigation. In some instances, departments

have already begun to make changes before or during CRT's formal investigation. If such is the case, CRT will acknowledge such progress and attempt to work with the department to build on these successes. Department cooperation can be recognized in letters from the CRT outlining investigatory findings. An excerpt from an investigatory findings letter to the Washington (D.C.) Metropolitan Police Department is illustrative.

> We recognize that in the past two years, MPD has achieved a significant reduction in the rate at which it uses deadly force and the rate at which its canines bite subjects. In 1998, eleven fatalities resulted from MPD's use of deadly force. Fatalities decreased to four in 1999 and to two in 2000. Due to important changes in its canine operations, over the same time period, canine bites have decreased from occurring approximately 70 percent of the time that canines are deployed to slightly over 20 percent.[13]

Stage 4: Determination of Action

Following the formal investigation, the CRT must determine whether a case is actionable. It makes this determination on the bases of the investigation's findings and the steps that departments may have already taken to remedy civil rights violations. Three basic determinations are possible:

1. No pattern or practice violation is found to exist at the time of the investigation.
2. A pattern or practice violation is found to exist and the CRT and law enforcement agency come to a negotiated agreement involving the government entity—municipality, county, or state—which funds and oversees the law enforcement agency.
3. A pattern or practice violation is found to exist and the CRT files a formal suit in federal court.

The vast majority of pattern or practice investigations that have resulted in a determination of actionable civil rights violations have been resolved through negotiated agreements in the form of either a consent decree or an MOA. At present, 14 jurisdictions have been signatories to 16 separate consent decrees or MOAs. Several agencies now operate under two federal agreements. In June 2003, the Detroit Police entered into two separate consent judgments—agreements analogous to consent decrees. One of these deals with issues regarding the use of force and one deals with arrest and detention policies and practices. In January 2004, the Prince George's County Police Department entered into an MOA regarding the general use of force and a consent decree with respect to use of canines as a force option.

To date, only one investigation—involving the Columbus (Ohio) Division of Police—has resulted in a formal suit. Before being adjudicated, however, that suit was set aside after a letter of resolution was submitted by the mayor of Columbus that specified numerous remedies that the police department would undertake. In this particular case, the remedies set forth in this letter were considered acceptable by the Assistant Attorney General for Civil Rights.

Consent Decrees and Memorandums of Agreement

Whether an investigation results in a consent decree or an MOA, the basic outcome is an extensive list of provisions with which the agency promises to comply and for which a federally approved monitor provides oversight for a specified time period. In general terms, an MOA is an agreement between the department and the CRT that details specific remedies to correct the patterns and practices of civil rights violations found during the investigatory stage. A consent decree results in a similar set of specific remedies, but takes the form of a judicial decree. As stipulated in both consent decrees and MOAs, the law enforcement agency admits no fault or liability, but in effect agrees to cease certain practices and to engage in specified remedies. On its part, CRT asserts within the agreement that it is acting pursuant to Section 14141 in seeking "declaratory or equitable relief to remedy a pattern or practice of conduct by law enforcement officers that deprives individuals of rights, privileges or immunities secured or protected by the Constitution or laws of the United States."[14]

In practice, the individual consent decrees and MOAs have been negotiated agreements involving the police agency, superseding government agency (e.g., the mayor's or city manager's office), and the Department of Justice. Some agreements, such as the MOA for the Buffalo Police Department, also include the police union as a signatory. Whether an investigation culminates in a consent decree or MOA may depend on a variety of factors. Included among these is the likelihood that compliance can be achieved cooperatively and with full support from within the department and city leaders. If an agency has demonstrated cooperation and progress in remedying problems during the investigatory phase, the CRT may determine that an MOA is a better vehicle to co-facilitate reform. Flexibility in this process of determination allows the CRT to respond to particular circumstances. In the case of the Prince George's County Police Department, for instance, the investigation of excessive force resulted in two agreements. An MOA was signed with provisions on general use-of-force policies, training, and accountability while a separate consent decree was signed to address policies, training, and accountability specifically related to canines as a use-of-force option.

Stage 5: Independent Monitoring

Consent decrees and MOAs generally establish a period of formal and systematic federal monitoring of the law enforcement agency investigated. In fact, all existing consent decrees and MOAs have resulted in such oversight. Ideally, the independent monitoring or auditing function is held by a mutually agreeable person. In the case of consent decrees, if parties cannot arrive at a mutually agreeable person within a reasonable period, the court determines the appropriate monitor from a list provided by the parties. In the case of MOAs, the process is similar, but is not decided by the court. For instance, the MOA may include provisions that an independent third party, rather than the court, should resolve any impasse in selecting a mutually agreeable monitor.

Because of the extensive authority, influence, and responsibility that this monitor will hold, the fact that an agency has a role to veto a monitor can be crucial. The authority and key responsibilities of the monitor include, but are not limited to, the following:

- The monitor is to be given access to all relevant documentation, including policy directives and training material bearing on the provisions.
- The monitor is to be given access to records and data systems to assess compliance and conduct quality assurance analysis. This may include access to use-of-force reporting forms and the early warning system.
- The monitor is to be given access to department personnel for purpose of assessing compliance.
- The monitor is to report on a regular basis regarding the agency's compliance with each provision articulated in the consent decree or MOA.

As with the investigatory process and the drafting of agreements, independent monitoring is guided by clear policies that allow for some level of flexibility. In several agreements the role of the monitor has included both oversight and consultative services. Indeed, technical assistance is often formally included as part of federal agreements. This is illustrated by the following excerpt from the Steubenville (Ohio) Police Department consent decree:

> The auditor shall offer the City technical assistance in coming into compliance with this Decree, including with: policy development, forms, training, management information systems. The auditor shall perform the policy review function specified in the Decree, and also shall audit and evaluate compliance with the Decree.[15]

An experienced monitor can help the department make sense of the complex and extensive provisions of the consent decree or MOA by breaking them down into a comprehensible and actionable set of steps. Most important, a cooperative and constructive relationship among the law enforcement agency, the independent monitor, and the Department of Justice can help set the foundation for continued accountability once the federal agreement has been terminated and monitoring is no longer taking place.

Duration of Federal Investigation and Oversight

Federal investigations and the resulting monitoring are labor-intensive for departments and for the CRT. Still, the Department of Justice seeks to complete investigations and its monitoring function in a responsible and timely manner. The DOJ web site, last updated in January 2003, states that the CRT will attempt to complete investigations within 18 months from the time it begins the formal investigation.[16] The document further states, however, that this length of time can be affected by the complexity of the case, the existence and quality of related documentation within the agency, and the degree of cooperation. In some instances, cooperation may actually serve to lengthen the investigatory phase. If the agency has begun to implement meaningful reforms that may bear on its patterns or practices, the CRT may wish to wait until those reforms have taken effect before concluding its investigation and making a final determination. Other factors may also lengthen the duration of an investigation. For instance, if separate criminal investigations are underway, the SPL may defer to that investigation and wait for it to be completed before commencing its investigation.

The minimal length of time for which monitoring must take place and the conditions that must be met before federal monitoring is terminated are specified in detail in the language of the consent decrees or MOAs. The exact conditions of monitoring have evolved over the time that pattern or practice have been in use. The first consent decree, signed in Pittsburgh in December 1999, established the following provisions regarding federal oversight:

> At any time after five (5) years from the date of entry of this Decree, and after substantial compliance has been maintained for no less than two years, the City may move to terminate this Decree. Any motion to terminate must detail all aspects of the City's compliance with each provision of this Decree, supported by affidavits and supporting documentation.[17]

While the next two consent decrees, those with the Steubenville (Ohio) Police Department and the New Jersey State Police, followed this precedent, subsequent agreements have reduced the minimal time of required oversight. For instance, the Prince George's County (Maryland) Police Department consent decree, signed in January 2004, stipulated a 3-year follow-up period with 2 years of substantial compliance.

The Potential Benefits of Federal Investigation and Oversight

The CRT's investigation and monitoring processes are structured but do afford a certain amount of fluidity that can be of benefit to individual agencies and prudent leaders. As civil rights violation investigations proceed, these investigations can develop into cooperative processes in which CRT staff and consultants with law enforcement expertise provide needed technical assistance to the agency. Some law enforcement leaders actually find that meeting the CRT half way and facing the realities of reform is a necessary and productive, though not necessarily easy, path. The Pittsburgh Bureau of Police was the first agency to emerge from federal monitoring under Section 14141. It has been widely acclaimed for its success. The study, *Turning Necessity into Virtue: Pittsburgh's Experience with a Federal Consent Decree*, chronicles how the department effectively managed the oversight process. This report found that Pittsburgh Bureau of Police went beyond the spirit of the agreement in its implementation of comprehensive early intervention system that improved policing practice and helped to ensure protection of civil rights.[18]

Additional Federal Assistance: The Community Relations Service

Other forms of federal assistance are available to agencies committed to addressing civil rights challenges, problems, or concerns. In fact, law enforcement agencies need not reach the crisis of a pattern or practice violation or a community demonstration alleging biased based policing before seeking out the aid of the federal government. Another division of the Department of Justice is empowered to assist individual law enforcement officials, community leaders, or advocacy groups to deal with civil rights-related issues

This division, the Community Relations Service (CRS), has had substantial experience in bringing police agencies and communities together where racial conflict, the potential for violence, or actual violence related to race, color, or national origin have inhibited cooperation. Since its inception more than 4 decades ago (1964), CRS has facilitated hundreds of mediation agreements designed to resolve civil rights conflicts between communities and local and state entities, including law enforcement agencies. CRS operates 10 regional offices and 4 field offices across the country. CRS services are free, neutral, and confidential. The work takes place in accordance with its mission statement, available on the CRS web site (www.usdoj.gov/crs):

> The Community Relations Service is the [U.S. Justice] Department's "peacemaker" for community conflicts and tensions arising from differences of race, color, and national origin. Created by the Civil Rights Act of 1964, CRS is the only Federal agency dedicated to assist State and local units of government, private and public organizations, and community groups with preventing and resolving racial and ethnic tensions, incidents, and civil disorders, and in restoring racial stability and harmony. CRS facilitates the development of viable, mutual understandings and agreements as alternatives to coercion, violence, or litigation. It also assists communities in developing local mechanisms, conducting training, and other proactive measures to prevent or reduce racial/ethnic tension. CRS does not take sides among disputing parties and, in promoting the principles and ideals of non-discrimination, applies skills that allow parties to come to their own agreement. In performing this mission, CRS deploys highly skilled professional conciliators, who are able to assist people of diverse racial and cultural backgrounds.[19]

Historically, CRS has been a low-profile agency. This is the result, in part, of a provision in its enabling legislation that requires the agency to provide conciliation assistance in confidence and without publicity. CRS work can become public when parties to the conciliation or mediation choose to make their agreements public. Mediation agreements between a law enforcement agency and a community based organization are sometimes made public as a demonstration of the agency's proactive community policing initiative. In the accompanying text box, this guide provides examples of successful community/police agreements that have become public.

> **Spotlight on the U.S. Department of Justice Community Relations Service**
>
> As mentioned in the introduction to this guide, the Community Relations Service (CRS) within the U.S. Department of Justice provides mediation and conciliation services to communities and to the local and state government agencies that serve these communities. In accordance with its mandate, CRS assists community and government agencies in addressing conflicts and tensions arising from differences of race, color, and national origin. CRS offices are geographically organized into regions, with regional and field offices as indicated in the map below. A list of the specific locations and contact information for these offices is available on the CRS web site and is provided in Appendix E of this guide. The CRS National Headquarters is located in Washington, D.C.

Protecting Civil Rights: A Leadership Guide

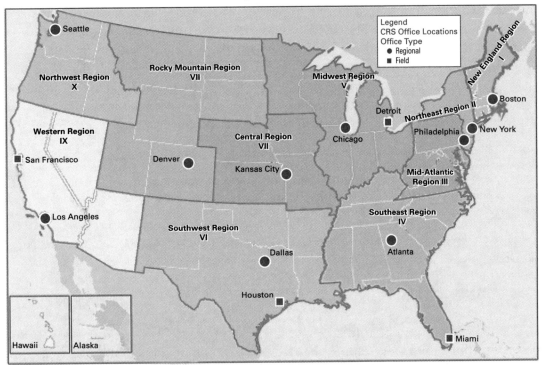

Map of Regional and Field Offices
Community Relations Service

~ Puerto Rico and the Virgin Islands are served by the Northeast Region
~ Guam is served by the Western Region

CRS offers its mediation and conciliation services when there is an underlying conflict between a local or state government entity and its residents; and also when there is a conflict between two different racial groups. CRS creates the opportunity for communities to reach voluntary conciliations through formal agreements. While CRS maintains a strict commitment to confidentiality, the parties to the conciliations often choose to make their agreements public. At least 13 agreements involving law enforcement agencies have been so publicized over the past few years, often in the form of a memorandum of understanding (MOU). CRS also intervenes and helps build relationships between community groups and government agencies such as schools and public institutions.

Given the CRS mandate to deal with issues of race, color, and national origin, many of the agreements involving law enforcement agencies were initiated in the aftermath of critical incidents involving allegations of excessive use-of-force within the minority community or pursuant to allegations or perceptions of racial profiling. The content of these agreements, however, may be far-reaching in scope and spirit. Agreements also may reinforce many of the concepts, strategies, and tools addressed in this guide.

In many ways, the agreements facilitated by CRS address the same substantive topics that appear in the consent decrees and memorandums of agreement that have resulted from investigations by the Civil Rights Division (CRT). The main difference between the agreements brokered by CRS and those implemented by CRT is that CRT's agreements stem from a determination or finding based on a "pattern or practice" investigation. These consent decrees have the force of law. Since CRS has no authority to enforce the law, agreements facilitated by CRS are between the parties that sign the agreement and are maintained voluntarily. To the extent that these agreements are voluntarily publicized with the consent of parties, the parties then have an additional vested interest to maintain and live up to the agreements. The map below shows the location of the 13 most recent publicized agreements. What follows below the map is a synopsis of three recent agreements.

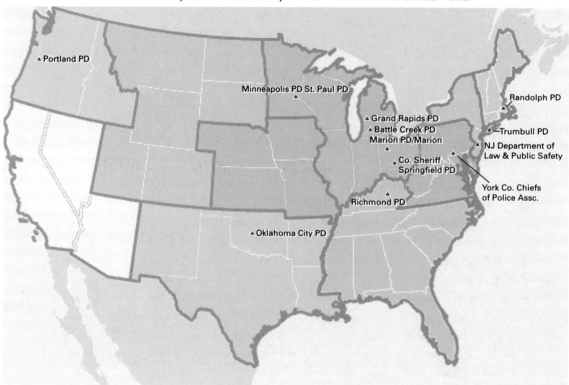

Publicized Agreements Involving Law Enforcement Facilitated by the Community Relations Service Since 1992

Richmond, Kentucky: The Richmond Police Department entered into a memorandum of agreement with various public officials and the local chapter of the NAACP and other community representatives in November 2004. At the core of this agreement was an acknowledgement that minority residents were fearful of the potential of police to misuse force. As a result, the Richmond Police Department agreed to revise its policy to better address these concerns, to define an administrative threshold for reportable use of force, and to enhance accountability. In the spirit of building bridges and trust with the community, he Department committed to establishing a police/community relations council that would serve as an advisory body, providing comment on police policy and training. The Department also reaffirmed its commitment to diversify its work force through recruitment and retention efforts as well as reaffirmed its commitment to engage in bias-free policing. In addition, the Department agreed to implement a wide variety of training programs that would promote outreach and civil rights.

Randolph, Massachusetts: In 2004, CRS worked with the Randolph Police Department to help it respond to allegations of police harassment and racial profiling by members of the Randolph, Massachusetts minority community. CRS worked jointly with the Randolph Fair Practices Committee and the Randolph Police Department to enable the police to change the community's perception of the police department and respond in a concrete way to allegations of disparity of treatment based on race. With CRS' help, the parties developed an MOU whereby the Randolph Police Department pledged to continue ongoing, mandatory cultural and racial diversity training for all police department personnel, established a monitoring system for police traffic stops to determine if racial profiling is taking place, and established an ombudsman program to focus on neighborhood issues surrounding race-based harassment of residents, among other detailed provisions. The primary purpose of this MOU is to establish a dialogue between the police department and local minority residents that better enables each party to work cooperatively. This is the goal of CRS mediation. It brings parties together in a neutral setting where issues from both parties can be discussed and resolved jointly.

Minneapolis, Minnesota: In December 2003, the Unity Community Mediation Team and the Minneapolis Police Department entered into a memorandum of agreement. This detailed and comprehensive agreement addressed improving police department responsiveness to and treatment of persons with mental illness and developmental disabilities. Other unique features of the agreement included a commitment by the police department to provide outreach material in the Spanish, Hmong, and Somali languages.

These highlighted agreements, and the others facilitated by CRS, address a broad range of community outreach and civil rights issues that have been addressed throughout this manual. A common thread in the agreements facilitated by CRS, but constructed by the parties involved, include frank acknowledgements of existing problems and concerns that are coupled with a commitment to building the trust, communication, and partnerships necessary to address underlying issues. While CRS is the vehicle for helping improve police community relations, clearly, CRS' mandate is not the same as the CRT regarding its procedural and legally binding approach. The scope of CRS' agreements, however, is similarly comprehensive and is focused on achieving the same goals. Law enforcement leaders committed to taking proactive approaches to protecting and promoting civil rights can learn a lot from the content of CRS agreements.

Although CRS' involvement on behalf of law enforcement agencies working through civil rights challenges is restricted—it cannot provide direct assistance to a jurisdiction unless there is some underlying conflict or allegation with respect to race, color, or national origin—CRS can refer interested parties to other sources for assistance. In addition, CRS is empowered to provide training to any law enforcement agency or community on general strategies for addressing civil rights issues or measures to prevent civil rights violations such as on the following topics responding to allegations of racial profiling; building trust between police and the community; law enforcement mediation; community dialogues; hate crimes; and others. Most training provided by CRS is accredited by state Police Officer Standards Training (POST) offices. All CRS training is free of charge.

Fulfilling its mission to undertake proactive actions to prevent or reduce racial and ethnic tension, CRS engages in outreach to law enforcement agencies and community groups. Often these actions include providing training to both law enforcement staff and community leadership. In the aftermath of the September 11 terrorist attacks, CRS developed a compelling and focused training symposium using locally based trainers from the Arab, Muslim, and the Sikh communities. This half-day symposium entitled *Arab, Muslim & Sikh Protocol Awareness Training Seminar* has been presented to numerous law enforcement agencies across the country. Many law enforcement agencies sponsor CRS training events and include community leadership in the classes. CRS training can also be tailored to specific local needs.

Another resource developed by CRS in response to September 11 is a police roll call video available on CD or DVD entitled, *The First Three to Five Seconds*, which is being used for training in law enforcement agencies across the country. This film, made for law enforcement audiences, familiarizes police with the Arab and Muslim cultures. The film stresses the vast diversity that exists within the Arab and Muslim cultures and provides practical advice for officers about traditional customs and beliefs. As a result of this training, officers are better able to interact with members of these communities in ways that are respectful and lessen the risk of engaging in behavior, often inadvertently, that might offend Arabs or Muslims within the communities they serve. Copies of the CD or DVD are available at no charge from CRS.

Distinct Roles of the Civil Rights Division, Special Litigation Section, and the Community Relations Service

While the SPL of the CRT and the CRS operate under the Department of Justice and both deal with civil rights issues, it is important to understand their distinct functions. Some in law enforcement have been confused by their respective roles.

CRS is a separate, independent agency within the Department of Justice. Its SPL has a narrowly defined legal mandate to bring remedy to patterns or practices that violate the Constitution or laws of the United States. It does this through investigations and potentially through litigation. Only CRT is empowered to investigate alleged pattern and practice violations, to authorize agreements as a remedy, or to litigate cases when other remedies have failed.

In contrast, the CRS's function does not involve investigations, enforcement, or litigation. CRS is empowered to facilitate collaborative agreements between departments and various community or advocacy groups on issues involving allegations of civil rights concerns. CRS

Protecting Civil Rights: A Leadership Guide

is not, however, a party to these mediation agreements that often take the form of MOAs. The parties to these MOAs facilitated by CRS are entirely free to walk away from the agreements without any legal repercussions. By contrast, consent decrees and MOAs developed by CRT are legally binding and strict accountability mechanisms are built into the process.

Proactively Protecting Civil Rights: Creating a Culture Bound by Rules

While law enforcement agencies confronting serious civil rights challenges should and do seek out federal assistance when necessary, hundreds of agencies are working internally—within their departments and in partnership with their communities—to ensure that their members adhere to ethical policing and protect the civil rights of the individuals they serve. These agencies work through two complementary strategies: first, they establish a policing culture that respects and protects civil rights and second, they establish sound accountability mechanisms. Of course, law enforcement agencies that establish both best succeed at protecting and promoting the civil rights of those individuals who live and work within their communities. Neither a culture-based nor an accountability-based approach alone is sufficient.

An ideal policing culture is one in which all officers are instilled with a respect and tolerance for diversity, a belief in the individual dignity of all persons, and a commitment to community service. While such a culture is a critical foundation for the protection of civil rights, it is, by itself, inadequate. Indeed, it is difficult to imagine a police agency—a complex organization with the broad responsibility to serve and protect the public under strict legal scrutiny—to function without the guidance of clear procedural rules, both internal and external to the agency.

Sound accountability mechanisms must consist of clear expectations, clear rules, and effective means by which to manage the performance of individual officers to ensure that they are meeting agency expectations and abiding by agency rules. Accountability mechanisms must also address problems as they arise through both corrective measures, such as counseling and retraining, and disciplinary processes. While relying solely on rules and accountability mechanisms may have some effect, this would likely result in resentment and disenfranchisement among officers. Rules are most likely to be embraced and adhered to when they are presented in the context of a policing culture. A core message of *Protecting Civil Rights*, then, is that law enforcement executives must be able to interweave the best of police culture and rule-bound accountability to provide effective law enforcement while protecting the civil rights of all.

The Evolution of Culture and Rules in Policing

Of course, policing cultures and rules evolve. Law enforcement, historically, has experienced shifts in its sense of mission as well as in its strategies for realizing its mission. The most recent shifts have occurred with the rise of community policing in the 1980s and the CompStat model of data-driven management in the early 1990s, led by the New York City Police Department. Although seen by some as competing approaches to policing, these popular and, now, rather fluid concepts have been molded to meet the needs of individual agencies and communities.[20] Indeed, many law enforcement agencies express a commitment to both community policing and CompStat—or a CompStat-*style* of—policing. And some police scholars do argue that community policing and CompStat are compatible.[21]

Protecting Civil Rights seeks to emphasize that there are elements of both strategies that can and do contribute to effective civil rights protections. In its first chapter, this guide will discuss the ways in which community policing philosophies and practices can help promote a policing culture that is sensitive and responsive to civil rights. In subsequent chapters, it will address the core elements of management that are essential to law enforcement executives who are working to protect and promote civil rights. This guide clearly advocates, for instance, that police leaders use the strategies of accountability, supervision, and information-driven management that are at the core of CompStat. Law enforcement executives can rely on these strategies to manage and reduce citizen complaints, the excessive use of force, and police misconduct in the same manner that they rely on them to reduce crime or increase productivity. This guide also advocates that agencies working to protect and promote civil rights adopt the proactive and preventive strategies that CompStat recommends for general agency management.

The incorporation of community policing and CompStat into law enforcement in general has been seen as revolutionary. *Protecting Civil Rights* suggests that invoking these strategies specifically in the service of law enforcement leaders, agencies, and officers dedicated to protecting and promoting civil rights will be just as revolutionary.

Overview of Chapters

Following this introduction, *Protecting Civil Rights* is divided into five chapters that are considered key building blocks for promoting and sustaining a commitment to civil rights protections. Each of the next five chapters addresses a major civil rights issue—community policing, early intervention, the complaint process, use of force, and racial profiling—that has been at the core of a pattern or practice investigation. While much of the material in these chapters is drawn from provisions embodied in federal consent decrees and MOAs, the chapters also rely on examples of illustrative policies and promising practices emerging out of a broad range of law enforcement agencies that have demonstrated a clear commitment to protecting civil rights. Each chapter ends with a series of recommendations. The concluding seventh and eighth chapters address personnel issues and issues of data collection, management, and analysis related to police efforts to protect civil rights. These chapters are outlined, in brief, below.

Chapter 2 – Sustaining Community Outreach and Engagement: The Intersection of Civil Rights and Community Policing

Exploring the connection between community engagement and civil rights protection, the chapter argues that effective community policing serves as a strong foundation from which agencies may protect and promote the civil rights of all community members. Acknowledging that community policing encourages the empowerment of citizens through participation in problem-solving partnerships with the police, this chapter emphasizes the need for community policing that is tailored to individual communities and that is institutionalized in individual agencies from the chief executive on down to the officer on the street. Of course, to best protect and promote civil rights, community policing strategies must engage the *entire* community. To this end, the chapter investigates strategies such as strengthening police-community relations in distressed neighborhoods, improving minority and immigrant outreach, and enhancing community understanding of policing through citizen academies. Repeatedly, the chapter underscores the reality that civil rights and community engagement are inextricably linked.

Chapter 3 – Developing an Early Intervention Strategy

The chapter will enhance law enforcement executives' understanding of early intervention systems—systems that analyze officer performance for the purpose of identifying and addressing potential problems before disciplinary action is required. The chapter is attentive to the commonalities of effective early intervention systems: the proactive focus on potential problems, the dependence on data collection, and the reliance on strong supervisory review. It also identifies some of the major differences in such systems—from the vast variety of performance indicators that agencies track to predict risk to the differing thresholds at which departments may determine that a review of an officer's performance is required. Through its attention to such details, this chapter suggests not only that early intervention is an appropriate tool for all agencies (not just large agencies with sophisticated data-management technologies), but that early intervention strategies can benefit individual officers, entire agencies, and whole communities by promoting a culture of accountability and emphasizing a commitment to ethical policing.

Chapter 4 – Managing the Complaint Process

An accessible, transparent, thorough, and fair citizen complaint process is not only a tool that instills public confidence, but a tool that improves a department's ability to be responsive to the community. Police executives who act on the substantiated concerns of the community members they serve garner the support of the public while enhancing their own policing. This chapter considers the challenges of managing an effective complaint process. Federal consent decrees and MOAs have revealed that complaint processes in some departments are inaccessible and ineffectual. This chapter addresses those concerns by investigating the complaint process in detail. From the initial filing of a complaint to its final adjudication, this chapter serves as a primer for executives looking to improve their agency's complaint process.

Chapter 5 – Managing Use of Force

The authorization to use force is a tremendous power that bears with it a tremendous a responsibility. Federal consent decrees and MOAs consistently require departments to modify their use-of-force policies, training practices, and accountability mechanisms to ensure that citizens' civil rights are protected. Accordingly, this chapter addresses departments' management of the use of force. It not only considers the most prevalent use-of-force options, but it explores executives' responsibility to ensure that the use of force is no greater than necessary to ensure public and officer safety, that excessive force is not tolerated, and that allegations of excessive or unlawful force are thoroughly investigated. This chapter stresses law enforcement leaders' responsibility to establish a policing culture as well as strong accountability structures that are intolerant of unlawful and excessive force. It also stresses the benefits to officer, agency, and community of keeping overall levels of force to a minimum while ensuring public and officer safety.

Chapter 6 – Addressing Racial Profiling: Creating a Comprehensive Commitment to Bias-Free Policing

The prevalence of racial profiling is a hotly contested topic among the media, the public, and police personnel. Addressing the community perception of racial profiling and taking proactive steps to prevent racial profiling deserves commensurate levels of attention from police leaders. This chapter focuses on the challenges law enforcement executives confront as they work to address and prevent racial profiling. The chapter begins by analyzing the role of race as a consideration in police discretion and decision-making. Against this backdrop, it considers law enforcement executives' efforts to establish clear policy directives against racial profiling, train staff on this complex and multifaceted issue, and establish sound accountability mechanisms. The chapter also considers the challenges that attend to racial profiling data collection and analysis. Its insights will be invaluable to law enforcement executives who currently collect data as well as those who are contemplating data collection in response to political and public pressures. Finally, the chapter offers insights into managing highly visible instances of perceived racial profiling in such a way as to build confidence with the public as well as within the department.

The chapters just discussed correspond to the core areas of concern addressed in the provisions of federal consent decrees and MOAs. In essence, these substantive areas are those for which prudent police chiefs are constantly refining their policies, training, and accountability. Several other issues such as personnel and data management, however, transcend these individual topics to demand the attention of law enforcement executives at every turn. The seventh and eighth chapters consider these issues.

Chapter 7 – Personnel Management Issues in the Context of Civil Rights

Personnel are the most valued resource in any police agency. They are also the most expensive and represent an agency's single most substantial investment. Law enforcement leaders must possess sufficient vision and skill to ensure that the right people with the right qualities are hired as officers. They must then train and hold on to these officers. This chapter identifies the strategies that make these goals achievable. It explores methods by which to maintain a diverse force that is reflective of the community; select officers committed to community service; and evaluate, reward, and promote officers on the basis of their community policing skills and their commitment to protecting civil rights. Finally, this chapter also considers the challenges facing chief executives who must hire excellent officers at a time when there is a scarcity of applicants.

Chapter 8 – Measuring and Evaluating Outcomes in the Context of Civil Rights

To evaluate the effectiveness of their personnel and to assess whether the agency is meeting its missions, executives rely on performance data. Data-driven management strategies have spread rapidly to law enforcement agencies of all sorts and sizes. Presently, law enforcement executives regularly collect, manage, and analyze data to gauge an agency's overall performance in preventing crime and operating efficiently. Increasingly, law enforcement agencies are using nontraditional performance data and analysis to assess their success in protecting and promoting civil rights. This chapter considers the benefits and challenges of effective data management. Although these issues are touched on in earlier chapters, this final chapter offers overall advice on data quality issues as well as systematic data collection, analysis, and interpretation. It also discusses the capacities and limitations inherent in using administrative data and suggests other avenues of data collection to supplement administrative data and to better assess both officer and agency performance with respect to civil rights.

Sources of Information

In the preparation of *Protecting Civil Rights*, IACP staff relied on several sources of information. These include the following:

- All publicly available information on civil rights pattern or practice investigations and agreements, including the content of all consent decrees and MOAs as well as publicly available documents providing technical assistance recommendations to departments under federal investigation.
- IACP–sponsored roundtable discussions with law enforcement leaders, both those involved in pattern or practice agreements and those from agencies known for exemplary civil rights practices.
- The expertise of staff at the COPS Office. This agency has provided federal support for community policing efforts through direct funding to local law enforcement and through an extensive array of publications, seminars, and trainings promoting fair and effective policing practices.
- Consultation with members of IACP's standing committees on civil rights and on professional standards. Committee members have been selected on the basis of their demonstrated commitment to enhancing the quality of policing and protecting civil rights. Several members serve as subject matter expert consultants to the Department of Justice in civil rights pattern or practice investigations.
- Roundtable discussions and focus groups of similar projects, most notably the Community Policing Consortium's technical assistance project on helping law enforcement agencies self-evaluate their policies and practices on civil rights.
- Consultation with several federal justice agencies, most notably two agencies within the Department of Justice: the Special Litigation Section of the Civil Rights Division and the Community Relations Service. These two agencies approach civil rights issues from different, but complementary perspectives.
- An extensive array of professional and scholarly literature available on the substantive issues addressed in this guide, including individual agency policy directives and model policies offered by professional associations and state oversight agencies.

Endnotes

1. Roosevelt, Franklin Delano. "Greeting to the American Committee for the Protection of the Foreign-born." Washington, DC. January 9, 1940.
2. International Association of Chiefs of Police. Law Enforcement Oath of Honor. www.theiacp.org/profassist/ethics/oath_honor_word.doc.
3. Pubic Law 103-322, title XXI, Sec. 210401, September 13, 1994, 108 Stat. 2071.
4. *International Brotherhood of Teamsters* v. *U.S.*, 431 U.S. 324, 336 n.16 (1977)
5. *Teamsters* v. *United States*, 431 U.S. 324 (1977)
6. Within the U.S. Department of Justice CRT is commonly used as the acronym for the Civil Right Divisions, while CRD is used to reference the Criminal Division.
7. The 12 sections are Appellate Section, Coordination and Review Section, Criminal Section, Disability Rights Section, Educational Opportunities, Section, Employment Litigation Section, Housing and Civil Enforcement Section, Office of Special Counsel for Immigration Related Unfair Employment Practices, Special Litigation Section Voting Section, and Administrative Management Section
8. "Overview." November, 22, 2002. U.S. Department of Justice, Civil Rights Division, Special Litigation Section. Retrieved November 13, 2005 from www.usdoj.gov/crt/split/overview.htm.
9. "Overview." November 22, 2002. U.S. Department of Justice, Civil Rights Division, Special Litigation Section. Retrieved November 13, 2005 from www.usdoj.gov/crt/split/overview.htm. Note that the receiving financial assistance provisions clause is limited to Omnibus Crime Control and Safe Streets Act of 1968. The Violent Crime Control and Law Enforcement Act of 1994 applies to all state and local agencies, whether or not they receive federal assistance.
10. "Frequently Asked Questions." January 31, 2003. U.S. Department of Justice, Civil Rights Division, Special Litigation Section. Retrieved November 13, 2005 from www.usdoj.gov/crt/split/faq.htm.
11. Brown, Shanetta C. "Introductory Remarks." Community Policing Consortium: National Civil Rights Symposium. Mayflower Renaissance Hotel, Washington, DC. June 12, 2005.
12. 42 USC § 3789d. § 3789d
13. "Department of Justice Investigation of Use of Force by the Washington Metropolitan Police Department." No date. U.S. Department of Justice, Civil Rights Division, Special Litigation Section. Retrieved November 13, 2005 from www.usdoj.gov/crt/split/documents/dcfindings.htm.
14. Law Enforcement Act of 1994, 42 U.S.C. § 14141
15. "United States v. City of Steubenville, Ohio Consent Decree. September 3, 1993. U.S. Department of Justice, Civil Rights Division, Special Litigation Section. Retrieved on November 11, 2005 from www.usdoj.gov/crt/split/documents/steubensa.htm.
16. "Frequently Asked Questions." January 31, 2003. U.S. Department of Justice, Civil Rights Division, Special Litigation Section. Retrieved November 13, 2005 from www.usdoj.gov/crt/split/faq.htm.
17. *United States* v. *City of Pittsburgh* Consent Decree. February 26, 1997. Retrieved November 13, 2005 from www.usdoj.gov/crt/split/documents/pittscomp.htm.

[18] Davis, Robert, Christopher W. Ortiz, Nicole J. Henderson, Michelle Massie, and Joel Miller. <u>Turning Necessity into Virtue: Pittsburgh's Experience with a Federal Consent Decree</u>. New York: Vera Institute of Justice, 2002.

[19] "Homepage." No date. U.S. Department of Justice, Community Relations Service. Retrieved November 18, 2005 from www.usdoj.gov/crs.

[20] Walsh, William F., and Gennaro F. Vito. "The Meaning of Compstat: A Theoretical Analysis." <u>Journal of Contemporary Criminal Justice</u> 20.1 (2004): 51-69.

[21] Magers, Jeffrey S. "Compstat: A New Paradigm for Policing or a Repudiation of Community Policing?" <u>Journal of Contemporary Criminal Justice</u> 20.1 (2004): 70-79.

[22] Funded by U.S. Department of Justice Office of Community Oriented Policing Services (COPS), the Community Policing Consortium (CPC) is a partnership of five professional police associations. They are the International Association of Chiefs of Police; National Organization of Black Law Enforcement Executives; National Sheriffs' Association ; Police Executive Research Forum; and the Police Foundation. These agencies, who have all committed to the philosophy of community policing, provide research, training, and technical assistance through the CPC to further the development of the community policing model and its adoption by law enforcement agencies across the country.

II. Sustaining Community Outreach and Engagement: The Intersection of Civil Rights and Community Policing

Sustaining Community Outreach and Engagement: The Intersection of Civil Rights and Community Policing

> [P]olice chiefs must know that the concepts of community policing and the concepts of protecting human and civil rights are inseparable. They are one and the same. And for law enforcement you can't have one without the other.[1]
>
> Chief Charles Gruber, South Barrington (Illinois) Police Department

Introduction

During the past 2 decades, law enforcement executives from all types of agencies—municipal police departments, sheriffs' offices, tribal agencies, state police departments, and special jurisdictional police departments—have adopted community policing strategies. The differences across these agencies—including variations in size, mission, management, and the nature of the communities they serve—mean that these leaders' implementations of community policing often look quite different. Despite these differences, however, community policing efforts are recognizable for several core commonalities. Most notably, for the purposes of this guide, they are built on partnerships with the community that promote trust, respect for diversity, and tolerance. These partnerships—the core of successful, genuine community policing strategies—have been credited with helping to resolve the us-versus-them mindset that too often has existed in agencies and communities alike.

The concept of community policing certainly is a familiar one to law enforcement leaders. Not all, however, may have considered the inextricable ties between the core tenets of community policing and civil rights protections as articulated in the above quote.

Chapter Overview and Objectives

This chapter explores the inextricable links between civil rights and community policing strategies. Following a brief definition of community policing, an assessment of evolving attitudes toward community policing in the aftermath of September 11, and an analysis of indicators of the prevalence of community policing, this chapter offers a review of five substantive community policing strategies for protecting and promoting civil rights. The chapter underscores each strategy by providing examples of innovative programs. Each example is notable for its success in using active community engagement and police-community partnerships to protect and promote civil rights and to better engage residents in the civic process.

A Definition of Community Policing

Many have described community policing as a philosophy of policing, rather than as a set of rules. The U.S. Department of Justice Office of Community Oriented Policing Services (COPS) defines community policing as: "[A] policing philosophy that promotes and supports organizational strategies to address the causes and reduce the fear of crime and social disorder through problem-solving tactics and community-police partnerships."[2]

Considering this conceptual definition, it is not surprising that there is no established programmatic checklist for what qualifies a department as practicing effective community policing. Each partnership is as unique as the community and police department that are part of it. While recognizing the uniqueness of each partnership, however, the following elements are often cited as key components:

- Adopting community service as the overarching philosophy of the organization
- Making an institutional commitment to community policing that is internalized throughout the command structure—from the chief executive to the officers in the streets
- Emphasizing geographically decentralized models of policing that stress services tailored to the needs of individual communities rather than a one-size-fits-all approach for the entire jurisdiction
- Empowering citizens to act in partnership with the police on issues of crime and more broadly defined social problems (e.g., fear of crime, disorder, decay, public nuisances, and quality of life)
- Using problem-oriented or problem-solving approaches involving police personnel working with community members.

In addition to enacting these key components, departments committed to effective community policing also work to increase levels of interaction between the police and community residents. They do this through practices and techniques that include the following:

- Holding regular (e.g., monthly), formal meetings with community members on a local level (e.g., "beat meeting" or "precinct meetings")
- Making greater use of citizen advisory groups or councils
- Directing outreach efforts toward key community leaders and stakeholders including those from business, educational, and faith-based communities as well as representatives from civilian associations such as neighborhood groups and tenant organizations
- Promoting geographic and functional decentralization by providing first-line supervisors and front-line officers with greater flexibility and discretion in dealing with the community
- Identifying and/or training selected officers and/or units to serve as liaisons with particular communities and interest groups (e.g., Hispanic outreach teams, senior citizen services teams)

- Increasing use of foot and bicycle patrol to allow officers to interact more frequently with community members
- Establishing and expanding citizen academies designed to offer community residents an operational overview of their police agency and its internal culture
- Increasing the use of civilian volunteers who provide assistance to the police.

As a whole, community policing strategies allow agencies the opportunity to establish more frequent contact and more meaningful relationships with a broad cross-section of their community. In addition, each practice described above provides police personnel of all ranks with more opportunities to engage with citizens in building trust, confidence, and partnerships. Community policing strategies not only make participants feel they are part of the policing process, they can actually increase overall levels of civic involvement. Achieving this goal successfully can actually serve to promote, rather than just protect, the civil rights of community members.

Law enforcement agencies, often in partnership with community members, have relied on the SARA model of problem-solving in many areas. SARA comprises *scanning* to identify the problems, *analyzing* as a means to study the problem and identify potential solutions, *responding* by using methods tailored to address the specific problem, and assessing problem-solving success through evaluation methods. Clearly, this model can be applied to civil rights issues as illustrated in several of the examples discussed later in this chapter.

The Evolution of Community Policing in a Post-9/11 Era

In the wake of the terrorist attacks of September 11, 2001, many analysts and observers have expressed concern about the future of community policing. When properly and fully implemented, community policing efforts can be time-consuming and resource intensive. Community policing and associated problem-solving strategies are, as political science Professor Wesley Skogan has suggested, difficult to sustain. He notes that they require "a great deal of training, close supervision, strong analytic capacity, and organization-wide commitment."[3]

Some community policing advocates fear that, in response to terrorism, police departments may feel that they have less time and fewer resources to devote to community policing efforts. On a practical level, departments are stretched to meet the new demands that confronting terrorism imposes including prevention, protective patrol, and preparedness. Challenges to maintain these efforts have become more acutely pronounced during times of shrinking municipal, state, and federal budgets and as police ranks and candidate pools are reduced through military call-ups to support war efforts. In response, some law enforcement agencies may feel the need to resort to a heavier reliance on, some may say retreat to, reactive strategies.

Sustaining Community Outreach and Engagement

Many community policing advocates, however, have become ever more assertive about the critical role of community policing in the aftermath of September 11. These advocates argue that community policing philosophies and strategies actually can enhance antiterrorism efforts and intelligence gathering. Director Carl R. Peed of the COPS Office suggests that as departments seek out the most effective ways to combat terrorism they will embrace community policing strategies:

> Since September 11, many state and local law enforcement agencies have sought new and effective methods of protecting our country's cities and counties, and have come to realize that community policing is more important now than ever before. Community policing encourages collaborative partnerships, employs problem-solving strategies, engages the community in its own protection, and requires organizational change within law enforcement to support effective decision making and efficient operations. Community policing can assist law enforcement agencies identify and respond to public concerns about terrorism, and help provide vital insight into a community's vulnerabilities and needs.[4]

While Director Peed underscores the effectiveness of community policing strategies for combating terrorism generally, others specifically emphasize the role community policing can play to enhance localized intelligence gathering. Decentralized management and accountability, as well as assignment of officers to specific beats on a more permanent basis, can result in stronger, more trusting relationships with the community. These relationships, in turn, can translate into greater vigilance—or extra eyes and ears—in reporting suspicious behavior and in enhancing intelligence-gathering efforts. As Drew Diamond, a former police chief, and his colleague Bonnie Bucqueroux suggest:

> Our goal should…be to provide as many opportunities as possible for people to tell police what they know, without singling themselves out for retaliation….We want people from all walks of life to trust police enough to place the call, and we also need officers who will listen. Neither will happen if the police become an occupying army….If we are to maintain recent reductions in violent crime and uncover the terrorists living among us, while preserving the civil rights that make our society special, we must insist on community policing now more than ever.[5]

Recognizing what police can obtain from a trustful community in terms of leads and alerts to suspicious behavior is only one side of the coin. Community policing emphasizes mutually beneficial relationships. Furthermore, new community needs have arisen following the terrorist attacks. Ellen Scrivner, deputy superintendent of the Chicago Police Department and former deputy director of the COPS Office, provided the following reminder of what communities may now need from police in a post-September 11 era:

> "Community fears when crime was spiraling out of control pales in comparison to the fears of suicide bombers and chemical attacks that kill innocent people going about their everyday lives."[6]

The Prevalence of Community Policing

Given that there are many varieties and definitions of community policing, it should not be surprising that a precise tally of law enforcement agencies engaged in community policing is difficult to establish. According to the 2003 Law Enforcement Management and Administrative Statistics Survey (LEMAS) conducted by the Bureau of Justice Statistics, an overwhelming majority—94 percent—of law enforcement agencies with 100 or more full-time sworn officers indicated that they practiced community policing in some manner. Percentages varied according to the type of agency surveyed. Overall, 99 percent of municipal police departments with 100 or more sworn personnel with arrest power indicated that they implemented community policing in some manner. By comparison, 92 percent of county police departments, 89 percent of sheriffs' offices, and 82 percent (39 of 48 responding) of state police agencies indicated that they had addressed community policing in some manner. The numbers of tribal and regional police agencies included in the survey were too few to make reliable estimates.

Methodological Note on Bureau of Justice Statistics Law Enforcement Data

The Bureau of Justice Statistics (BJS) administers both a census and survey of law enforcement agencies, both conducted on a periodic basis, as part of its **Law Enforcement Management and Administrative Statistics** (LEMAS) program. The two most recent LEMAS efforts are the census conducted in 2000 and the survey conducted in 2003.

The Census of State and Local Law Enforcement Agencies provides a baseline tabulation of the nation's police agencies operating in the U.S. and contains basic information about personnel, operational capacity, technological capacity, key equipment, and policies and programs.

BJS administers the LEMAS survey every 3 or 4 years. This survey captures more detailed information than is captured through the census. The survey is targeted to all law enforcement agencies with 100 or more full-time equivalent sworn personnel, as well as a representative sample of smaller agencies. This sampling strategy results in a nationally representative sample of 2,859 agencies that represent the approximately the 18,000 publicly funded state and local law enforcement agencies (determined by the census) that operate on a full-time basis in the U.S.

The data presented in this guide are drawn from the 2000 census and 2003 survey. A subset of questions in the survey were only asked of agencies with 100 sworn officers, while others were asked of all sampled agencies regardless of size.

For the survey-based analysis and comparisons made in this and other chapters of the guide, readers should be aware that the number of responses for agencies with less than 100 sworn officers are based on randomly selected agencies. As a result of the BJS stratified–random

> sampling processes, however, these analyses provide scientifically reliable estimates when sufficient numbers are included in the categories compared. For some less common agency types (e.g., tribal police), too few agencies were included in the sample for reliable comparisons to be made across agency-size categories. More information on the survey methodology can be found on the BJS-LEMA web site (www.ojp.usdoj.gov/bjs/lawenf.htm).

The concept of community policing, of course, may be implemented in a variety of ways. The LEMAS survey allowed responding agencies to identify one of three ways in which they implemented community policing.[7] The most common form of implementation reported was a *specific community policing unit with full-time staff*. This accounted for 55 percent of responding agencies. The other two methods, each accounting for 19 percent of responses, were implementation by *dedicated community policing personnel* (but no unit) and by *other means*.[8]

In the LEMAS survey, prevalence of community policing implementation, as well as methods of implementation, varied by agency size. In general, the likelihood of implementation increased with agency size. And, while the clear majority of agencies (regardless of size) implemented some type of community policing, the method of implementation for municipal agencies and sheriffs' offices varied according to the size of the agency. These results are indicated in the charts below.

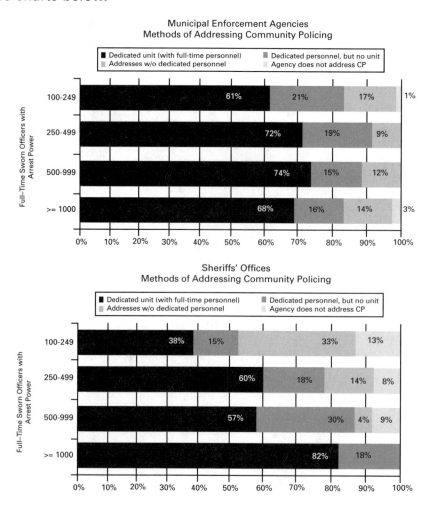

Sustaining Community Outreach and Engagement

While the LEMAS survey determined that the overwhelming majority of agencies report that they implement community policing in some manner, this self-reported index should not be interpreted as a definitive measure of the prevalence of community policing among the nation's law enforcement agencies. This response to the questionnaire says little about the depth of commitment or the degree to which community policing is institutionalized and internalized across the command structure and in operational contexts. The LEMAS survey itself, contains a series of other questions addressing community policing implementation and the prevalence of other components (e.g., use of problem-solving strategies and the citizen police academies) by which to assess variations in community policing in more detail. Any attempt to characterize a law enforcement agency's philosophical and organizational approach requires in-depth assessment.[9]

Promising Practices: Protecting and Promoting Civil Rights through Community Policing Strategies

The high prevalence of community policing reported among law enforcement agencies across the nation is an encouraging sign if one maintains that comprehensive community policing initiatives and civil rights protections are inseparable, as is a core tenet of this guide. Far from suggesting that community policing strategies can be applied mechanically or that that there is a single or most preferred way to implement community policing, however, this guide recognizes that implementation may vary widely. In the following sections, this chapter illustrates five strategies that are consistent with the core tenets of community policing. The programs used to illustrate these strategies are just a small sampling from among many successful implementations of community policing strategies that protect and promote civil rights.

Each of these programs illustrates the variety of ways that local agencies implemented community outreach strategies to fit local needs. Of course, the reader should realize that many of the examples are multifaceted. That is, they may address community policing and traditional policing strategies simultaneously. Moreover, the five strategies outlined here are not mutually exclusive. Indeed, most of the promising practice examples presented here simultaneously address several of these strategies.

Strategy One: Improving Police-Community Relations in Distressed Neighborhoods

Law enforcement leaders who have embraced community policing and problem-solving approaches recognize that partnerships are vital, yet not all communities have equal capacity to organize themselves. Many agencies have diverse jurisdictions, including some areas of affluence and other areas that are impoverished, run down, and lacking adequate resources. These latter areas are frequently those in which police presence is most critical, but in which police-community relations, unfortunately, have been most strained. Many police executives have recognized that they can take the lead in developing partnership strategies to reduce neighborhood stress, enhance the quality of life, and empower residents. Through these comprehensive outreach strategies, the police agencies are more likely to be perceived as partners and allies rather than indifferent bureaucrats, preservers of the status quo, or even "occupying forces." Through such strategies, police officers learn to work effectively with law-abiding residents—the overwhelming majority of residents in these areas—not only to reduce levels of victimization but also to improve the overall quality of life.

The following examples are only two of many such programs that have been successfully implemented across the nation.

Robert Hartley Housing Complex Project[10]

The Robert Hartley Housing Complex Project was initiated by the New Rochelle (New York) Police Department in the early part of 1999. This project, which is still in progress, began as the police and the community used the problem-solving technique of scanning to identify a six-block area as the area with the most recurring problems of concern to the public and the police. Comprising mostly municipal housing buildings, the area is centrally located in New Rochelle, the seventh largest city in New York with a population of 72,500.

Drug dealings, shootings, assaults, and robberies were prevalent in this area. As a result, residents not only experienced a good deal of fear, but made increased calls for police services. Regrettably, community members felt a pervasive distrust of the police on whom they relied. They perceived the police to be insensitive and lacking understanding of the needs of the community.

These circumstances were only complicated as the city of New Rochelle, always ethnically diverse, experienced population increases in Blacks and Hispanics. These increases resulted in racial tensions as the composition of neighborhoods altered. They also resulted in problems for police who addressed these tensions while managing increasingly complex police-community relations issues.

In March 1999, local clergy, community leaders, and the New Rochelle Police Department responded to the distrust of police and increasing racial tensions by partnering to create Citizens for a Better New Rochelle. Upon its formation, the group adopted the following mission statement:

"The police and community working together to provide a mutually respectful relationship through open lines of communication and cooperation."

Citizens for a Better New Rochelle consists of members from the New Rochelle Police Department, the clergy, the NAACP, the New Rochelle Municipal Housing Authority, the Youth Bureau, the City Council, the United Tenants Council, the Community Action program, and private citizens. With the Citizens for a Better New Rochelle in place, the police formulated a multifaceted response plan to deal with distrust and racial tension that included the following components:

- Training for a Neighborhood Watch Patrol
- Assignment of housing officers to patrol the area on foot
- Assignment of beat officers to patrol the area on foot and bicycle
- Assignment of Critical Incident Unit officers to park and walk patrol during hours of past criminal activity as well as to patrol Lincoln Park during summer basketball league
- Establishment of Community/Police Liaison Office to provide local residents with an immediate bridge to the department
- Involvement of department's community resources coordinator to provide crisis intervention services to residents experiencing serious family and personal problems through information referral and counseling.

The New Rochelle Police Department conducted an assessment by collecting pre-response and post-response data to determine whether their goals were being met. They determined that their project effectively and efficiently scanned, analyzed, responded and assessed (SARA) the recurring problems of distrust and racial tension. Their assessment also demonstrated that the police and the community attained the specified goals of the Robert Hartley Housing Complex Project.

Agency Profile: Population 72,500; Officers 179

Community Action Team [11]

In 1998, the El Paso (Texas) Police Department collaborated with various community and police organizations to form the Community Action Team. The Community Action Team works to decrease crime and improve the quality of life in El Paso. The purpose and the practices by which the team realizes this purpose are detailed in a mission statement on the programs web page and reproduced below. (www.elpasotexas.gov/police/yip_cat.asp):

Function: The mission of the Community Action Team is to work in partnership with the community, the police regional commands and various community agencies. Together, areas of high crime and quality-of-life issues will be identified and targeted to reduce the fear and incidence of crime, and restore the neighborhood's pride and commitment, while employing the department's community policing and problem solving tactics.

Strategies: The concept requires the establishment of a team, consisting of six officers and one sergeant. The team will work to resolve the crime and quality of life issues that exist within each predetermined neighborhood.

The duties of the team will extend well beyond an officer's normal duties. The concept requires the officers and supervisor to work as a team (with the community), identify crime indigenous to a neighborhood, and employ problem-solving tactics. In addition, the team will address the quality-of-life issues that are apparent and those that are brought to its attention by citizens or other sources.

The team will employ a wide-range of tactics to accomplish its objectives. The team must also remain flexible due to the various range of problems present in each of the targeted neighborhoods. For example: officers will conduct neighborhood surveys, speak with residents to determine their concerns and thoughts, conduct foot patrol in neighborhoods, identify new problems, conduct surveillance of suspected criminal activity, initiate community involvement through neighborhood watch and other community programs, and, where applicable, initiate the abatement process.

Agency Profile: Population 650,000; Officers 1,126

Strategy Two: Reaching Out to Engage Minority Communities

Strained relationships between minority communities and the police may seem, to some, as ubiquitous. Many police departments, however, have built bridges to diverse community groups through effective community policing strategies. While such outreach strategies are often associated with major urban cities, or particular distressed inner-city neighborhoods, many departments use a broader strategy recognizing that minority populations are themselves diverse in socioeconomic status, culture, religion, and other characteristics. The concerns of minority members in smaller or rural communities may be quite distinct, as is demonstrated in the following example.

Building Community Bridges[12]

In 2001, under the chief of police at the time, the Camillus (New York) Police Department started an outreach program called Building Community Bridges. The program was intended to improve access to the Camillus Police Department for minority groups and other segments of the population that felt their needs were not understood as thoroughly as the needs of other segments of the Central New York community.

In a bold and proactive effort, Chief Perkins and his department invited representatives of diverse groups directly into department planning sessions where they were given an excellent opportunity to have their concerns heard. Organizations such as the Onondaga Commission on Human Rights, the NAACP, the New York Civil Liberties Union, and the Inter-Religious Council of Central New York have attended these meetings as have elected officials from Camillus, the Spanish Action League of Syracuse, and the Syracuse Model Neighborhood Facility.

By bringing together all segments of the community—the residential population, visiting shoppers, and the commuting workforce—this effort is building a law enforcement agency of which the whole community is proud.

Agency Profile: Population 23,000 (Town of Camillus including Village of Camillus); Officers 19

Sustaining Community Outreach and Engagement

Strategy Three: Reaching Out to Engage Immigrant Communities

Although police may attempt to reach out to all groups within their community, they may not succeed in engaging all equally. Immigrant groups can be among the most difficult for police to engage because of the unique challenges they confront, including limited English proficiency. Police also may struggle to engage immigrant groups where a large number of group members are themselves struggling to overcome negative perceptions of the police that are the result of realities in their home countries. It is important for police to understand that many immigrants come from countries where police are perceived, often with good reason, as coercive agents of the government. These immigrants must first shed their inherent distrust of police before they can begin to appreciate the positive role that police may play in their new communities in this nation. Besides language and trust issues, challenges may be exacerbated by the lack of organizational capacity of recent immigrants and the existence of undocumented workers. While it may seem nearly impossible for law enforcement agencies to forge significant partnerships with these groups, successful efforts are becoming more common.

Dedicated and concentrated effort by police can win the trust of immigrant groups. Departments that have proactively reached out to immigrant communities through language immersion and cultural awareness programs have begun to build partnerships that departments that expect immigrant groups to take part in police programs or services of their own initiative will never realize. The following examples illustrate how several departments have organized to respond to the needs of immigrants. In one example, a department found success in reaching out to multiple immigrant communities spread over a wide geographic area by establishing a specialized unit. In another department, the agency responded to a need that they identified for a particular immigrant group.

International Relations Unit[13]

In 2000, the Charlotte-Mecklenburg (North Carolina) Police Department established the International Relations Unit to serve as the department's liaison when dealing with issues associated with the international community. The ultimate goal was to enhance the quality of life within the international community in Charlotte-Mecklenburg. This program consists of the following key components and principles:

Mission Statement

The International Relations Unit (IRU) of the Charlotte-Mecklenburg Police Department is a countywide resource committed to improving the quality of life, reducing crime, and fostering mutual trust and respect with members of the international community.

Personnel

The IRU is composed of six full time officers and one sergeant who have fluency in a second language and or an understanding of a second culture. Currently, the IRU is composed of members who speak Spanish, Vietnamese, Laotian, and Thai. These officers facilitate communication and improve understanding between police and members of the International community.

Unit Priorities
- To assist the international community, patrol officers, and police detectives with finding solutions to problems and concerns
- To conduct training within the international community and public/private organizations to improve service and reduce the number of victims
- To conduct language and cultural awareness training within the police department
- To provide assistance with police investigations that affect the international community
- To use specialized training, expertise, and experience to improve relationships with the international community
- To participate in community events that directly affect the international community
- To assist with the recruitment of culturally diverse and bilingual officers
- To act as a liaison between the police department and the international community.

Agency Profile: Population 746,500; Officers 1520

Operacion Apoyo Hispano (Operation Hispanic Outreach)[14]

A surging Hispanic population posed a challenge to the Clearwater (Florida) Police Department. The Hispanics were hesitant to approach the police and many long-time residents were suspicious of their new neighbors. Those attitudes have changed thanks to a truly unique collaboration between the police department and the YWCA. The comprehensive program encompasses everything from crime concerns to social and economic opportunity for Hispanics. Housed in a city-owned building, the one-stop center has an active outreach component and provides immigration and child care services along with interpretation and victim advocacy. Hispanics now come forward and report crimes to the police, resulting in a number of successful prosecutions. In 1 year, more than 175 Hispanic residents received crisis intervention and counseling at the center.

Agency Profile: Population 109,000; Officers 264

Strategy Four: Helping Residents Understand Police Operations and Culture

Law enforcement agencies engaged in genuine and effective community policing regularly engage their officers in cultural awareness training to learn more about the particular communities they serve. As police better understand the cultures—the value systems, taboos, and social rituals—of the communities that they serve, they are able to interact more respectfully and effectively with individuals from those communities. By the same token, citizens can benefit from learning about their law enforcement organization that, in many ways, has a culture of its own. The formation of Citizen Academies has become an effective vehicle for achieving this goal. As explained the National Citizens Police Academy Association's web site:

> [A]gencies have formed Citizen Police Academy programs that create an expansion of their community based efforts. These programs are intended to open the lines of communication between the Community and the Police Department. Generally, the relationship between the police and the citizen is one of "love/hate". To the Citizen, it may frequently appear that the police are not doing their job or are exceeding their boundaries. By allowing citizens a firsthand look at what rules, regulations and policies the police follow, some of the misunderstanding may be alleviated. The objective of the Citizen Police Academy is not to train an individual to be a "Reserve Police Officer" but to produce informed citizens. The Citizens and Police Officers meet each other face to face in a neutral, friendly setting and each becomes a person to the other. In the past, citizens have simply seen a uniform, now they have an understanding about the person behind the badge.[15]

Sustaining Community Outreach and Engagement

As indicated in the following examples, many departments successfully tailor their citizen academies to particular populations, including youth groups or immigrant groups.

The Beaverton Police Department's Student Academy[16]

The Beaverton (Oregon) Police Department formed its Student Academy to provide high school students with a better understanding of law enforcement's role in society. Like many law enforcement agencies across the nation, the Beaverton Police Department had seen a decreasing amount of respect for authority among some of its younger residents. Children's ideas of what police officers do are more often based on what they see on television shows and in the movies than on actual positive interactions with police officers.

The Beaverton Police Department embraced the philosophy of community policing in 1993. As part of that effort, the Beaverton Police Department established a Citizens Academy as a tool to bring community members and law enforcement officers together. This program experienced great success. As a result, the department developed its Student Academy on similar ideals. Designed to reach out to young people, the Student Academy uses the strategies of communication, education, and hands-on experience.

Strategy #1 – Communication: The goal of the Student Academy is to break down barriers to communication by providing an opportunity for police and students to work together. It is difficult to build bridges with young people when their initial perception of law enforcement is negative. During the Student Academy, young citizens and officers are able to spend quality time together and learn more about each other.

Strategy #2 – Education: Students are educated on the need for proper procedures in law enforcement. These procedures are explained to students in order to combat the perception that police officers "pick on" them. Students are told what can happen to police officers, perpetrators, victims, or innocent bystanders when police procedures are not followed.

Strategy #3 – Hands-On Experience: Students attend mini workshops that provide them with basic education and hands-on experience with topics such as traffic, forensic science, and use of force. Students participate as well in simulated scenarios.

The Beaverton Police Student Academy is a positive forum for young citizens and police officers alike as it provides accurate information about the role of law enforcement.

Agency Profile: Population 80,000; Officers 117

Hmong Finish Course on Policing In Minnesota

The following Associated Press article regarding the success of the Hmong Course on Policing in St. Paul appeared in the *Minneapolis-St. Paul Star-Tribune* on March 31, 2005.

ST. PAUL (AP) -- Several Hmong residents completed a citizens academy designed to give them a better understanding of the police and how they do their jobs.

The graduates Wednesday, most of them Hmong community leaders, said their new understanding of the Police Department will help them resolve disputes within the community.

"This will really help us to learn the different departments in the police," said Bao Yang, who attended the academy with her husband.

A majority of the class members were from the Hmong 18 Council, the historical leaders of the Hmong community. The council represents each of the 18 Hmong family clans and typically resolves family disputes that arise from divorce, adultery, runaway children or domestic abuse.

St. Paul has one of the largest Hmong populations in the country.

The 11-week academy, not an accredited law enforcement course, is free to anyone aged 21 or older.

Police Chief John Harrington said the graduates may now qualify to serve on the Police Community Internal Affairs Commission, which currently does not have a Hmong member.

Some of the graduates said they appreciated simply learning who the police were.

Vue Chu said he plans to begin a citizens patrol in his East Side neighborhood. Brandon Moua said he wants to enter the police academy.

While the students were learning, they taught police officers a few things about the Hmong 18 Council, said Sao Lee, of St. Paul, who attended the academy with his wife.

"They didn't know how the Hmong 18 Council works, so now (the relationship) is much closer," he said.

Agency Profile: Population 275,000; Officers 579

Strategy Five: Cooperative Approaches to Addressing Racial Profiling Concerns

One of the reasons that law enforcement agencies have embraced community policing strategies is because they realize that they can be more efficient and effective by working cooperatively with the community rather than working alone. Increasingly, police departments are adopting this same principle as they strive to deal with the issue of racial profiling. One such strategy is described below.

Addressing Racial Profiling through Building Trust[17]

Enhancing trust between the citizens of Wichita, Kansas and the Wichita Police Department has been an aspiration of the department since its transition to a community policing philosophy in the mid 1990s. A desire to proactively address the issue of racial profiling and community concerns about race-based policing led the Wichita Police Department to undertake the Building Trust Initiative.

In May 2000, the Wichita Police Department joined with the community to develop a comprehensive plan to address the issue of racial profiling. From the beginning, it was apparent that the term "racial profiling" did not adequately describe the community's concerns. The core issue was trust. Using the SARA model, the department relied on its philosophy of community involvement in problem solving.

The Kansas Region of the National Conference for Community and Justice served as the community facilitator to gather community input on the initiative's three major components: collecting data on traffic and pedestrian stops, increasing the ease and opportunities for community members to voice their concerns about police activity, and developing cultural diversity and customer service training for all members of the department.

As a result, the department integrated committee recommendations and the analysis from its stop study—composed of 37,000 traffic and pedestrian stops—to promote a change in departmental police culture. Innovations included revising the traffic stop policy, simplifying and publicizing the citizen complaint process, creating a regulation on racial profiling, designing and implementing training on customer service and cultural diversity, and diversifying recruiting practices.

The Building Trust Initiative has resulted in positive, sustainable change. Racial profiling complaints have dropped significantly from 2001 to the present. Trust relationships have grown and positive organizational change has occurred because policies, practices, and training now reflect the department's core values. Citizens accurately perceive that the Wichita Police Department is truly community oriented and is not afraid to examine its organization for potential weaknesses. The Building Trust Initiative has created a model to address racial profiling issues that can be easily replicated by other law enforcement agencies.

The Building Trust Initiative has not come to its final conclusion. Strategies to sustain changes and to measure ongoing success include the collection and analysis of a second set of data on pedestrian/traffic stops (2004), a critical review of the state of Kansas's racial-profiling study, continued customer service training for new employees, and a review of professional standards complaints regarding racial profiling. While pleased with the outcomes of its Building Trust Initiative, the Wichita Police Department recognizes that the issue of race-based policing requires constant vigilance.

Agency Profile: Population 380,000; Officers 646

Conclusion

This chapter has asserted that law enforcement agencies that adopt community policing philosophies and that use the types of strategies highlighted in this chapter can better succeed in their critical mission of protecting and promoting civil rights. This is not intended to suggest that community policing is a panacea or that law enforcement agencies that do not officially embrace community policing are not able to ensure that they enforce the law while protecting civil rights. Building bridges throughout the community that a law enforcement agency serves, under any philosophical banner, is a critical cornerstone of protecting civil rights. These efforts, of course, can be made stronger by systematic analysis and adoption of a problem-solving approach. While customer-service orientations embraced by departments are highly valuable, they must be reinforced by the types of policies, training, practices, and accountability tools discussed in the rest of this guide.

Suggestions for Further Reading

Many publications addressing community policing exist in the literature. More information about those supported through the U.S. Department of Justice Office of Community Oriented Policing Services can be found at www.cops.usdoj.gov/Default.asp?Item=118.

A short list of resources relevant to community policing and its nexus with the enhancement of mutual respect and the protection and promotion of civil rights are listed below.

Davies, Heather J., and Gerard R. Murphy. Protecting Your Community From Terrorism: Strategies for Local Law Enforcement – Volume 2: Working with Diverse Communities. Police Executive Research Forum, Washington, DC; 2004.

Ethics Toolkit: Enhancing Law Enforcement Ethics in a Community Policing Environment presented by The International Association of Chiefs of Police and the U.S. Department of Justice Office of Community Oriented Policing Services. www.theiacp.org/profassist/ethics.

Khashu, Anita, Robin Busch, and Zainab Latif. Building Strong Police-Immigrant Community Relations: Lessons from a New York City Project, Vera Institute of Justice, New York, NY; 2005. www.cops.usdoj.gov/mime/open.pdf?Item=1576.

Peed, Carl R. Making a Mark: Police Integrity in a Changing Environment. Police Executive Research Forum, Washington, DC; 2002. www.cops.usdoj.gov/mime/open.pdf?Item=781.

Scrivner, Ellen. Mutual Respect in Policing: Lesson Plan. Police Executive Research Forum, Washington, DC; 2006. Including VHS tape @ 22:47 minutes.

Endnotes

1. Gruber, Charles. "A Chief's Role in Prioritizing Civil Rights." The Police Chief. November 2004 Available on web at www.policechiefmagazine.org/magazine and selecting "Archive."
2. What is Community Policing. November 2000. Office of Community Oriented Policing Services. Retrieved on November 1, 2005 from www.cops.usdoj.gov/default.asp?Item=36.
3. Skogan, Wesley, and Lynn Steiner. CAPS at Ten: Community Policing in Chicago; An Evaluation of Chicago's Alternative Policing Strategy. Chicago/Evanston IL: Chicago Community Policing Evaluation Consortium, 2004.
4. Peed, Carl. "Applying Community Policing Principles Post 9/11." Making a Mark. Introductory Letter. January 16 2003. Retrieved November 1, 2005 from www.cops.usdoj.gov/mime/open.pdf?Item=780.
5. Diamond, Drew and Bonnie Bucqueroux. Community Policing Is Homeland Security. policing.com. October 30, 2005. Available on the web at www.policing.com/articles/terrorism.html.
6. Scrivner, Ellen. "Building Training Capacity for Homeland Security: Lessons Learned from Community Policing." The Police Chief October 2005. www.policechiefmagazine.org/magazine select "Archive."
7. For this question, "community policing" was part of a list of programs and tasks. For each task, respondents were requested to answer, "How does your agency address the following problems/tasks?" Response categories for all programs and tasks were the same. The response selections were: (1) "Agency HAS specialized unit with FULL-TIME personnel to address this problem/task" or, under the general heading of " Agency DOES NOT HAVE a specialized unit with full-time personnel" choices were (2) "Agency has dedicated personnel to address this problem/task," (3) "Agency addresses this problem/task, but does not have dedicated personnel," or (3) "Agency does not address this problem/task" (emphases in original).
8. "Other means" may include a broad diversity of implementation strategies. The use of this response by the Chicago Police Department provides an illustrative example. Chicago is recognized widely as having an ambitious community policing strategy. Rather than making community policing the task of a particular unit or designated personnel, the department expects community policing to be the responsibility of every officer. Other survey respondents who also have indicated that they implement community policing trough "other means" do not necessarily follow the Chicago model.
9. See for instance McGuire, Edward R. Organizational Structure in American Police Agencies: Context, Complexity, and Control. Albany, NY: SUNY Press, 2003.
10. This program was an applicant in the 2002 IACP Webber Seavey Award for Quality in Law Enforcement and an applicant for the Herman Goldstein Award for Excellence in Problem Oriented Policing, also in 2002. Text is derived from the Webber Seavey program abstract.
11. This program received the Herman Goldstein Award for Excellence in Problem Oriented Policing in 2000, was a finalist for the 2001 IACP Webber Seavey Award for Quality in Law Enforcement, and was an applicant in the 2002 Innovations in American Government Program. More information on this program is available at www.innovations.harvard.edu and on the department's web site at www.eppd.org
12. Perkins, Lloyd, and Thomas Winn. "Crime Prevention and Community Programs: Building

Bridges." <u>The Police Chief</u> October 2005. The text was adapted from the article.

[13] The text above was obtained from the programs web page at www.ci.charlotte.nc.us/Departments/Police/Crime+Info/International+Relations/Home.htm. The publication "Law Enforcement Services to a Growing International Community." The manual is available on CMPD's web site at www.cmpd.org and the North Carolina Governor's Crime Commission's web site at www.ncgccd.org.

[14] This program was a semifinalist for the IACP 2005 Weber Seavey Award for Quality in Law Enforcement. The text was adapted from the award publication available on the web at www.theiacp.org/awards/webber/2005WSAbstracts.pdf.

[15] "Frequently Asked Questions." The National Citizens Police Academy Association (NCPAA). Retrieved November 15, 2005 from www.nationalcpaa.org/faq.htm

[16] This program was a semifinalist for the IACP 2003 Weber Seavey Award for Quality in Law Enforcement. The text was adapted from the award publication available on the web at www.motorola.com/governmentandenterprise/contentdir/en_US/Files/General/WebberSeavey2003Winners.pdf.

[18] This program was an applicant in the 2003 IACP Weber Seavey Award for Quality in Law Enforcement. The text was adapted from the award submission submitted to the IACP.

III. Developing an Early Intervention Strategy

DEVELOPING AN EARLY INTERVENTION STRATEGY

> The costs associated with hiring and training a police officer run in the thousands of dollars. It is in the officer's and our best interest to intercede when an officer is struggling personally or professionally. Without early intervention, we risk losing personnel from our ranks that we might well have been able to keep with intervention.[1]
>
> James Hussey, Chief of Cohasset (Massachusetts) Police Department

Introduction

When carefully designed and implemented, early intervention systems can benefit individual officers, police departments, and the community. Increasingly being integrated into broader personnel assessment or risk-management systems, early intervention management strategies provide a means of identifying officers who may be headed for trouble. This strategy offers a crucial opportunity to intervene on behalf of these officers, their departments, and their communities. At the individual level, early intervention can save officers' careers and potentially save lives. Police departments justifiably devote considerable resources and offer extensive training to prevent on-duty deaths and injuries. Nevertheless, at least twice as many law enforcement officers are lost each year to suicide as are killed in the line of duty.[2] Properly implemented early intervention strategies can provide the assistance that officers working in a highly stressful profession urgently may need.

Individual officers, police departments, and their communities benefit when departments succeed in addressing the factors that contribute to officers' risk for errors in professional judgment, alcohol abuse, and suicide as well as other personal and professional problems. To be fully effective, early intervention must be accepted by officers, supervisory personnel, and communities as an important alternative and complement to disciplinary systems. Through early intervention policies and practices, departments benefit from proactive prevention and actually reduce the need for reactive discipline. When well designed, early intervention programs stress positive performance. The same focused supervisory techniques used to identify the first signs of a problem can also be used to identify and encourage officers whose performance is markedly above average. Communities benefit from a law enforcement agency that has enhanced its commitment to accountability, both internal and external.

Chapter Overview and Objectives

This chapter offers a working definition of early intervention, in part, by drawing on information about early intervention from federal consent decrees and memorandums of agreement (MOA) as well as from promising and innovative early intervention efforts from police departments throughout the nation. It explores a range of practices commonly associated with early intervention and addresses both its benefits and its challenges.

This chapter acknowledges that, much like CompStat and problem-oriented policing, early intervention is a data-driven management strategy. Early intervention efforts are only as effective as the information that is gathered and the managers who use it. The most technologically sophisticated early intervention systems will be severely compromised if data that inform decisions are not collected systematically and if managers are not motivated and trained to take advantage of this tool. Although more and more departments are using early intervention systems, clear data standards and uniform practices have yet to be established.

This chapter deliberately considers early intervention within the context of police departments' other operations. Early intervention efforts do not exist in a vacuum. They must be considered in a broad context, i.e., as part of an integrated agencywide management approach. Early intervention must be coordinated with many areas of police practice. It must be deployed in ways that are consistent with department policies, field operations, supervisory practices, personnel practices, data management practices, and community outreach strategies.

Finally, this chapter argues that early intervention is cost-effective. Although early intervention requires a considerable commitment of department resources and personnel, its effectiveness in identifying indicators of risk among police officers is being demonstrated in a growing number of departments. While the sheer number, variety, and complexity of early intervention systems prohibit a precise cost-benefit analysis at this time, many departments are recognizing that the short-term costs of implementing early intervention, though significant, are less than the long-term costs they will incur without such a system in place.

A Definition of Early Intervention

Early intervention refers to a series of interrelated personnel management processes that help supervisors identify, assess, and evaluate employees' performance for the purposes of addressing potential concerns in a timely manner. Early intervention allows supervisors to address problems in officers' performance before these problems escalate to the point of requiring disciplinary action. Samuel Walker, professor of criminal justice at the University of Nebraska Omaha specializing in police accountability, defines early intervention systems as the "systematic collection and analysis of data on officer performance for the purpose of identifying problems that need to be corrected."[3]

The Evolution of Early Intervention

Early intervention strategies are continually evolving. Paralleling the development of improved management techniques and technological innovations across all operational areas of law enforcement, early intervention strategies are becoming more prevalent and more sophisticated. Leading examples of early intervention systems include those at the Los Angeles County Sheriff's Department, the Miami-Dade Police Department, the Phoenix Police Department, and the Pittsburgh Bureau of Police.[4] While all four of these model systems are located in large departments, law enforcement agencies of various sizes and various jurisdictions—municipal, county, state, and special—are now adopting early intervention systems and tailoring them to meet their own needs.

The spirit of early intervention is similarly evolving. Initially, many early intervention systems were designed primarily to detect, and even remove, officers who constituted a risk to their department. Now, these systems tend to be more far-reaching and refined. Today's early intervention systems are designed to identify—at the first sign of a potential problem—officers who might benefit from assistance in the form of counseling, retraining, and other forms of nonpunitive intervention. In this way, early intervention is realizing the vision of those forward-thinking law enforcement leaders who first recognized the value of nonpunitive approaches to promoting police integrity and spearheaded some of the first early intervention efforts.

Indeed, many departments are expanding their use of early intervention systems to identify and reward exemplary officers. The same data systems and management techniques that allow departments to identify officers who may benefit from nonpunitive intervention allow departments to identify officers who are exemplary performers. Early intervention systems may be used to identify an officer who, for example, may be working on highly active and risky details such as drug or gang interdiction units where suspect complaints are commonplace, but who receives very few citizen complaints or use-of-force citations. Departments are also using early intervention systems to identify officers who receive public commendations or awards.

Early intervention systems are expanding in other ways as well. Many departments are using early intervention to enhance management and performance assessment of nonsworn personnel.

> **Early Intervention: Terminology with a Purpose**
>
> The terms "early intervention," "early warning," "personnel assessment," and "risk management" are often used interchangeably for early intervention systems. The federal consent decrees and MOAs generally refer to "early warning" or "risk management" systems or adopt the name of the specific system that was in use in the jurisdiction at the time of the agreement, e.g., The Personnel Performance Management System by the Washington, D.C., Metropolitan Police or TEAMS II by the Los Angeles Police Department.
>
> When discussing specific systems, this guide, like the consent decrees and MOAs, uses the term used by the specific agency. When discussing these systems generally, however, this guide uses the term "early intervention" exclusively. As Samuel Walker suggests, the term "early intervention" better conveys the nondisciplinary and corrective characteristics of these systems while the term "early warning" has connotations that appear more ominous to police personnel.[5] An early intervention process based on objective screening and careful supervisory assessment followed by intervention strategies chosen to meet the specific needs of an individual officer is consistent with a management philosophy that advocates professional development and assistance over management based solely on compliance and punishment.
>
> Terminology can make a major difference. Relying on the term "early intervention" instead of "early warning" is a better reflection of the true aim of these systems and may help impart a less threatening image to personnel and police unions.

The Prevalence of Early Intervention

There is some difficulty in determining the prevalence of early intervention strategies in law enforcement agencies. Part of the problem is that most of the attention has been paid to discussing the front end of the system—data collection and setting thresholds—and little attention to the back end—the role of supervisors in contextually assessing indicators and determining interventions. Consequently, the assumption remains that early intervention systems are by definition computerized. A broader definition might reveal that many more departments, particularly smaller departments, are engaging in early intervention systems in their day-to-day practices without the benefits (or the need) for computerized system.

Results from the 2003 Sample Survey of Law Enforcement Agencies (LEMAS) conducted by the Bureau of Justice Statistics provide an opportunity to assess the prevalence of *computerized* early intervention systems. Only departments with 100 or more sworn personnel with arrest powers were asked about such a system.[6] Details about LEMAS methodology and data are in the text box on page 31 in Chapter 2.

LEMAS results revealed that 32 percent of municipal departments and 22 percent of sheriffs' offices of that size reported having computerized early intervention systems in 2003. Approximately 33 percent (16 of 48) responding state police agencies and approximately 56 percent (18 of 32) of county police agencies reporting having such a system.

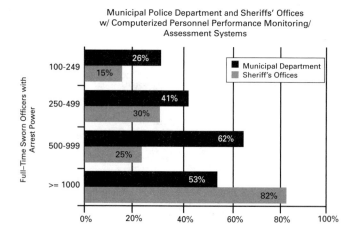

The graph presented here illustrates findings across municipal police departments and sheriffs' offices by agency size. Among municipal police departments and sheriffs' offices, the likelihood of an agency having a computerized early intervention system generally increased with size. Except for the largest category, early intervention systems are more common in municipal departments than in sheriffs' office of similar size.[7]

The Benefits of Early Intervention

When properly implemented and managed, early intervention offers numerous benefits to law enforcement agencies. The benefits associated with early intervention include the following:

- Enhancing police integrity
- Promoting a culture of accountability and reconciling the ideals of internal and external accountability
- Emphasizing the department's commitment to ethical policing
- Decreasing reliance on negative sanctions and punitive actions

- Providing supportive intervention to sustain, revive, and advance individual careers
- Supporting and increasing efficiency of first-line supervisors
- Promoting clearer and more consistent communication between supervisors and subordinates across the organization
- Improving staff retention, thereby limiting the costs associated with staff turnover and lost investments in recruitment and training
- Increasing overall management efficiency
- Improving officer morale
- Decreasing liability and costs of civil suits associated with misconduct and use of force
- Enhancing community relations, particularly when community generated data are made part of the early intervention system
- Reinforcing problem-oriented policing (POP) approaches for both internal and external problems
- Underscoring the department's commitment to information and data-driven management strategies.

Core Principles of Early Intervention

Although early intervention systems vary in scope and complexity according to agencies' size, mission, and management priorities, three core principles are critical to successful early intervention.

1. Effective early intervention identifies potentially problematic behaviors in individual officers rather than identifying and removing problematic officers.

Successful early intervention proactively identifies and addresses precursors to misconduct rather than imposing sanctions for actual misconduct. As the expression "early intervention" implies, these systems seek to recognize potentially problematic behaviors early on, when nondisciplinary, corrective actions will have the greatest likelihood for success. When early intervention systems indicate a need for intervention, these systems seek to problem-solve with the goals of redirecting and enhancing an officer's performance, rather than isolating or ostracizing that individual for the purposes of discipline or termination.

> The Gladstone (Missouri) Department of Public Safety emphasizes the necessity for identifying problematic behaviors early on in order to ensure a problem-oriented versus a person-oriented approach in its description of the "Personal Early Warning System":
>
> The Personnel Early Warning System [is] a time-sensitive system effectively designed to organize critical performance and evaluation data in a format conducive to promptly identify early indicators of certain performance and/or stress related problems and to facilitate any necessary or appropriate follow-up activities.
>
> Source: Gladstone (Missouri) Department of Public Safety's Policy Manual
> Agency Profile: Population 23,246; Officers 42

Developing an Early Intervention Strategy

Through such an approach, early intervention not only assists individual officers, but also benefits an entire agency by sending the message that positive reinforcement, professional development, and education are favored over negative sanctions. To send this message unequivocally, management must emphasize and ensure that early intervention focuses on detecting problematic *behaviors* in officers rather than identifying, labeling, and weeding-out problematic *officers*. This latter task should remain the function of the disciplinary system, which ideally would be used as a last resort only if early intervention fails.

2. Effective early intervention depends on the collection of relevant data and the use of that data in decision making.
Many law enforcement departments have embraced data-driven strategies—including problem-solving and CompStat-style management—to fight crime and maintain public order. Early intervention is predicated on the same commitment to data-driven management. Prudent police managers recognize the power of data-driven management practices in improving public safety. They are now recognizing that these same strategies can be focused inward to improve personnel performance and integrity and to manage risk.

While it is critical that departments demonstrate a commitment to the collection of relevant data and the use of that data in decision-making processes, early intervention systems do not require sophisticated information technology systems. Small and medium-sized departments can achieve the same objectives as larger, more technologically advanced agencies by relying on consistent and comprehensive record-keeping practices. The federal MOA between the Department of Justice and the Villa Rica (Georgia) Police Department indicates that early intervention can succeed even when a computerized database is not used:

> The VRPD [Villa Rica Police Department] shall develop a formal system to monitor officer conduct. This system shall include information on investigations, complaints (including civil lawsuits), uses of force, training histories, supervisory reviews, and disciplinary and other corrective actions. The VRPD's system *need not be computerized*, but shall contain triggers set to detect behavior which raises concerns and requires supervisory review. The VRPD shall require supervisors to review the data regarding officers under their command on a regular basis, and should establish guidelines regarding the specific events that require additional supervisory review and consideration of corrective action.[8] (Emphasis added.)

While early intervention can succeed with or without sophisticated computerized systems, technology does provide the benefit of allowing supervisors to access large volumes of organized data by automating certain processes. For example, supervisors' direct observations of and interactions with officers may be augmented by reference to an early intervention database. In addition, department personnel may set specific criteria by which the database automatically indicates an individual officer as exhibiting potentially problematic behavior.

3. Effective early intervention requires strong and effective supervisory review.
Early intervention succeeds as thoughtful and thorough supervisors make appropriate use of the data at their command. Early intervention systems are only a tool, not a substitute, for strong and effective supervisors. The critical importance of supervision to successful early intervention efforts is emphasized in many department policies as well as in federal consent decrees and MOAs. The Rock Hill (South Carolina) Police Department explicitly identifies supervisors' responsibilities within its Personnel Early Warning System:

1. First and second level supervisors will familiarize themselves with their subordinates and routinely observe their demeanor, appearance, and conduct.
2. Supervisors will remain alert for indications of behavioral changes or stressors that may affect a Department member's performance.
3. When supervisors perceive or determine that a Department member has problems or is causing problems, they will assess the situation and take appropriate action in accordance with this general order and the other policies and procedures of the Department, including referral to the City Employee Assistance Program or a police chaplain, informal counseling by a supervisor, and other remedial action.

Source: Rock Hill (South Carolina) Police Department General Orders Manual
Agency Profile: Population 50,000; Officers 107

Under the consent decree of the Detroit Police Department, the department is required to develop a "Review Protocol" for commanders and supervisors using the department's Risk Management System. The consent decree requires that commanders and supervisors "promptly review records of all officers recently transferred to their sections and units" and further stipulates that commanders and supervisors "be evaluated on their ability to use the risk management system."[9]

Law enforcement executives can increase the likelihood that these systems will be effective and accepted if they ensure that early intervention occurs in a preventive, timely, and problem-oriented (versus reactive) manner that it is data-driven and is seen as a tool (rather than a substitute) for good supervision.

Basic Components of Early Intervention Systems

The fact that the scope and complexity of early intervention systems and their associated administrative features vary widely by agency and the fact that these systems are constantly evolving make a thorough review of early intervention systems challenging. Nevertheless, the basic components of these systems are identifiable. These components receive detailed discussion in the early intervention policies of individual police departments, the language of the consent decrees and MOAs, and the professional and academic literature describing these systems.

The following discussion presents the basic components of early intervention systems and provides an overview of these components as documented by agencies and in the language of consent decrees and MOAs.

Indicators: The Foundation of Early Interventions Systems

Early intervention systems are built on a foundation of performance indicators that are believed to be indicative of potentially problematic behavior. While early intervention systems vary widely because of the number and scope of performance indicators used, the most commonly included indicators are citizen complaints, use-of-force reports, and firearm discharges. Although performance indicators are the foundation of early intervention systems, very little assessment of the relative strengths and weaknesses of the various indicators in predicting risk have occurred. To date, there is little standardization of which indicators should be used, but there is growing interests among agencies to share experiences as the use of these systems continues to evolve.

As early intervention systems become more prevalent and more sophisticated, the number of indicators is growing. Today, early intervention systems commonly include incidents of resisting arrest, instances of civil litigation, vehicle pursuits, accidents/vehicle damage, sick days, and secondary employment as performance indicators. Some early intervention systems are even incorporating more particularized indicators to predict risk. For instance, while many departments simply specify use-of-force incidents as an indicator, others count only use-of-force incidents that exceed a certain level of force or consider use-of-force ratios that statistically account for variations in arrest activity. Similarly, while many departments merely tabulate sick days and then assess them against fixed-threshold or department-wide standards, others specifically flag sick days that are contiguous to vacations or holidays for greater scrutiny.

The following text box lists the performance indicators used in the Phoenix Police Department's Personnel Assessment System (PAS) and the Pittsburgh Police Bureau's Performance Assessment Review System (PARS). The performance indicators used in these systems are among the most comprehensive in the nation. Both systems can be used to identify officers exhibiting behaviors indicative of risk. Both systems can also be used to identify officers who are exemplary performers because their performance indicators include commendations and citizen compliments. Finally, it is important to note that, for both systems, many of these performance indicators are not indicators per se, but sources of information that are used for contextual reference. For instance, both the Phoenix and Pittsburgh systems track arrests as an indicator although a mere count of arrests is not indicative of any risk. Rather, the number of arrests can be used to put other indicators in context (e.g., use-of-force ratios relative to activity such as arrests, field interrogations, or citations).

Indicators Tracked by the Phoenix Police Department's PAS[10]

- Assignment history
- Discipline
- Employee use of force
- Firearms qualification data
- Suspect use of force
- All O.T. worked and % paid & held
- All citizens, supervisory, & PSB employee requested notes
- Complaints
- Police accidents
- Refer to driving analysis
- Interrogations
- Significant event radio codes from CAD
- Industrial Injuries
- Use-of-force ratios
- Industrial exposures
- Department reports
- Training records
- Employee summary report
- Leave time history & balances
- PAS contact information
- Police Shootings
- Employee photo
- Work-hour summary
- Threshold summary report
- Arrests
- Employee assistance options
- Discretionary arrest codes
- Peer support
- Citations, traffic & criminal
- Critical Incident Stress Team
- Pursuits
- Chaplains
- Internal audits
- Mental health professionals
- Off-duty work data
- 24/7 crisis lines
- Commendations, awards, & letters of appreciation

Indicators Tracked by the Pittsburgh Police Bureau's PARS[11]

- Accidents
- Arrests
- Counseling
- Civil claims
- Complaints
- Criminal investigations
- Discipline
- Lawsuits
- Missed court dates
- Traffic stops
- Weapons discharge
- Search and seizure
- Use of force
- Sick time
- Other absences (e.g., suspensions)
- Grievances
- Secondary employment
- Injuries
- Citations, traffic and criminal
- Pursuits
- Off-duty work data
- Discretionary arrest codes (false information, escape, resisting arrest, disorderly conduct, no identification)

Developing an Early Intervention Strategy

When departments rely on more comprehensive performance indicators, their ability to predict risk and identify exemplary performers may be enhanced, but there may also be an increased tendency for individual officers to be indicated as exhibiting potentially problematic behavior. As these data-driven systems expand, it is increasingly imperative to ensure strong and effective supervision. The existence of "indicated" behavior does not necessarily mean that potentially problematic behavior exists. Managers and supervisors must not fall into the trap of assuming that a complicated risk-indicator system, based on a sophisticated statistical algorithm, represents a magic formula that automatically and precisely determines risk. Both the Phoenix Police Department's PAS and the Pittsburgh Police Bureau's PARS rely on standardized statistical reports that are regularly reviewed by supervisors, but that also allow for ad hoc reporting and analysis. The need for the careful review of performance indicators by experienced and well-trained supervisors who assess information within the context of the precipitating event and the individual officer's career cannot be overstated.

Acting on Indicators: The Workings of Early Intervention Systems

Having established a foundation of performance indicators, early intervention systems succeed as supervisors respond to indications that officers may benefit from intervention. This process generally occurs in four steps. First, early intervention identifies officers who may require intervention. Second, early intervention requires a mandatory supervisory review to determine if intervention should occur. Third, early intervention requires supervisors to identify and implement the most appropriate form of intervention. Fourth, early intervention recommends post-intervention monitoring. Drawing, again, on consent decrees, MOAs, successful early intervention systems, and professional literature, the following discussion reviews the means by which various early intervention systems accomplish these steps.

Step One: Identifying Officers Who May Require Intervention

The first step for successful early intervention is to identify officers who may require intervention. Standard management practices across all agencies should ensure that supervisors remain continually aware of officers' behavior. Frequent—ideally daily—contact and periodic reviews of officer performance on a systematic basis should enable superiors to identify and direct increased attention to officers who are exhibiting potentially problematic behaviors or whose behavior does not appear to comply with agency expectations or standards maintained by their peers.

Early intervention offers the added advantage of augmenting supervisors' direct interactions and observations based on reference to an objective set of performance indicators. An individual department typically will organize these performance indicators according to a specified threshold. Whenever officers' behaviors reach this department-established threshold, supervisors review their records and assess officer performance to determine whether intervention is appropriate. A variety of thresholds are currently in use. For example, a threshold may be reached once a certain number of indicators—such as use-of-force incidents—occur over a certain period, such as 3 months. Other methods of using statistical thresholds may involve calculations that are more complex. This section will review the most prevalent types of early intervention thresholds.

Fixed Threshold Alerts

Fixed thresholds are the most straightforward. Fixed thresholds are reached whenever a certain number of indicators occur over a specified period. Below is a hypothetical version of text adapted from several early intervention system policy directives (which have since been updated).

> ### Early Intervention System Criteria
>
> Officers will be targeted for review by the early Intervention system if he or she is found to have an accumulated total of *four incidents* from the following categories *within a 6-month period* the officer's name will be placed on the early warning system review list for attention.
> 1. Vehicle pursuits initiated by officer.
> 2. Preventable vehicle accidents.
> 3. Uses of force determined NOT to be in compliance.
> 4. Citizen complaints filed.
> 5. Any instance of department discipline.

Most departments that implement these thresholds require that officers who meet a fixed threshold receive required mandatory supervisory review to determine if intervention is warranted.[12]

Point System Threshold Alerts

Compared to fixed thresholds, point system thresholds are a slightly more complex method of triggering mandatory supervisory review. In point systems, different performance indicators are given different point values. Officers are indicated for review when they reach a certain number of points within a specified period. The Greenville (South Carolina) Police Department uses a point system for specific performance indicators in its Personnel Early Warning System, as follows:

> Complaint = 2 points
> Disciplinary action = 2 points
> Use of force = 1 point
> Vehicle pursuit = 1 point
> Vehicle collision = 1 point
>
> Source: Greenville (South Carolina) Police Department's policy manual
> Profile: Population 56,000; Officers 184

Department thresholds are reached if an officer receives six points in a 3-month period or 20 points in a year.

Peer-Based Threshold Alerts

Peer-based thresholds acknowledge the reality that different officers are more or less likely to reach a fixed threshold or a point system threshold given their assignment. Officers working on a specialized gang or drug unit or in a high-crime district, for instance, are more likely to be the subjects of citizen complaints or experience more situations where use of force is warranted. Accordingly, peer-based thresholds are adjusted to acknowledge the risk inherent in officers' various assignments. Officers who are being assessed relative to a peer-based threshold, for instance, may be indicated if they are one standard deviation above the mean of their peers for specified performance indicators. Peers are defined by a variety of criteria. For example, an officer's peers may be defined as those working the same zone and same shift. As a result, these thresholds adjust for different risk levels associated with different assignments.

The Pittsburgh Police Bureau pioneered the use of early intervention peer-based thresholds when developing its *Performance Assessment and Review System* in response to the 1997 consent decree with the Department of Justice. In developing this peer-based threshold, Pittsburgh actually went well beyond the scope of requirements specified in the consent decree. Today, that system is a model for other departments, including many under federal consent decrees and MOAs. A Prince George's County (Maryland) Police Department *Consent Decree Status Report* specifically credits Pittsburgh's system as exerting a major influence over its system.[13]

Single-Event Threshold Alerts

As various thresholds become increasingly sophisticated, many departments still recognize that certain incidents should automatically indicate an officer for review. A mandatory supervisory review is in order whenever a death, whether of a suspect, bystander, or fellow officer, results from the actions of a police officer or whenever an officer uses force defined as deadly. The implication of such a review is not that the officer's behavior was necessarily problematic. Instead, a review is performed in recognition of the fact that deaths, injuries, or shootings that result from officers' actions are traumatic experiences for which counseling or other forms of intervention may be advisable.

Alerts not Based on Automated Threshold

The use of thresholds, which provide crucial alerts for mandatory supervisory review, is a key feature of early intervention systems. Departments that use early intervention, however, quickly recognize that intervention sometimes may be warranted before a threshold is reached. Supervisors should act when they observe signs of potential problems rather than waiting for a problem to manifest itself in statistically indicated behavior. Supervisors may be aware of stresses in officers' personal lives such as marital discord, illness, or problems with children. Supervisors may observe sudden changes in personality, such as when a normally quiet and reserved officer suddenly seeks out attention or when an outspoken officer appears unusually quiet. Such behavioral cues should be heeded as signs of problems that may affect an officer's performance or judgment on the job. These may be signs that the officer might later "act out," on or off the job, in career-ending ways. Department thresholds—no matter how extensive or nuanced—will not always alert supervisors to the myriad problems that officers may experience. Alert, conscientious, and diligent supervisors are the critical component in even the most technologically sophisticated early intervention strategy.

In the experience of the Phoenix (Arizona) Police Department, nonthreshold alerts have come from supervisors, peers, family members, and officers themselves. Supervisors in Phoenix see this as an encouraging trend suggesting that officers and their families recognize the Phoenix Police Department's PAS as a genuine effort to assist employees.[14]

Benefits of Timely Indicators
Early intervention can be most effective if it is administered in a timely manner. Thus, it deserves note that computerized early intervention systems can offer the additional advantage of generating an automatic notification whenever an officer has crossed a department-defined threshold. The sooner supervisors learn of potentially problematic behavior, the sooner they can review this behavior and take steps, if necessary, to prevent escalation. In many manual and some automated systems, agencies tabulate performance indicator data on a quarterly basis. This standard compromises the timeliness of early intervention efforts. Data recorded and reviewed in real time is the most useful. Departments with fully automated systems may alert supervisors as soon as an officer crosses a threshold. These automated alerts may take the form of briefing reports submitted to appropriate supervisors or automated e-mail notifications.

Step Two: Mandatory Supervisor Review for Indicated Officers
Once an early intervention system "indicates" an individual officer, most departments require a mandatory supervisory review to determine whether the indicated officer is, indeed, in need of intervention.

It is important to emphasize again that supervisors are making a critical decision at this point. The fact that an officer is indicated does *not* automatically mean that he or she is in need of intervention. While early intervention systems are an effective tool to indicate officers in need of intervention, legitimate police activity can and does indicate officers who do not require intervention. Indicated officers should not be projected in a prejudicial or negative light. Instead, supervisors must remember that indication is the first step in a multistep process and is not in itself determinative of the need for intervention. Supervisors must play the critical role in determining whether intervention is warranted.

Understandably, supervisors may prefer to err on the side of caution. Early intervention exists to identify and address potentially problematic behavior before escalation. Departments, however, must rely on a supervisor's experience and insight in determining if, in fact, there is need for intervention. Being indicated does not mean that intervention is imminent. Indeed, in certain circumstances, the decision not to intervene may be the appropriate decision.

While the review requirement is almost universal, there are no widely established criteria or precise protocols for performing this review. There should be absolute consensus, however, that supervisors play *the* critical role in the decision process. The computerized alert is simply a tool.

Developing an Early Intervention Strategy

Text from the Colorado Springs (Colorado) Police Department manual suggests the breadth of information and experience on which supervisors will need to draw:

> The analysis of the facts should include consideration of the totality of circumstances surrounding each incident and/or complaint, drawing on knowledge of human behavior, department polices and procedures, and the insight of the involved supervisors and managers.
>
> Source: Colorado Springs (Colorado) Police Department manual
> Agency Profile: Population 315,000; Officers 501

Indeed, supervisors' experience, training, and direct working knowledge of their officers at this stage of the process are especially critical. By considering the context in which the indicating events occurred, supervisors are best able to use their personal knowledge of the officer and his or her professional judgment of the officer's behavior to determine whether intervention is required. Department policies should identify factors that reviewing supervisors should consider in their decision regarding intervention. The following discussion investigates these factors.

<u>*Supervisors should ascertain whether the indicating events reflect a pattern or an isolated incident or incidents.*</u> Behaviors that reflect a pattern may require intervention where isolated incidents may not. For instance, an officer may have been indicated because of four citizen complaints within a 1-week period. Upon assessment, the supervisor may determine that all the complaints were generated by members of a family alleging that the office was rude to a specific person in the family, a person that the officer lawfully arrested. Noting that the officer has never had a citizen complaint for rudeness or for any other reason in his 5-year career, the supervisor may decide that no intervention is needed even though the indicator threshold was met.

<u>*Supervisors should determine whether there are links between the indicating events.*</u> Similar events may be indicative of underlying problems. A string of complaints in which an officers is alleged to have been using foul and discourteous language, may be related to personal problems the officer is experiencing. Seemingly dissimilar indicators may also have a common link. For instance, a supervisor may need to determine whether an inordinate use of sick days or missed courts dates are related to an officer's secondary employment.

<u>*Supervisors should consider the full context in which indicating events occur.*</u> In supervisors' efforts to assess an officer's behavior and performance, context is critical. Supervisors should always seek to determine if there are factors, including factors outside the department, contributing to an officer's behavior. For instance, an officer may be experiencing marital problems, a death in the family, or problems with children that influence work performance. Understanding the critical factors, both on and off the job, will help supervisors decide when to intervene and to tailor needed interventions to individual officers' needs.

Developing an Early Intervention Strategy

Supervisors should ascertain whether deficiencies in policies or training might have contributed to indicating events. In a thorough assessment of indicating events, a supervisor may determine that unclear policies or inadequate training contributed, in part or in whole, to the problem. Police work is remarkably complex; policies and training cannot anticipate every situation. If novel situations expose problems with existing policies or training, supervisors should respond by providing feedback to appropriate department personnel. If either unclear polices or inadequate training is a major contributing factor in indicating an officer, the supervisor may well decide that no intervention for that officer is needed.

Supervisors should determine what, if anything, should or could have been done differently to prevent the indicating events. Supervisors may prevent unfortunate events in the future by fully understanding how officers might have acted differently in the past. For instance, if an officer is indicated for crossing a use-of-force threshold or a single event threshold for excessive use of force, the supervisor should review how these situations might have been handled differently. If intervention is needed, discussing different ways of handling the situations may become an important part of that intervention.

Supervisors should document their reviews of indicated officers. Just as there are no widely established criteria or precise protocols for performing mandatory supervisory reviews, there are no hard and fast guidelines governing the documentation of these reviews. Some departments require formal written reports in which supervisors are required to respond with highly specific detail. Other departments are much less formal. Departments should determine what purposes the required documentation of reviews would serve. The requirements for the highly detailed, formally written reports used in the Early Intervention Program at the Colorado Springs Police Department follow:

> The report of the [Early Intervention Program] analysis will include a brief summary of the facts of each incident and/or complaint that qualified the employee for the EIP. This report should include the findings and conclusions based on the supervisor's analysis, as well as a recommended assistance. Suggested assistance may include, but is not limited to:
>
> 1. Assessment that no problem behavior exists.
> 2. Need for remediation or training.
> 3. Referral to the department psychologist for counseling or further referral to Employee Assistance Program [EAP].
> 4. Peer training/assistance.
> 5. Change of working environment.
> 6. Documentation of an approved performance plan.
>
> This performance plan will be designed to assess further and correct any identified performance concerns, and may include any or all of the above corrective measures. This performance plan may include progressive discipline for any failure to meet the stated requirements. In reference to use of force incidents, supervisors should address the following when documenting their review of the initial investigation:
>
> 1. Supervisor notification.
> 2. Photos taken of the suspect.
> 3. Detailed description of the suspect's actions.
> 4. Detailed description of the employee's actions.

5. Documentation of all employees involved.
6. Listing of all officers and witnesses present.
7. City of Colorado Springs listed as the victim in all resisting, interference, and obstructing cases.
8. Employee listed as the victim in all Assaults on a Peace Officer cases.
9. Statement of when/if resistance stops.
10. The employee's job assignment(s) during the reporting period.
11. The employee's Internal Affairs and Staff Resources Section records.
12. The number of arrests made during the reporting period.
13. Any other information or statistics that may be pertinent.

Final Review of EIP Analysis Report

The report, with the recommended assistance, will be completed by the officer's supervisor and presented to the involved Lieutenant. The Lieutenant will review the recommendation and provide any necessary insight and/or recommendation(s). The Division Commander will then review the summaries and provide any necessary insight and/or recommendation(s). The Division Commander will make the final decision on any recommended action as a result of an EIP Analysis Report. The original EIP Analysis Report will be delivered and maintained by the Office of Professional Standards, Internal Affairs Section, and a copy placed in the employee's EIP file. The completed EIP Analysis Report will be delivered to the Internal Affairs Section within thirty days of the initial notification that an employee has qualified for the EIP. The Division Commander of the affected employee will ensure that:

1. The employee is fully informed of the findings and disposition of this analysis.
2. All final recommendations are fully implemented.
3. A copy of this analysis may be retained in the employee's evaluation file.

Source: Colorado Springs Police Department Manual
Agency Profile: Population 315,000; Officers 501

Step Three: Selecting and Implementing Appropriate Intervention

When supervisors determine that intervention is warranted, they are given considerable leeway in deciding what form that intervention should take. Intervention ranges from the very informal, such as a discussion of the indicating event with a supervisor, to the more formal, such as a referral to psychological counseling, stress management, or substance abuse programs through a department's employee assistance program (EAP). The most common intervention options available for officers include the following:

- Training/retraining in specific problem area
- Transfer/reassignment
- Counseling
  o By supervisors
  o By peers
  o By mental health professional
- Alcohol/substance abuse counseling
- Referral to EAP.

While intervention options may vary from department to department, all interventions should share two characteristics. First, interventions should be designed to assist the officer in correcting the problem. Intervention must be undertaken with the goal of creating a response that will benefit the officer, the department, and the community in a proactive, not punitive, way. Second, interventions should be tailored to the needs of the individual. In contrast to the disciplinary process, early intervention is not intended to be a quid pro quo system. Two officers indicated for similar events (e.g., an inordinate number of use-of-force incidents when compared with their peers) may be experiencing different underlying problems. While retraining may be an appropriate intervention for one, the other may require retraining and counseling. Supervisors should expect that interventions could vary widely.

Step Four: Post-Intervention Monitoring

Precise protocols for post-intervention monitoring are as uncommon as they are for intervention itself. In this step, supervisors benefit from flexibility and informality as they monitor their officers. As with intervention, the success of post-intervention monitoring depends on the experience and skill of supervisors who may tailor their monitoring to the needs of the individual officer. During post-intervention monitoring, the supervisor's efforts should focus on the officer. For instance, if an officer is indicated because of three use-of-force incidents in a year, any subsequent use-of-force incident should be reviewed thoroughly. Increased supervision, including random roll-bys to observe the officer's performance in the field may also be warranted.

In addition to monitoring individual officers, supervisors must monitor their own success in managing early intervention efforts alongside disciplinary procedures and in sustaining the viability of the early intervention system in the minds of their officers.

<u>Supervisors should clearly understand the difference between early intervention strategies and disciplinary strategies and distinguish between the two. Supervisors should also expect monitoring of these efforts by their superiors.</u> Early intervention is meant to identify and address problematic behavior at its first appearance rather than waiting until disciplinary action is required. Wisely and increasingly, police executives are adopting early intervention

strategies because of their preventive benefits. Early intervention can ensure that officers are not punished for effective, active, and appropriately aggressive policing. It can also ensure that disciplinary action remains a tool of last resort. Still, early intervention does not supplant the appropriate use of discipline. Departments' policies must remain clear in recognizing that some behaviors require discipline and are best handled through the standard disciplinary process.

Departments using early intervention alongside their traditional disciplinary system are likely to see disciplinary proceedings take place for at least two reasons. First, disciplinary systems remain necessary in cases of alleged official misconduct and in instances when officers allegedly violate criminal law. This is the case in departments with or without early intervention. Second, disciplinary systems are necessary in cases in which early intervention was attempted but unsuccessful because an officer refused or was unable to comply. Ideally, the effective use of early intervention strategies will result in a corresponding decrease in disciplinary measures.

Police executives are ultimately responsible for ensuring that their departments achieve the proper balance between early intervention and traditional disciplinary protocols. The discretion granted to first-line supervisors under early intervention strategies is critical. It necessitates a heightened level of review by command staff to guard against misapplication, either intentional or unintentional. Supervisory decisions should be reviewed frequently and systematically by the chain of command to ensure that early intervention is not used in cases where discipline is mandated by a department's policies. Review procedures should also guard against the opposite: instances in which disciplinary procedures are used where early intervention is more appropriate.

Supervisors should monitor their efforts to preserve the credibility of early intervention.
Although it is now common practice for a department to keep early intervention strategies conceptually and operationally distinct from its disciplinary system, this does not obviate the need for employee safeguards when implementing early intervention. In keeping with ethical and professional personnel management practices, many departments adhere to standards of confidentiality and policies that promote employee access. Not only are these standards ethical, but they also can contribute to officers' confidence in early intervention.

Maintaining Confidentiality
Departments commonly specify that early intervention data files, whether electronic or manual, be held in confidence. Data is shared only with immediate supervisors and the chain of command directly involved in decisions regarding intervention. Supervisors should only be permitted to view data regarding officers serving beneath them in the chain of command. When formal reports or memorandums are issued as a result of supervisory review, departments generally treat these documents as confidential. The chief, however, may exercise discretion and make reports or memorandums available to appropriate supervisors for further review or when it serves the interests of the department.

Allowing Employee Access
Increasingly, departments also specify that officers' early intervention data be accessible to them. Accessibility offers several benefits. First, open access policies increase the transparency of the system and underscore the message that early intervention exists to assist

employees. Second, open access offers officers the opportunity to challenge or amend critical information used in early intervention, thereby providing an additional layer of checks and balances. Access may be given to both individuals who have been indicated and those who have not. The latter individuals may simply wish to know how close they are in coming to a threshold in order to take self-directed action to avoid being indicated.

Integration of Early Intervention Systems into Comprehensive Personnel Assessment Systems

Increasingly, law enforcement agencies are turning to personnel assessment or risk-management systems instead of more narrowly focused early intervention systems. These more comprehensive systems typically contain the elements of early intervention systems, but provide other personnel management functions as well. These systems track officer performance data (e.g., responses to calls for service, arrests, and citations issues) including indicators of positive, neutral, and negative connotation. Through standardized report procedures and ad hoc queries, such systems yield consistent and reliable measures of performance. Increasingly, departments are using these systems to inform and support a wide range of personnel issues. Many departments routinely and systematically will assess performance indicators anytime an officer is transferred, promoted, or reassigned. Such indicators can be of invaluable assistance to supervisors when they receive transferred officers. Also, broadly focused personnel assessment systems can be useful tools for annual performance assessments and promotional decisions. The fact that these systems are broad enough to capture positive, neutral, and negative data means that these systems are more likely to be accepted by rank-and-file officers. The fact that they are now often used to manage both sworn and nonsworn personnel may contribute to a sense that the system is more evenly applied and inherently fairer.

The Challenges of Complex Personnel Management Systems: Dealing with Data

The growth of early intervention systems and the development of more comprehensive personnel management systems require departments to manage increasing amounts of data. Fortunately, the need for effective data management parallels a greater reliance on data-driven strategies in policing generally. Data technology throughout law enforcement is increasingly comprehensive and sophisticated. More and more agencies are developing enterprisewide or gateway data solutions that make them more efficient in data-collection efforts while avoiding needless duplication.

In simple terms, a gateway data system draws information from discrete data systems in ways that are transparent to the user. For instance, rather than storing all indicator data on a database system dedicated exclusively to early intervention, a gateway system pulls relevant data from systems designed for other purposes. For instance, an early intervention system that tracks sick days and use-of-force incidents may rely on a gateway system that pulls sick day information from a centralized city database that keeps track of city employee timesheets and use-of-force data from a police department database maintained on an internal server.

Developing an Early Intervention Strategy

This same early intervention system may also pull data from the agency's records management system to determine the ratio of use-of-force incidents to felony arrests for a particular officer.

Consistent with this data integration approach, many departments treat their early intervention data as part of their broader data-collection system. For instance, the Pittsburgh Bureau of Police and the Phoenix Police Department both rely on gateway data systems for their early intervention efforts.

Identifying Exemplary Performers

Departments that capture positive, neutral, and negative data in their early intervention or personnel assessment systems have begun to rely on these indictors not only to identify officers in possible need of intervention, but also to identify exemplary performers. Recognizing and rewarding officers for exemplary performance can serve as an incentive for others, provide opportunities for peer mentoring, and reinforce the message that early intervention truly assists officers. The Pittsburgh Bureau of Police relies on PARS to assess which officers are worthy of promotions as well as to decide whether to accommodate officer-initiated requests for duty transfers or outside training. For instance, if a patrol officer requests a transfer to the traffic division, PARS can be queried to determine whether that officer made traffic stops a priority as a patrol officer and whether the officer performed satisfactorily in these duties (e.g., did the officer routinely show up in traffic court?). PARS is effectively used as part of broad personnel performance assessments.

Moving Beyond Individual Assessment

While early intervention systems and even more comprehensive personnel management systems have been advocated mainly as a tool to assess individual performance, prudent managers have realized that these systems allow analysis of entire units, entire agencies, and of individual, unit, and agency performance over time.

Unit and Agencywide Assessment

Just as early intervention and personnel management systems allow for the analysis of individual officers' behavior, these systems allow for the analysis of unit and agency activity. For instance, although precincts 1 and 2 may have similar demographics, crime problems, and land-use profiles, an early intervention or personnel management system might reveal that precinct 1 has far more citizen-generated complaints and use-of-force incidents than precinct 2. Once in possession of these facts, managers will want to determine whether these disparities require action. Is one unit managed more effectively than the other? Are there differences in staffing levels? Are the relatively high levels of complaints and use-of-force incidents in precinct 1 evenly distributed or are these levels more attributable to a particular shift or even a particular officer or group of officers? Early intervention and personnel management systems enable agencies to answer such performance questions.

Assessment over Time

Similarly, early intervention systems and personnel management systems can be used to assess trends over time. For instance, managers may use simple line charts to compare use-of-force incidents across months or quarters. Through such analysis, they may assess whether the introduction of a new technology or procedure had an impact on use-of-force incidents and whether that impact varied across units. Similarly, managers who invite citizens to file complaints or commendations over the agency's web site may rely on data from an early intervention or personnel management system to determine whether this policy change had an impact on the volume of complaints and commendations as well as whether this impact was more or less pronounced for some geographic units compared to others. Managers might even compare performance indicators across different generations of academy graduates or determine whether trends in use-of-force incidents correlate with periodic refresher courses. These managers might decide to readjust a 3-year training cycle if indicators reveal dramatic increase in incidents 2 years after training.

While early intervention systems and more comprehensive personnel management systems allow managers to address these questions effectively, they must remain vigilant in their management of data and their supervisory efforts. As with individual assessments, unit and agencywide assessments and assessments made over time must be made in context. For instance, a department that publicizes its complaint process in a series of public forums and then begins to allow community members to file complaints on the agency web site should expect a rise in complaints. Rather than perceiving an agencywide surge in complaints as a problem, the department may well point to this as an indicator of the effectiveness of its strategy. Only after such a change is in effect for some time would tracking of complaints once again become a meaningful indicator of public perception and officer performance.

Recommendations

Based on assessment of federal consent decrees and MOAs, as well as the preceding discussion, the IACP offers the following recommendations. The International Association of Chiefs of Police (IACP) reminds readers that these recommendations may require periodic revision because early intervention systems and related management strategies are evolving rapidly. The IACP also reminds readers that any department's ability to implement early intervention strategies may be affected by local laws and collective bargaining agreements.

The recommendations below correspond sequentially with the goals of creating an early intervention system, implementing the system, and promoting the system to relevant stakeholders.

1. Organize a working committee that involves a broad cross-section of participants in the planning, development, and implementation of early intervention.

Executives, managers at all levels, line officers, and administrative staff will have a vested interest in early intervention strategies. The performance of sworn and nonsworn personnel may be monitored by the early intervention system and many individuals and units will be required to contribute data to or use the data within the early intervention system. As a result, departments planning, developing, and implementing an early intervention system should organize a broadly representative working committee. Even after the early intervention system is implemented, this working committee should remain intact to monitor the system, make necessary adjustments to the system, and assess the impact of new or revised policies on the system.

2. Involve relevant government bodies in the planning and implementation processes.

Municipal, county, and state governments have a clearly vested interest in early intervention systems that are used in their law enforcement agencies. The reputation of these government entities depends in large degree on the performance and reputation of their law agencies. Prudent government leaders will recognize the benefits that can come with meaningful early intervention strategies and will understand that an investment in early intervention strategies can reduce liability and costs in the long run. Government bodies fund these systems and stand to benefit from them. They should be involved in their planning and implementation.

3. Involve police unions, whenever possible, in the planning and development of early intervention.

Unions have a keen interest in any system that has a potential impact on their members. To date, union reaction to early intervention has been mixed. This is the result of the vast diversity of early intervention systems now in operation. Differences also exist because some departments developed early intervention systems reactively, such as under the requirement of federal consent decrees or MOAs, while other departments developed early intervention on their own initiative. At a minimum, police unions should be informed about the planning and development of early intervention. Whenever possible, union representatives should be brought into the planning and development process as active participants. Departments should emphasize the differences between an early intervention system and the disciplinary system as well as the potential benefits of early intervention to officers.

4. Inform the community about the planning and development of early intervention and involve them in planning, when appropriate.

Departments should inform community stakeholders about the development of early intervention. Departments may even choose to involve community stakeholders in the development process. Community involvement may range from a simple review to active participation in the working committee. Involvement of community stakeholders may be warranted if similar processes had already been successfully completed. For instance, if the department has successfully used community input in designing its citizen complaint process, they may invite involvement again. Departments may consider developing community surveys to determine which indicators are of most concern to the community. The survey results may help department personnel decide which indicators should be included in the system or what thresholds the department should use for various indicators.

5. Determine the scope of early intervention that is most appropriate for a department.

Early intervention requires that an agency engage in a regular review of officers' performance along a defined set of indicators. Each agency should determine the scope of the system that best serves its needs. Many smaller departments with reasonable ratios of first-line supervisors to rank-and-file officers may already engage in early intervention strategies without a formal program or model. For some of these departments, the formalization of these efforts into policies or directives may be all that is needed. Many larger departments, however, may realize that their early intervention should be developed as part of a more comprehensive and automated personnel management system that draws on existing data systems. The decision regarding the scope of early intervention should be based on the size, function, and existing data technology of the individual agency. Design of early intervention systems should take advantage of what similar agencies have already experienced.

6. Involve information technology (IT) staff, data systems operators, and end users of existing data systems in the planning, development, and implementation of early intervention.

Any early intervention system that involves computerized data must involve representatives from the IT staff, data systems operators, and end users of existing data systems that may feed into the early intervention system. Whether designing a dedicated early intervention data system or deploying a gateway system that draws from a variety of existing data systems, IT staff will need to create appropriate query and report capabilities that meet end users' needs. End users of other data systems (e.g., the records management system or the personnel system) will be able to provide critical input on the quality of that data and can help assess whether existing data collection practices will be sufficient for the early intervention system. Data input operators can provide critical information about current data quality issues, particularly as they relate to paper forms generated in the field.

The development of early intervention is likely to occur while improvements are being made in data management systems. IT staff and data systems operators will be critical in considering compatibility issues as they update computer-aided dispatch systems, web sites, records management system, and other data systems.

7. Carefully assess other agencies' early intervention systems and experiences.

Although there is no such thing as one-size-fits-all early intervention, there is no reason that a department should start from scratch when designing its early intervention system. Agencies that have developed large-scale early intervention systems have charted new territory in policy, data system design, data management, and changes to supervisory practices. Managers should learn from the challenges that had been faced by peers in other departments rather than learning through trial and error.

Departments, regardless of size or function, should familiarize themselves with model early intervention systems. These include the following:

- Pittsburgh Bureau of Police—Performance Assessment Review System, www.city.pittsburgh.pa.us/police
- Miami-Dade Police Department—Employee Identification System, formerly Employee Profile System, www.mdpd.com
- Los Angeles Sheriffs' Department—Personnel Performance Index, www.lasd.org
- Phoenix Police Department—Personnel Assessment System, www.phoenix.gov/police/pas.html
- Charlotte-Mecklenburg Police Department—Early Intervention System, www.charmeck.org/Departments/Police/Services+A-Z/Home.htm (select "directives" then select "300-018 Performance Review and Development.PDF").

Departments should also use other agencies' web sites as well as published material to explore the variety of systems in operation. Departments may solicit input from colleagues across the nation through IACPNet or web-based list-serves. At a minimum, departments should consider what early intervention systems are in use in neighboring jurisdictions.

Although departments tend to borrow best practices from early intervention systems in other departments, they seldom adopt other systems in their entirety. Early intervention systems generally rely on indicators driven by local supervisory practices that vary across departments. As a result, few commercial off-the-shelf (COTS) systems are available. While it is doubtful that any department could simply use another department's early intervention database, there may be portions of a software program that could be modified to meet the needs of another department. In such an instance, the agency's IT staff or qualified software development consultants should play a role. Any consideration of standard software, including COTS software, should carefully assess the extent to which that system conforms to the agency's data collection efforts and the extent to which the software can be customized to meet the agency's particular needs.

8. Ensure that supervisors have the appropriate experiences, skills, and training to perform their early intervention responsibilities.

Supervisors must be qualified to perform their early intervention responsibilities. In departments with a strong history of close supervision and ongoing feedback, the need for additional training for supervisors may be negligible. If these are not in place, however, considerable support and training of supervisory personnel may be warranted. Depending on the complexity and sophistication of the early intervention system, supervisors may require training in collecting data, querying the system, assessing early-indicator data in context, writing reports to document decision-making processes, and intervention, intervening, and follow-up monitoring. Departments planning and implementing an early intervention strategy should be aware that it might warrant reassessment of the way supervisory personnel are selected, trained, and evaluated.

9. Ensure that early performance indicators are well-established, clearly understood, and fair.

Using performance indicators that are not collected consistently and reliably can be counterproductive and may compromise early intervention system efficacy and fairness. This is a particular area of concern for highly discretionary police actions. For instance, some early intervention systems use field interviews (sometimes called field interrogations) as an early intervention system indicator. Use of indicators such as these would be advisable only if there was a consistent definition of the term and only if supervisors are assured that all officers consistently fill out these forms. If officers conduct field interviews but can avoid recording them so they can fly under the radar screen, it compromises both the fairness and utility of the early intervention system

10. Ensure that early intervention data are collected and entered in a timely manner.

In addition to being reliable, early intervention data must be timely if the system is to identify potentially problematic behavior and intervene as needed. Implementing an early intervention system may require an agency to commit resources for timely data collection and entry as well as take measures to assure data quality.

11. Carefully consider how to best document supervisors' early intervention decisions and selection of interventions.

While selection of performance indicators and mechanisms for tracking indicators and setting thresholds for mandatory supervisory review have received ample attention in policing literature, far less attention has been paid to early intervention review processes and documentation of those reviews. Some departments with early intervention systems require early intervention review reports that follow a specific protocol while others are entirely silent on the issue of reports.

Departments that require periodic review using early intervention performance data (e.g., quarterly reviews) typically will require specific report formats to ensure compliance by supervisors and to ensure consistency in the review process. Recognize that these reviews should be used address exemplary behavior as well as indicate the need for intervention.

The department should consider that heavy reliance on formal protocols and stringent reporting requirements that deal only with indicators of problem performance may lead some to believe that the early intervention process is just another format of the disciplinary process. While individual departments may differ in organizational culture and the documentation processes, documentation processes should in no way compromise the benefits of a truly nonpunitive early intervention program and inhibit informal intervention options being used when appropriate.

12. Continually review and refine early intervention indicators and thresholds.

To work effectively, early intervention must respond to changing conditions within the department and community. Managers must regularly review and refine early intervention indicators and thresholds. Departments that introduce new use-of-force options may need use-of-force thresholds. Similarly, departments that make their citizen complaint process more accessible and more transparent may need to adjust their citizen complaint thresholds.

13. Ensure that early intervention policies and practices do not conflict with other department policies and practices.

Early intervention systems and personnel management systems may be far-reaching and complex. As a result, early intervention policies and practices must be carefully reviewed to ensure that they do not conflict with other policies and practices. For instance, departments that rely on a point system to quantify their officer productivity should handle high-discretion arrests (e.g., resisting arrest or disorderly conduct without other charges) appropriately. It would be confusing and contradictory, for instance, if high-discretion arrests are treated positively for accumulating productivity points but are used as an indicator of risk in early intervention.

14. Establish the differences between early intervention and the disciplinary process through a separate written policy for early intervention systems.

To distinguish early intervention from the disciplinary system, departments should have a formal written policy. Departments may consult neighboring jurisdictions' written policies, relevant standards published at the state level, Commission on Accreditation for Law Enforcement Agencies (CALEA) standards (standard 35.1.15), or the IACP Model Policy on Early Warning Systems (volume 5, number 82).

15. Clearly articulate the differences between early intervention and the disciplinary process in day-to-day communications and operations by making early intervention an integral part of the standard supervisory process.

Departments deploying early intervention must understand and clearly articulate the differences between the two systems, both in policy and day-to-day practice. The proactive and preventive nature of early intervention should never be confused with the reactive, punitive measures of the disciplinary system. If early intervention is perceived as an extension of the disciplinary system, it will be resisted by the officers and steadfastly opposed by the union. While the disciplinary system may be administered by a special unit, often the internal affairs unit, early intervention strategies are best administered through the normal chain of command, with first-line supervisors assuming primary responsibility. Emphasizing the facts that individual officers can access the system and that data will be made available only to the officer's immediate chain of command will help to establish the differences between early intervention and the disciplinary system. It must always be recognized, however, that early intervention efforts may be used alongside disciplinary actions in certain circumstances. In cases where discipline is warranted or required as a matter of policy, individuals may still benefit from assistance provided through the early intervention process.

16. Educate rank-and-file officers about early intervention.

Early intervention is designed to promote and protect the well-being of individual officers. The introduction of early intervention to a department, however, can be challenging. The introduction of early intervention can be perceived as a change to the department's organizational culture and viewed as a threat to the status quo. Managers must educate rank-and-file officers about the purpose and workings of the early intervention system, making sure to emphasize its intent to assist officers.

17. Educate community groups and community leaders about early intervention.

When properly designed, implemented, and managed, early intervention can be an effective public relations tool and can enhance public confidence in the police. Community groups and community leaders should be educated about early intervention.

One of the most effective and economical means of educating the community is to present information about early intervention on the department web site. The web site should articulate the differences between early intervention and the disciplinary system. The web site should explain the general purposes of the early intervention system and discuss specifically how it relates to citizen-generated complaints and excessive force allegations. The web site should identify the ways in which early intervention benefits the community, the department, and the individual officer.

The Phoenix (Arizona) Police Department uses its web site to offer a comprehensive and clear introduction to its PAS. The following is an excerpt from its web page:

> **Early Intervention and Personnel Assessment System FAQs**
>
> The Personnel Assessment System, (PAS), is the Phoenix Police Department's Early Identification and Intervention System. PAS was originally created to make our employees more successful. It is a non-disciplinary system designed to identify possible problematic behaviors with employees, and to offer assistance using intervention options to modify those behaviors before discipline is required.
>
> This program will also assist in reducing future police department liability using risk management programs and techniques already in place. The department also found that by using an extensive case management system within PAS, supervisor accountability is being held to a higher standard.
>
> On January 1, 2004, the Phoenix Police Department fully implemented PAS and began to send out Intervention Reviews. Many department employees have received training, which is an ongoing process and crucial to the success of this program. PAS is available for review to all departmental employees.[16]
>
> Source: Phoenix (Arizona) Police Department Manual
> Agency Profile: Population 1,321,045; Officers 2,626

Conclusion

Early intervention is a management strategy, not just a technological solution. The concepts of early intervention must be seen primarily as a supervisory strategy and not as a technologically driven panacea. Early intervention strategies and technological solutions are evolving rapidly and the experiences of several agencies suggest that they have tremendous potential, They can save individual careers, help safeguard a department's investment in training and career development, help personnel get the services they need, reduce agency liability, and identify and reinforce exemplary performance. While tech-savvy agencies may benefit from sophisticated data-driven early intervention alerts, smaller agencies can benefit from incorporating similar concepts into their supervisory routines. Law enforcement executives should look to what other agencies of similar size are doing in this area and determine how those practices might be adapted to their departments.

Suggestions for Further Reading

As early intervention systems and related supervisory practice are becoming more prevalent, a growing number of publications and resources are becoming available. This is a partial list.

Davis, Robert C., Nicole J. Henderson, Janet Mandelstam, Christopher W. Ortiz, and Joel Miller. <u>Federal Intervention in Local Policing: Pittsburgh's Experience with a Consent Decree</u>. Vera Institute of Justice, New York; 2006. (includes discussion of the role of the Pittsburgh Bureau of Police's early intervention strategy as part of the agency successfully coming to terms with a federal consent decree) www.cops.usdoj.gov/mime/open.pdf?Item=1662.

DeCrescenzo, Dino. "Focus on Personnel: Early Detection of the Problem Officer." <u>FBI Law Enforcement Bulletin</u>; April 2005: 4. Available on the web at www.highbeam.com (Use the keyword/title search).

Jacocks, A. M., and M.D. Bowman. "Developing and Sustaining a Culture of Integrity." <u>The Police Chief</u>. April 2006:4. www.policechiefmagazine.org/magazine (Select through "Archives").

Walker, Samuel. <u>Early Intervention Systems for Law Enforcement Agencies: A Planning and Management Guide</u>. Police Executive Research Forum, Washington, DC; 2003. www.cops.usdoj.gov/mime/open.pdf?Item=925.

Walker, Samuel, Stacy Osnick Milligan with Anna Berke. <u>Strategies for Intervening with Officers through Early Intervention Systems: A Guide for Front-Line Supervisors</u>. Police Executive Research Forum, Washington, DC; 2006. www.cops.usdoj.gov/mime/open.pdf?Item=1671.

Walker, Samuel, Stacy Osnick Milligan with Anna Berke. <u>Supervision and Intervention within Early Intervention Systems: A Guide for Law Enforcement Chief Executives</u>. Police Executive Research Forum, Washington, DC; 2005. <u>www.cops.usdoj.gov/Default.asp?Item=1634</u>.

Walker Samuel. <u>The New World of Police Accountability</u>. Sage Publications Inc., Thousand Oaks (California); 2005

Endnotes

1. Hussey, James, Chief of Cohasset (Massachusetts) Police Department. Personal Correspondence. December 1, 2005.
2. Violanti, John M., John Vena, and James Marshal. "Suicides, Homicides, and Accidental Deaths: A Comparative Risk Assessment of Police Officers and Municipal Workers." American Journal of Independent Medicine 1996: 99-104.
3. Walker, Samuel. The New World of Police Accountability. Thousand Oaks (California): Sage Publications, 2005.
4. "Interview of Samuel Walker." Best Practices Review (Publication of the Police Assessment Resources Center) October 2002: 14-17.
5. Walker, Samuel. The New World of Police Accountability. Thousand Oaks (California): Sage Publications, 2005.
6. The full text of the relevant question on the LEMAS survey is, "Does your agency have a currently operational computer-based personnel performance monitoring/assessment system (e.g., early warning or early intervention system) for monitoring or responding to officer behavior patterns before they become problematic?"
7. There is slight anomaly in this pattern for municipal departments: 52 percent (20 of 38) of the largest municipal agencies (>= 1000 sworn officers with arrest power) responding to the survey versus 62 percent (21 of 34) of the next largest category. In addition, the 82 percent figure for the largest sheriff's office is based on a limited number of respondents. There were only 11 sheriffs' offices of that size among the respondents and nine reported having an early intervention system.
8. *United States* v. *City of Steubenville, Ohio* Consent Decree (09/03/97) Available on the web at www.usdoj.gov/crt/split/documents/steubensa.htm.
9. *United States of America* v. *City of Detroit, Michigan and the Detroit Police Department* Consent Decree (06/12/03). www.usdoj.gov/crt/split/documents/dpd/detroitpd_uofwdcd_613.pdf.
10. "Early Intervention and Personnel Assessment System FAQ's." Phoenix Police Department. Retrieved February 01, 2006 from www.phoenix.gov/POLICE/pas1.html.
11. Information obtained from site visit to Pittsburgh Bureau of Police on February 22, 2005.
12. Correspondence with several departments that had previously used fixed thresholds, reveal that they have replaced them with what they consider more flexible methods that rely more heavily on supervisory skills.
13. Third Quarter Status Report. Prince George's County Police Department & the U.S. Department of Justice, 2005. www.goprincegeorgescounty.com/Government/PublicSafety/Police/pdfs/Consent_Decree_1-7-05.pdf.
14. Comments made by Detective Toye Nash of the Phoenix Arizona Police Department at May 10, 2005. Symposium on Early Intervention System Workshop at the Police Executive Research Forum in Washington, DC.
15. Vaughn, Michael S., Tab W. Hunter, and Rolando V. del Carmen. "Assessing Legal Liabilities in Law Enforcement: Police Chiefs' Views." Crime and Delinquency 2001, 3-27.
16. "The Personal Assessment System." Phoenix Police Department. Retrieved October 10, 2005 from www.phoenix.gov/POLICE/pas.html.

IV. Managing the Complaint Process

Managing the Complaint Process

> A simple declaration that all complaints against any member of the police department will be received and investigated leaves little room for dispute. It also prevents the age-old problem of certain complaints being discounted or rejected for purely subjective reasons. It is difficult to explain to a citizen why one complaint was accepted and one rejected for basically the same offense. It puts supervisors in awkward positions when a peer has accepted a complaint that they have rejected in the past.[1]
>
> **Chief Beau Thurnauer, Coventry (Massachusetts) Police Department**

Introduction

An accessible, fair, and transparent complaint process is a hallmark of police responsiveness to the community and is consistent with the goals of community policing. In addition, a thorough assessment of all allegations of police misconduct—whether these allegations are initiated externally by civilians or internally by other department personnel—offers police managers an opportunity to proactively address concerns from a problem-solving perspective. Too often, the processing of complaints has been viewed simply as an adjudicative process in which complaints are investigated and in which dispositions and disciplinary sanctions are applied. Under this traditional approach, the principal parties are the aggrieved person making the allegation and the officer whose behavior is in question. An emerging perspective, however, recognizes that the community and the department as a whole are important stakeholders in the complaint process. Under this more comprehensive view, the civilian complaint process serves not only to redress grievances; it also serves as a management tool, a forum to address public concerns and to enhance public relations, and an opportunity to refine policies and training.

Chapter Overview and Objectives

Drawing on federal consent decrees and memorandums of agreement (MOA) as well as on promising and innovative efforts from police departments across the nation, this chapter explores the benefits and challenges of civilian complaint processes. In its introductory paragraphs, the chapter offers a working definition of the civilian complaint process. This definition is followed by an analysis of the ways in which the civilian complaint process is evolving as well as an overview of the prevalence of civilian complaint processes currently in use in law enforcement agencies.

Moving beyond these introductory materials, the chapter explores the core principles of the civilian complaint process. The chapter asserts that the civilian complaint process succeeds to the extent that it is—and is perceived as being—comprehensive, accessible, fair, and transparent. To the extent that civilians feel able to file a complaint with reasonable convenience, feel sure that every complaint receives a fair investigation resulting in a timely resolution, and feel aware of the workings and rulings of the civilian complaint process, this process will build community confidence in the police department's determination to serve ethically and efficiently.

From its exploration of core principles, the chapter turns to a consideration of the basic components of the civilian complaint process from the initial filing of complaints to their final adjudication. It explores the standards that emerged from the federal agreements regarding the handling of complaints, as well as those that have been enacted proactively in different departments across the nation.

Finally, this chapter offers a series of recommendations to police departments establishing and implementing a civilian complaint process. Like the chapter's discussion of the civilian complaint process itself, these recommendations result from the careful consideration of federal consent decrees and MOAs, as well as practices from police departments across the nation.

A Definition of the Civilian Complaint Process

The civilian complaint process is the series of steps by which law enforcement agencies accept, investigate, and adjudicate allegations of misconduct or incompetence on the part of police personnel.[2] In the language of the consent decrees and MOAs, such complaints may address "any action or inaction by [agency] personnel which the source considers to be contrary to law, proper procedure, good order, or in some manner prejudicial to the individual, the [agency], or to the community."[3] While such complaints are, in fact, filed mostly by civilians, complainants may also arise from agency personnel or anonymous sources.

The Evolution of the Civilian Complaint Process

Residents, business persons, and other civilians are consumers of police services. When they perceive that they have been aggrieved by acts ranging from discourteous treatment to criminal misconduct on the part of police personnel, they have the right to be heard and to seek remedy. In recognition of this right, police executives have facilitated the acceptance and timely resolution of individual grievances. When warranted, they have acknowledged the mistakes of their agency personnel.

While this civilian complaint process has long existed, police executives' attitudes toward the process are changing. Although police executives once tended to focus narrowly on the adjudication of alleged misconduct and, as a result, to view civilian complaints entirely in a negative light, many are now using civilian complaints as a barometer of public satisfaction and as a general management tool. By engaging in a comprehensive, accessible, fair, and transparent civilian complaint process, police executives are enhancing their agencies' image as professional and ethical organizations while underscoring their commitment to addressing community concerns. By regarding civilian complaints as critical pieces of a data-driven management strategy, police executives are gauging the performance of individual officers, seizing important opportunities to modify policies and procedures, and better guarding against future misconduct on the part of police personnel.

On the level of the individual officer, many police executives rely on civilian complaints as an important indicator by which to gauge officer performance in early intervention systems. For instance, an inordinate number of civilian complaints about an individual officer can alert supervisors to potentially problematic behavior that could benefit from nondisciplinary intervention. Serious and substantiated civilian complaints may also identify instances in which disciplinary action is required.

At aggregate levels, an analysis of civilian complaint trends can be used to determine whether the agency as a whole or particular units within the department are moving in the right direction. If, for instance, one precinct's civilian complaints are trending up while all others are dropping, the police chief and commanders may want to determine what factors are contributing to such an anomaly and what actions, if any, need to be taken. Conversely, if one precinct's civilian complaints are trending down while all others are holding steady or rising, police executives would want to determine the reason for the precinct's apparent success and take steps to assure that similar successful management practices could be transferred to other precincts.

Police executives who proactively use civilian complaint data from a management perspective can use the process to fine-tune agency performance and enhance community trust. An open and constructive approach to handling civilian complaints, instead of a reactive and defensive approach, casts that agency in a positive light.

Publicizing a Positive Attitude About Civilian Complaints

Increasingly, police departments rely on effective complaint processes to inspire public confidence and reinforce community relations. While many of these departments recognize that discouraging civilian complaints can seriously undermine community relations—particularly in minority and other communities that historically have felt disenfranchised—others recognize that their departments actually benefit by publicizing their openness to the complaint process. Police departments of varying sizes and types across the nation are realizing the benefits of comprehensive, accessible, fair, and transparent complaint processes on their web sites and in their official policies. The following three examples from departments of different sizes are illustrative of this type of approach.

Example 1
Many employees view the internal affairs function as strictly negative. Quite the opposite is true. When properly run, the internal affairs function will protect the innocent employee from untrue allegations while maintaining citizen confidence and trust. To ignore or treat citizen complaints with anything less than the utmost of concern will increase the number of complaints, cause a loss of trust and result in demands for citizen review boards.

Source: Midvale (Utah) Police Department's Policy Manual
Agency Profile: Population 28,000; Officers 45

Example 2
Citizen Complaint Process: The mission of the Portland Police Bureau is to maintain and improve community livability by working with all citizens to preserve life, maintain human rights, protect property, and promote individual responsibility and community commitment. Our goals state that our employees must be guided by the principles that every individual has infinite dignity and worth and that we must show respect for the citizens we serve and for the men and women of the Bureau.

A citizen complaint, and its subsequent investigation, causes police to examine the service that we provide to our community and to make necessary improvements in the way we provide services.

Source: Portland (Oregon) Police Bureau web site (www.portlandonline.com/police)
Agency Profile: Population 509,610; Officers 1,028

Purpose and Intent: It is the guiding principle of the Waite Park Police Department that _all_ allegations of employee misconduct or criticism of its services be acknowledged and addressed. To succeed in this endeavor, this order establishes a comprehensive departmental process to respond to such inquiries and complaints. Its purpose is to provide citizens with a fair and effective avenue to voice their legitimate grievances against the actions of the Police Department, yet to protect departmental employees from false charges of misconduct and wrongdoing.

OBJECTIVES:
a) To maintain the community's support and confidence in its Police Department by providing a process that assures responsiveness to citizen's inquiries and complaints.
b) To create a process for dealing with inquiries and complaints, whether originating internally or externally, that permits police managers to monitor departmental compliance with established departmental rules, procedures, and norms.
c) To clarify employee rights and the due process protection that will be afforded departmental employees in the investigation of inquiries and complaints.

Source: Waite Park (Minnesota) Police Department's Policy Manual
Agency Profile: Population 7,562; Officers 12

The Prevalence of the Civilian Complaint Process

Major benchmarks for police standards, including the Commission on Accreditation for Law Enforcement Agencies (CALEA) and International Association of Chiefs of Police (IACP) Model Policies, call for policies and procedures for the civilian complaint processes. CALEA standards for complaint processes, for instance, are imbedded with its section on Internal Affairs (52), recognizing that larger departments may have specific internal affairs units, whereas a smaller agency may have to designate this responsibility to an individual officer.[4] As is discussed in subsequent sections, some agencies rely, if full or in part, on civilian review boards to review civilian-generated complaints.

Without exception, all the federal pattern or practice agreements related to law enforcement agencies address the complaint process. The language within the consent decrees and MOAs related to the complaint process is extensive and addresses both civilian complaints and internal complaints.

The foundation of any complaint process, whether conducted by internal affairs, designated personnel within the department, or by civilian boards is the establishment of clear policy directives. Results from the 2003 Sample Survey of Law Enforcement Agencies (LEMAS) conducted by the Bureau of Justice Statistics (BJS) provided an opportunity to assess the prevalence of policy directives on civilian complaints by department size and type. Details about LEMAS methodology and data are available in the text box on page 31 in Chapter 2.

As the LEMAS results below indicate, across agencies of all sizes, the vast majority of municipal departments and sheriffs' offices reported having civilian complaint policies. While the likelihood of having such a policy was higher in larger departments, these policies are still the norm even in the smallest departments. Among agencies surveyed, about three in four municipal departments with four or fewer full-time officers had such a policy. Based on the LEMAS survey data, all state police agencies, all county police agencies, and all regional police agencies had civilian complaint policy directives.[5]

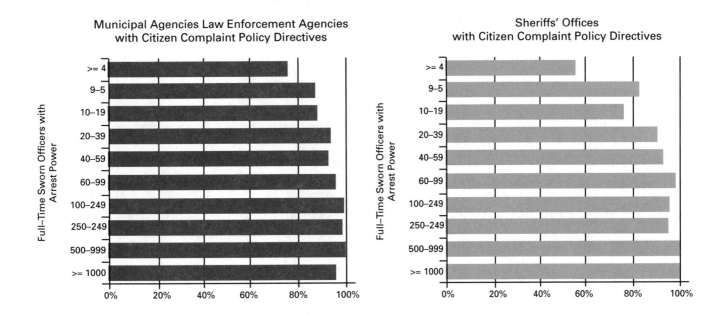

The Benefits of the Civilian Complaint Process

When police executives recognize that the civilian complaint process may serve as an important management tool and a critical component to creating community trust, they begin to realize the following benefits:

- Enhancing the investigative process to assess officer culpability and to assess the agency need to enhance policies and training
- Rendering clear findings in individual cases
- Identifying individual officers who may be in need of intervention, either nondisciplinary or disciplinary, as appropriate
- Identifying pockets of risk within the department
- Providing opportunities to modify and improve policies and training
- Developing strategies to reduce or prevent misconduct
- Enhancing organizational efficiency
- Ensuring accountability within the agency
- Ensuring responsiveness and accountability to the community
- Enhancing community trust as well as building and sustaining community relations.

The Core Principles of the Complaint Process

Effective policing depends on the trust and confidence of the community. Police rely on individuals within the community to report crimes, serve as witnesses, and occasionally offer assistance. From a community policing and service-oriented perspective, the community's satisfaction with police services is of paramount importance. This satisfaction is the result, in part, of how police handle the discrete instances of dissatisfaction that are brought to their attention through civilian complaints. The civilian complaint process may turn dissatisfaction into confidence as police adhere to four core principles that underlie an effective complaint process.

1. An effective complaint process must be comprehensive. It must accept and act on <u>all</u> civilian complaints. The system should also integrate complaints from other sources, including internal complaints as well as alleged acts of misconduct that arise in the context of civil or criminal proceedings against agency personnel.

Across departments, the preponderance of misconduct allegations are made by civilians—nonpolice personnel—who have had contact with the police. These contacts may involve individuals who seek police assistance; are crime victims; are crime suspects; are witnesses, or potential witnesses; and those who have been stopped for traffic violations. While an agency's complaint process must treat these civilian complaints seriously, it must not discourage or ignore the complaints that arise from other sources.

Another significant source of misconduct complaints is department personnel themselves. Historically, some observers have argued that police maintain a "blue wall of silence" and that officers who observe misconduct among their fellow officers are reluctant to report it. Many departments, however, have implemented strict stipulations that hold police officers accountable for knowingly failing to report misconduct of fellow officers. By expanding the scope of their complaint process to address not only civilian complaints but also the complaints of officers themselves, departments underscore their commitment to ethical policing and strict accountability.

The language of federal consent decrees and MOAs expresses an unwavering commitment to addressing internal complaints. These agreements stipulate that officers are required to report other officers' misconduct. For instance, the consent decree with the Pittsburgh Bureau of Police underscored the department's existing polices and practice: "the City shall continue to require officers to report misconduct by other officers. Misconduct by fellow officers shall be reported directly to OMI [Office of Municipal Investigations] or through an officer's chain of command."[6]

The MOA of the Buffalo Police Department expresses a similar requirement and, although it acknowledges the limitations imposed by the local collective bargaining agreement, enjoins the department to attempt to surmount these limitations:

> To the extent allowed under the applicable collective bargaining agreement in force on the effective date of this Agreement, the City shall require officers to report misconduct by other officers. To the extent not already allowed under the applicable collective bargaining agreement in force on the effective date of this Agreement, the City shall initiate negotiations and shall bargain in good faith for the right to require officers to report misconduct by other officers.[7]

While the most common sources of misconduct allegations are civilian complaints and the reports or allegations of other officers, there is a growing recognition that a comprehensive complaint process should address complaints arising from other, nontraditional sources. For example, allegations of misconduct may emerge during internal investigations, or instances of alleged misconduct may come to light through civil or criminal suits filed against officers or through media reports. Federal consent decrees and MOAs stress the importance of investigating all misconduct complaints, regardless of source. For instance, the Los Angeles Police Department (LAPD) consent decree requires that the city inform the police department whenever "a person serves a civil lawsuit on or files a claim against the City alleging misconduct by an LAPD officer or other employee of the LAPD."[8] This consent decree also stipulates that the department will "require all officers to notify without delay the LAPD whenever the officer is arrested or criminally charged for any conduct, or the officer is named as a party in any civil suit involving his or her conduct while on duty (or otherwise while acting in an official capacity)." Other federal agreements go further to stipulate that such notifications are required regardless of whether this behavior occurs while the officer is on or off duty.

This comprehensive approach is advocated not only in federal consent decrees and MOAs, but also in the language of individual police agency policies, in state standards, and in professional standards such as CALEA and IACP model policies. The IACP Model Policy on Standards of Conduct, for instance, requires that "officers who are arrested, cited, or come under investigation for any criminal offense in this or another jurisdiction shall report this fact to a superior as soon as possible."[9]

2. An effective civilian complaint process must be accessible. Civilians must understand, have easy access to, and feel comfortable with complaint filing procedures.

In addressing the civilian complaint process, federal consent decrees and MOAs are consistent and unequivocal on the need for accessibility. In general, these consent decrees and MOAs require that filing a complaint be reasonably convenient. They also set a tone of inclusiveness rather than exclusiveness by requiring that, at a minimum, all complaints must be accepted and afforded some level of investigatory review.

In many of the pattern or practice investigations leading up to consent decrees and MOAs, the access to civilian complaint processes were found to be inadequate. Several of these investigations found that police were taking actions to actively discourage or effectively preempt certain civilian complaints. Some disincentives to reporting complaints are inherent within complaint forms themselves. For instance, language on complaint forms sometimes stipulates that a civilian complaint will not be accepted unless notarized. When followed by language stating that knowingly making false, untrue, or malicious complaints will be subject to criminal prosecution, some would-be complainants may be intimidated.

In response to these conditions, the language of consent decrees and MOAs seeks to establish civilian complaint policies, procedures, and actions that ensure that no civilian is intimidated, discouraged, or impeded from making a complaint and that *all* complaints are taken seriously.

When considered together, the federal consent decrees and MOAs, recommendations from professional organizations such as CALEA standards and IACP Model Policies, and policies of individual departments provide a clear picture of the evolving standard. It is not enough that civilians who come in contact with the police merely be given an opportunity to file complaints. Departments under federal agreements were required to develop proactive public outreach strategies to inform the community of their right to file complaints. The general intent of these strategies is to enhance accessibility by creating greater awareness regarding the complaint process. The specific public outreach requirements stipulated in the federal consent decrees and MOAs include the following:

- Establish public information campaigns about complaint filing procedures
- Establish methods for filing complaints other than formal written complaints including:
  o Telephone hotlines
  o Web-based filings
  o E-mail filings
  o Fax submissions
- Post information about complaint filing procedures on the agency's web site
- Provide complaint notifications, complaint filing instructions, and complaint forms in multiple languages, as appropriate, considering the particular jurisdiction's population.

While the common thread through federal consent decrees and MOAs is that the complaint filing process should be accessible, these agreements vary substantially because they are responsive to individual investigations and are tailored to the specific circumstances and organizational capacities of different departments. The following sections of the MOA between the Washington, D.C., Metropolitan Police Department (MPD) and the U.S. Department of Justice provide an illustrative example of the specific requirements made on the department to ensure open and broad access to file civilian complaints.

> 92. Within 90 days from the effective date of this Agreement, MPD shall make it possible for persons to initiate complaints with MPD in writing or verbally, in person, by mail, by telephone (or TDD), facsimile transmission, or by electronic mail. MPD shall accept and investigate anonymous complaints and complaints filed by persons other than the alleged victim of misconduct. MPD shall ask anonymous and third-party complainants for corroborating evidence. MPD shall not require that a complaint be submitted in writing or on an official complaint form to initiate an investigation.
>
> 93. Within 120 days from the effective date of this Agreement, the City shall institute a 24-hour toll-free telephone hotline for persons to call to make a complaint regarding officer conduct. The hotline shall be operated by OCCR. The City and MPD shall publicize the hotline telephone number on informational materials and complaint forms. The City shall tape record all conversations on this hotline and shall notify all persons calling the hotline of the tape recording. The City shall develop an auditing procedure to assure that callers are being treated with appropriate courtesy and respect, that complainants are not being discouraged from making complaints, and that all necessary information about each complaint is being obtained. This procedure shall include monthly reviews of a random sample of the tape recordings.[10]

3. An effective civilian complaint process must be fair and thorough. The investigation of civilian complaints must proceed according to high standards.

In their discussion of the investigation of civilian complaints, federal consent decrees and MOAs consider a broad range of issues including standards of proof, thoroughness of investigations, supervisory roles, and quality of data. While these agreements impose specific requirements on specific departments as a result of findings from individual investigations, a standard of fairness is common across the agreements. In general, federal consent decrees and MOAs require that departments give civilian complaints thorough, rigorous, unbiased, and timely investigation. Indeed, in many ways, federal consent decrees and MOAs call for investigatory procedures that parallel criminal investigations.

4. An effective civilian complaint process must be transparent. Departments should keep complainants apprised of specific complaint proceedings and the community apprised of summary information regarding the civilian complaint process.

The federal consent decrees and MOAs are resolute in requiring that the civilian complaint process be transparent both at the level of the individual complainant and of the community as a whole. In general, consent decrees and MOAs require that complainants be periodically informed of the progress of the complaint investigation. They also require that complainants

Managing the Complaint Process

be notified of the outcome at the conclusion of this process. These requirements are in keeping with standards established by professional organizations including the CALEA policy on internal affairs standards:

> The agency keeps the complainant informed concerning the status of the complaint, to include at a minimum: (a) verification of receipt that the complaint has been received for processing; (b) periodic status reports; and (c) notification of the results of the investigation upon conclusion.[11]

Federal consent decrees and MOAs establish the transparency of the civilian complaint process at the community level by requiring monitoring of the process by independent auditors and by requiring departments to "maintain and periodically disseminate to the public a statistical summary report regarding complaints files and resolution of those complaints." Many departments routinely include this summary information in their annual reports or on their web sites. Ensuring the transparency of the civilian complaint process by providing summary information is sound public policy.

Variations in the Civilian Complaint Process

The nature of the civilian complaint process varies considerably by department. This is the result, in part, of the varying roles that civilians play in overseeing the process. In some departments, civilian complaint review boards are composed entirely of civilians and are empowered to conduct investigations and issue subpoenas independently. In many departments, particularly smaller departments, the responsibility for overseeing the civilian complaint process is internal. Many departments have civilian complaint processes that fall somewhere in between independent civilian review boards and strictly internal processes.

The following discussion considers, first, the varying levels of civilian involvement in the civilian complaint process; second, the basic components of the process—filing, investigation, and resolution—that occur whether civilians or police department personnel oversee the handling of civilian complaints; and third, the actions taken by departments to ensure both internal accountability and accountability to the public they serve.

Assessing Civilian Involvement in the Complaint Process

Increasingly, police executives recognize the advantages of taking proactive steps to establish civilian complaint processes that are comprehensive, accessible, fair, and transparent. Historically, the impetus for establishing a civilian complaint process has emerged both from within and without departments. Law enforcement leaders continually must balance pressures from within the department and police unions versus outside the department—through politicians, activists, and community groups—in assessing how involved civilians should be in the processing of complaints.

In the absence of meaningful internal oversight, or in response to processes that were perceived as ineffectual, civilian groups and advocacy organizations have felt compelled to call for an external complaint process and demand an active role in its oversight. Prudent police executives understand that taking the initiative—rather than reacting to others' dissatisfaction—offers them the best opportunity to design and implement an effective civilian complaint process. In particular, making decisions regarding civilian involvement in that process provides police executives with the opportunity to address important matters of public concern in a proactive, forthright manner, rather than in reaction to some crisis or in response to adverse public sentiment.

Making decisions regarding the structure of civilian complaint processes and the degree of civilian involvement is remarkably complex. While numerous arguments exist both for and against civilian involvement in the civilian complaint process, it is beyond the scope of this guide to examine these arguments in depth or make recommendations. Instead, readers should consult the IACP Ethics Toolkit article, "Police Accountability and Citizen Review: A Leadership Opportunity for Police Chiefs," which offers several critical tools for department decision makers.[12]

As a brief overview, the article offers essential action steps for assessing a department's need for civilian involvement in the complaint and misconduct resolution process:

- Assess whether a problem exists
- Examine existing literature and practice regarding forms of citizen review and their impacts
- Confer with constituencies that must be involved in the decision to establish a citizen review device
- Work with citizens and government officials to understand how the review process may affect them
- Understand possible/probable outcomes of citizen review
- Complete a preliminary cost analysis to determine the financial impact on the department and the city.

A Typology of Complaint Processes Based on Citizen Involvement

In many jurisdictions, complaint procedures arise out of complex political processes and sometimes in response to publicized incidents of police misconduct. Not surprisingly, there are countless variations of the theme. Again, it is beyond the scope of this chapter to review all of these; however, the following classification from the IACP Ethics Toolkit helps put the range of options in perspective.

> **Class I: Citizen Review Board.** Citizen complaints are reviewed and investigated, and recommendations for disciplinary or policy action are made by a board comprised wholly of citizens. The board may or may not have subpoena power. Under this model, a citizen review board handles each step on the continuum from original complaint through review, investigation and recommendations for sanctions. This is the most independent citizen review model.
>
> **Class II: Police Review/Citizen Oversight.** Complaints are reviewed and investigated, and recommendations for disciplinary or policy action are made by law enforcement officers, with oversight of each case by a citizen or board of citizens.

Under this model, the steps on the complaint continuum are handled by the police. A board of citizen reviewers, or a single individual, reviews those actions/determinations. Since law enforcement conducts the initial fact-finding investigation, the Class II model is considered less independent than Class I.

Class III: Police Review/Citizen-Police Appeal Board. Complaints are reviewed and investigated by law enforcement officers in the Internal Affairs Unit, which recommends disciplinary action to the chief. Complainants who are not satisfied with outcomes of investigations can appeal for review to a board composed of both citizens and sworn officers.

Under this model, the complaint process is handled by the police. In the event a complainant is not satisfied with the outcome of his or her case, a board that includes police officers undertakes review of how the case was originally investigated. Citizen participation is limited to appeal review only.

Class IV: Independent Citizen Auditor. An independent citizen auditor or auditor system reviews the law enforcement agency's internal complaint review process (IA) and makes recommendations as needed.

Under this model, the complaint process is fully in the hands of the police. However, an auditor or audit team has access to that process and reviews it for effectiveness and accuracy of findings, making recommendations to improve the process as needed. The auditor reviews completed complaint cases and contacts complainants to assess satisfaction with outcome.

Considerations for Civilian Review in Complaint Processing

Law enforcement leaders must weigh carefully both the advantages and disadvantages of civilian review, considering factors such as the local political climate. Demands by the public, by special-interest groups, and by politicians can often put the police executive in a difficult position. Calls for civilian involvement in the process often will have to be weighed against the opposition of the rank-and-file and the police union. If civilian review is seen as a viable option, determining the level of civilian involvement—from far-reaching investigatory and subpoena power to a limited advisory function—is a decision that police executives will want to consider carefully.

Decisions about civilian review must be made in consideration of many factors. The article mentioned above from the IACP Ethics Toolkit addresses multiple considerations in this process, particularly as they relate to department size and existing police-community relations.

> Not all police departments need or would derive substantial value from formalized citizen review. In jurisdictions where community trust is solid and durable, strong police-community bonds exist, community access is institutionalized, and misconduct is not frequent nor egregious, citizen oversight is neither likely to emerge as an issue nor to have a profound impact on existing conditions. Smaller departments, in particular, have the advantage of constant informal interaction with citizens to maintain close ties and receive information and guidance. As communities and police agencies grow in size, lines of citizen/police contact may need strengthening through formality. Community leaders may suggest a citizen review mechanism to ensure involvement in problem resolution at the officer and/or department level. Even in these cases, alternative interventions may satisfy needs.[13]

Statistical Snapshot of Civilian Involvement in the Complaint Review Processes

Given the variations in local practice, it is difficult to assess the level of civilian involvement in the complaint process; however, greater civilian involvement tends to be associated with larger departments.

The 2003 Sample Survey of Law Enforcement Agencies (LEMAS) addresses the question of whether law enforcement agencies with 100 or more full-time sworn officers with arrest powers have within their jurisdictions a civilian complaint review board or agency that is empowered to investigate use of force complaints. (The LEMAS survey contains no corresponding questions about whether civilian review boards/agencies exist for other types of civilian complaints.)

Considering the specificity of this question, the LEMAS survey reveals that approximately 19 percent of municipal law enforcement agencies with 100 more sworn officers with arrest power use some form of civilian review in which civilians are empowered to review use-of-force complaints. The comparable figure for county police departments is 25 percent and for sheriffs' departments is 6 percent. None of the 49 state police agencies indicated they had such civilian review process for use-of-force complaints.

As the charts below indicate, for municipal police departments and sheriffs' offices, the likelihood of civilian review for use of force generally increases with agency size. Based on these data, it would appear that in municipal departments some level of civilian involvement occurs in the slight majority of departments with more than 500 sworn officers with arrest powers.

Municipal Police Departments and Sheriffs' Offices Percent with Civilian Review Boards/Agencies Empowered to Review Use-of-Force Complaints

The LEMAS survey further revealed that, overall, about one in four of these civilian review boards had independent investigative authority with subpoena powers.

The Basic Steps in Handling Civilian and Internal Complaints

Whatever level of civilian involvement a department may establish, the basic steps necessary for the handling of complaints remain the same. These include the filing of complaints, the investigation of complaints, and the resolution of complaints. While different departments may handle these basic operations differently, the following discussion offers an overview of important commonalities.

Step One: The Complaint Receipt and Filing Process
Although federal consent decrees and MOAs impose specific requirements on specific departments, they enjoin all departments to establish an accessible civilian complaint process. Making the civilian complaint process accessible depends on a number of organizational, community, and public relations considerations. The single most important factor, though, may well be the demeanor and behavior of officers on the streets. Notifying civilians about

their right to file a complaint is the critical gate-keeping event. The willingness of officers to meet this requirement, therefore, is critical to an open and successful civilian complaint process.

To ensure accessibility, the federal consent decrees and MOAs consistently issue the following requirements regarding officer conduct in the complaint filing process:

- Officers are to provide their name and badge number to civilians on request.
- Officers are required to provide complaint procedure information to civilians on request.
- Officers are required to have complaint forms available for civilians on request.

To underscore the importance of an accessible complaint process, consent decrees and MOAs stipulate that departments must hold officers accountable when they fail to provide notification of complaint filing procedures or when they, in any way, inhibit the civilian complaint process:

- The agency should have policies and procedures for disciplining officers who fail to notify a civilian of the complaint process when the civilian indicates a desire to file a complaint.
- The agency should have policies and procedures prohibiting any act that impedes or intimidates a civilian from making a complaint; these policies should contain disciplinary actions.

Such policy requires many departments to initiate separate investigations against officers who fail to notify civilians of their right to file a complaint. The LAPD consent decree is clear on this point:

> The LAPD shall initiate a Complaint Form 1.28 investigation against (i) any officer who allegedly fails to inform any civilian who indicates a desire to file a complaint of the means by which a complaint may be filed; (ii) any officer who allegedly attempts to dissuade a civilian from filing a complaint; or (iii) any officer who is authorized to accept a complaint who allegedly refuses to do so.[14]

As noted in the discussion of core principles, entire departments as well as individual officers must accept the responsibility of ensuring accessible civilian complaint processes. Federal consent decrees and MOAs consistently urge departments to take the following measures:

- Departments should have an open and accessible process by which they accept complaints in multiple formats (e.g., in person, by mail, and by e-mail).
- Departments should allow complaints to be filed in different public or private facilities and should specifically assure that complainants have options other than having to go to a police facility to file a complaint.

In addition to offering directives to officers and departments regarding the filing of complaints, the federal consent decrees and MOAs also stipulate a number of conditions and behaviors by personnel that are aimed at making the initiation process open and unbiased. Specifically, the consent decrees and MOAs set a tone of inclusiveness rather than exclusiveness regarding complaints. They insist that all complaints be taken seriously. Among the measures regarding the intake of complaints that ensure that the complaints are treated seriously are the following:

- Officers who perform complaint intake are prohibited from making assessments about the complainant's mental capacity or about the veracity of the allegations (they may, however, make factual comments about the complainant's demeanor or physical condition).
- Third-party complaints (e.g., those by witnesses) are allowed.
- Anonymous complaints are allowed.

While the consent decrees and MOAs thus work toward inclusiveness, they do not stipulate that certain complaints, such as anonymous complaints, should necessarily have the same weight as other complaints throughout the process. For instance, while the LAPD consent decree stipulates that anonymous complaints must be received and investigated, it also stipulates that an anonymous complaint that is not substantiated should not be used against an officer as a basis for discipline or to deny promotion.

Beyond merely making the complaint process accessible, some department policies expressly acknowledge the right of individuals to file complaints and contain language that helps facilitate complaints. The following excerpt illustrates this approach.

> If the complainant needs assistance completing the form, offer whatever assistance is required. Refusing to provide an initial complaint form is a violation of state law and of department guiding principle and procedure.
>
> Attempting to screen or discourage those who ask for forms is not an option. As soon as a form is requested, it needs to be provided. Contacts do not have to justify their request for a form.
>
> Source: Waite Park (Minnesota) Police Department Guiding Principles
> Agency Profile: Population 7,562; Officers 12

Step Two: The Complaint Investigation Process
The federal consent decrees and MOAs require that departments give complaints—specifically civilian complaints—full and rigorous investigatory attention. To do this effectively and appropriately, complaints first must be categorized.

Categorization of Complaints
Police executives, administrators, and civilian reviewers have long recognized that not all civilian complaints are of the same gravity or require the same type of investigation or

intervention. Civilian complaints range from gripes to allegations of felony offenses. To be clear, this does not mean that certain types of low-level complaints can be summarily dismissed.

Because the procedures for investigating complaints depend on the nature and seriousness of the allegation, many departments define multiple categories of complaints. These categories often will determine, particularly in larger departments, the administrative processes type of misconduct hearing that will take place.

Complaints usually are categorized according to the seriousness of the allegation. For instance, the Boise (Idaho) Police Department identifies less serious allegations as Class II complaints, which are defined as "those involving allegations of driving violations, demeanor complaints, and minor enforcement complaints." Class I complaints are defined as those that allege more egregious behaviors. They are specifically defined as "all other allegations including serious allegations of policy or criminal conduct." In addition to these classes, the Boise Police Department also categorizes some complaints as "Citizen Inquiries."[15] Although civilian inquiries may be generated like other complaints, they are commonly questions about whether procedures were followed or generalized comments that are not directed at an individual officer or employee.

Other departments use similar classification schemes. For instance, the Missouri City (Texas) Police Department categorizes complaints into two classes quite like to those of the Boise Police Department. In Missouri City, Class I allegations refer to "violations of federal, state or local laws, use of force, or incidents of potential public concern/outcry." Class II allegations involve other types of complaints, including complaints of rudeness/discourtesy, inadequate/incomplete case investigation, and improper tactics/procedures.[16]

Some departments opt for more detailed classification schemes. For instance, the Tempe (Arizona) Police Department and the Prince George's County (Maryland) Citizen Complaint Oversight Panel each rely on multiple category schemes. These are illustrated below.

> **Complaints received will generally fall into one of the following categories:**
>
> (1) **Serious Misconduct**—allegations which may constitute a violation of criminal law or conduct that could result in suspension, disciplinary pay reduction, demotion, or termination.
>
> (2) **Minor Misconduct**—allegations which do not appear to be a violation of criminal law and which would not result in suspension, demotion, disciplinary pay reduction, or termination.
>
> (3) **Policy Infraction**—allegations which are not of a serious nature, but involve some infraction of department policy.
>
> (4) **Inquiry**—those complaints against department policy.

(5) **Administrative Investigation**—initiated at the direction of the Chief of Police and conducted by the Internal Affairs component.

Source: Tempe (Arizona) Police Department's Policy Manual Agency
Profile: Population 165,000; Officers 327

COMPLAINT CLASSIFICATION

All incoming complaints are assigned to the following investigative categories based on the most serious allegation in the complaint:

Special Investigations (SI): Complaints that allege a criminal act or could result in a criminal charge or investigation, such as domestic violence, DWI/DUI, theft, unauthorized access to a criminal data base, uses of force that result in injury and all discharges of firearms. A special investigation team within the police department investigates these complaints.

Internal Affairs Investigations (IA): Complaints alleging use of abusive, derogatory or inappropriate language, most uses of force that do not result in injury, and certain types of misconduct.

Field Cases Investigations (FC): Complaints alleging offenses such as unbecoming conduct, unreported misconduct, process violations, minor uses of force, and failure to attend to duty. These complaints are referred directly to district commanders for investigation.

Police Supervisory Investigations (PS): Complaints initiated by police supervisory staff regarding an officer's performance of or failure to perform his assigned duties.

Source: Prince George's County (Maryland) Citizen Complaint Oversight Panel: 2003 Annual Report[17]
Agency Profile: Population 795,000; Officers 1,400

Investigatory Procedures for Categorized Complaints
As discussed, legitimate complaints are most often categorized according to their level of seriousness. Not surprisingly, complaints of differing levels of seriousness are handled through different investigatory procedures. Commonly, less serious complaints are reviewed by the chain of command while more serious complaints are reviewed by specialized units within the department or external boards or commissions that have various degrees of independence from the department. For instance, the policy of the Tempe Police Department calls for supervisory and command personnel to resolve complaint allegations involving minor incidents or inquiries. The policy, however, requires that more serious allegations be recorded on the department's Employee Complaint/Commendation Report and be brought to the attention of the chief of police for further processing that may include referral to Internal Affairs.

While allowing for variation according to the needs of different departments, the federal consent decrees and MOAs nevertheless are firm in the requirement that all departments give all complaints—particularly civilian complaints—thorough, rigorous, unbiased, and timely investigation. In their discussion of the investigatory process, the agreements explore a wide range of issues including the thoroughness of investigation, standards of proof, quality of data, the role of supervisors, and timeliness of dispositions. In considering these issues, the agreements are deliberately prescriptive and proscriptive—addressing both what departments ought to do and ought not to do.

Thorough Investigations
The federal consent decrees and MOAs establish the following conventions to ensure the thoroughness of complaint investigations:

- Involved officers and witness officers are obligated to appear for investigative interviews.
- Supervisors and command staff who were at the scene of the relevant incident should be interviewed.
- Photographs of officers' and complainants' injuries should be taken, if applicable.
- All related audio and visual recordings (e.g., from in-car cameras) should be reviewed for evidentiary content.
- Investigators are required to canvas the scene for relevant evidence, if applicable.
- Investigators are required to actively seek out witnesses, if applicable.
- Investigatory processes should assess the consistency of information across statements by complainants, officers, and witnesses.
- Investigatory processes should be documented in standardized reports.

Rigorous Legal Standards
The federal consent decrees and MOAs establish the following conventions to ensure the integrity of complaint investigations from a legal perspective:

- The evidentiary standard for complaint resolution is preponderance of evidence.
- A finding or admission of guilt by the complainant on criminal charges related to the incident should not be considered evidence weighing against the complainant.

- Unavailability of the complainant or withdrawal of the complaint should not automatically result in the complaint investigation being dismissed.
- During the complaint filing and investigation process, no civilian can be required to waive his or her right to sue for police misconduct unless he or she has a lawyer present.

In many ways, the language of the consent decrees and MOAs calls for investigatory procedures that parallel the rigor and legal standards required in criminal investigations.

Unbiased Investigations
The federal consent decrees and MOAs establish several evidentiary and investigatory conventions to ensure that investigations are not conducted in a manner that allows biases in favor of the police. These are particularly germane to internal investigations.

- Officers' statements should never receive automatic preference over the complainants' statements.
- Group interviews of complainants, witnesses, and indicated officers are prohibited.
- Leading questions are prohibited during investigatory processes.
- Officers named in the complaint should not be materially involved in the investigation.
- Officers not named in the complaint but who nevertheless supervised, approved, or were directly involved in the conduct that is the subject of the alleged complaint should not be materially involved in the investigation.
- Officers not named in the complaint but who may be party to the complaint investigation (e.g., required to give an investigatory interview) should not be materially involved.

Timely Investigations
Although the federal consent decrees and MOAs establish the clear expectation that complaint investigations must be timely, the actual timelines established for the completion of complaint investigation differ across departments. The most common timeline for complaint investigation completion, stipulated in agreements with Buffalo, Cincinnati, Washington, D.C., and Montgomery County, was 90 days. The New Jersey State Police agreement, however, stipulated 45 days while the Steubenville, Ohio agreement stipulated 30 days. In the LAPD agreement, the "expected" timeline to complete complaint investigation was 5 months, but this directive was couched in the following language:

> All investigations of complaints shall be completed in a timely manner, taking into account: (a) the investigation's complexity; (b) the availability of evidence; and (c) overriding or extenuating circumstances underlying exceptions or tolling doctrines that may be applied to the disciplinary limitations provisions (i) applicable to LAPD officers and (ii) applicable to many other law enforcement agencies in the State of California. The parties expect that, even after taking these circumstances into account, most investigations will be completed within five months.[18]

As the LAPD agreement makes clear, the timeliness of an investigation must be defined considering several factors, including the number of complaints a department must investigate, the resources it has to dedicate to investigations, and the complexity of each complaint. Departments should also consider the impact of state laws or collective bargaining agreements on their ability to investigate complaints in a timely manner. All departments should establish and adhere to a reasonable timeline. They also should stipulate that there may be exceptions to these timelines when exceptional circumstances arise. Certainly, the fairness and comprehensiveness of complex complaint investigations should not be compromised by time constraints.

Step Three: The Complaint Resolution Process

The federal consent decrees and MOAs stipulate that the resolution of any complaint must be based on an investigation that is thorough, rigorous, unbiased, and timely and that adheres to a preponderance of evidence standard. The agreements also address the appropriate methods by which the resolutions of complaint investigations are made known.

Disposition

All complaint investigations must be resolved with a disposition or "conclusion of fact." Although the terminology varies slightly across consent decrees and MOAs, these dispositions range from full exoneration of the officer to the full substantiation of the complaint allegation. The dispositions most commonly stipulated in the consent decrees and MOAs fall into the following four categories with their accompanying definition:

- **Sustained**: Preponderance of the evidence shows that misconduct or inappropriate behavior occurred.
- **Unfounded**: Preponderance of the evidence shows that misconduct or inappropriate behavior did not occur.
- **Exonerated**: The conduct described by the complainant or other referral source occurred, but did not violate the agency's policy and/or relevant laws.
- **Not Sustained/Not Resolved/Insufficient Evidence**: There is insufficient evidence to determine whether the alleged misconduct occurred.

Record of Disposition

The federal consent decrees and MOAs stipulate that complaints should be resolved in writing. While the agreements do not prescribe a particular format for these reports, they do stipulate that the reports should contain both the disposition of the complaint and the grounds for that decision. Some agreements further stipulate that the report identify any apparent inconsistencies among statements of complainants, witnesses, and officer interviews that became apparent during the investigation. All reports should explain any sanctions imposed on the officer who is the subject of the complaint, including disciplinary and nondisciplinary actions. Finally, the consent decrees and MOAs are resolute in requiring that complainants be notified of the outcome at the conclusion of the process.

Ensuring Accountability in the Complaint Process

Departments of all sizes and jurisdictions dedicate significant resources to establish and operate civilian complaint processes. The federal consent decrees and MOAs seek to ensure that these resources are expended productively by demanding accountability both within the department and for the benefit of the public the department serves.

Internal Accountability

The federal consent decrees and MOAs seek to ensure accountability for the civilian complaint process within departments through careful stipulations regarding supervisory roles. These stipulations govern the way individual supervisors handle individual complaints as well as they way departments as a whole supervise the complaint process in general. For instance, consent decrees and MOAs require that an officer's direct supervisor should be notified as soon as possible anytime an officer is named in a civilian complaint or is subject to an internal misconduct allegation. These agreements also clearly delineate supervisory authority in general. For instance, consent decrees and MOAs decree that the authority for resolving a complaint investigation—often dependent, as noted earlier, on the nature and seriousness of the allegation—generally rests with the supervisor or a specifically designated investigatory officer, such as one assigned to the department's internal affairs unit. In general, the federal consent decrees and MOAs stipulate that the chief and supervisor have an oversight role and may call for the involvement of specifically designated investigatory officers, as needed, to ensure a fair investigation.

In addition to these stipulations, which guarantee the careful handling of individual complaints, the consent decrees and MOAs stipulate a general monitoring of the overall progress, timeliness, and completeness of all complaint investigations. Depending on the agency size and the jurisdiction of complaint review (e.g., by chain of command or within internal affairs), managers are responsible for the overall monitoring. As a part of this monitoring process, some departments were required to engage external auditors or monitors to conduct audits of the complaint investigations. These audits should be designed to determine whether the complaint process is upholding standards of thoroughness, rigor, and timeliness. Similar internal auditing regimens, often under the auspices of a professional standards are common, particularly in larger departments.

The complaint process audit outlined in the Pittsburgh consent decree is representative of the substance and scope that the agreements seek to establish for departments' auditing processes generally:

> 71. The auditor shall perform quality assurance checks of OMI investigations. The City shall provide the auditor with full access to all OMI staff and records (including databases, files, and quarterly statistical summaries), the automated early warning system described in Paragraph 12, all information regarding officer use of force and searches and seizures (including the use of force reports required by Paragraph 15, and the search and seizure reports required by paragraph 15), all information required in Paragraph 16, and all relevant City manuals of policies and procedures that the auditor deems necessary to fulfill his or her duties, as defined

below. The auditor shall review and evaluate the following information, and issue a quarterly report to the parties and the Court describing the review and analysis: a. All OMI final reports as described in Paragraph 63, and all remedial training and disciplinary records described in Paragraphs 41 and 21(c). The City shall forward all OMI final reports and all disciplinary and training records to the auditor immediately upon their completion. b. The substance and timeliness of at least 50% of all OMI investigations completed during each quarter of the City's fiscal year. c. Statistical information on the number and types of complaints of PBP misconduct, the timeliness of the investigations, the disposition, and any remedial training, counseling, discipline, transfers, or reassignments. d. Discipline, remedial training, mandatory counseling, transfers, and reassignments actually imposed as a result of each complaint. e. Officer use of force, searches and seizures, and traffic stops.[19]

The Role of Internal Affairs

In most departments, internal affairs units play a role in the complaint investigation and resolution process. In some departments, particularly smaller departments, internal affairs units may play the primary role in investigating serious complaints or all complaints. While adjudicating complaints in a fair and equitable manner is a clear mandate, internal affairs units must attend to a broader range of concerns than just the adjudication on individual cases. As with external oversight bodies, they must demonstrate a commitment to enhance public trust and assess whether deficiencies in department policies, procedures, or training may have contributed to the problematic behavior. These objectives apply whether internal affairs plays the sole role in investigating complaints or works in tandem with civilian oversight.

Accountability Through Data Management

Federal agreements establish provisions that promote individual and departmental accountability for the civilian complaint process through the effective collection and management of complaint data. Provisions common across the consent decrees and MOAs include the following:

- The department is to assign a tracking number to each unique complaint.
- The department should establish a written protocol for use of the complaint information system.
- The department should take appropriate steps for linking and integrating complaint data with the early intervention (risk-management or personnel assessment) system.
- The department is required to maintain complaint data for a specified period of time for the purpose of maintaining complaint histories on individual employees or summary reports by agency or unit. (the period of time, which varies by department, may reflect the influence of factors such as state law or collective bargaining agreements).

Taken together, these provisions aid agency management in using complaint data to enhance accountability. Many agencies have proactively adopted similar data-management strategies, including integrating complaint data into their early intervention systems, and publishing summary data as a means of keeping their communities informed.

Managing the Complaint Process

Public Accountability

The federal consent decrees and MOAs also seek to ensure accountability of the civilian complaint process by stipulating that departments make summary reports of misconduct complaints available to the public. The agreements impose the following requirements:

- The department is to maintain summary reporting ability, including the ability to create complaint history summaries by individual officer or by unit.
- The department is to maintain and periodically disseminate to the public a statistical summary report regarding complaints files and resolution of those complaints.

While the agreements impose the requirements across departments, departments share summarized information on the filing, investigation, and resolution of complaints with the public in various ways. Some departments routinely include this information in their annual reports. Other departments post this information on their web sites.

While the sophistication and level of detail of these summary reports vary considerably by department, providing such reports is sound public policy. The very availability of this summary information sends an important message of transparency and accountability to the public. With summary information in hand, the public can better understand the workings of the complaint process. If the summary report contains monthly, quarterly, or yearly comparisons, then the public is able to assess whether complaints are generally on the rise or dropping. If the summary report breaks down particular types of complaints, such as rudeness or excessive force, by time period, then the public is able to make similar assessments at a more detailed level.

Departments are holding themselves accountable to the communities they serve by offering these summary reports in clear and informative formats. For instance, the table below, available on the web site of the Seattle (Washington) Police Department (SPD), provides information regarding trends of complaint allegations during 6 years.

Type of Allegation	1997	1998	1999	2000	2001	2003
Unnecessary Force	79	64	61	94	105	80
Conduct Unbecoming on Officer	39	35	50	65	85	105
Violation of Rules	42	48	36	21	71	82
Misuse of Authority	39	39	21	20	19	20
Improper Language	45	34	8	5	6	5
Failure to Take Appropriate Action	23	29	20	12	12	14
Violation of Law	7	5	15	12	15	8

Source: Seattle Police Department Office of Professional Accountability
Annual Report Fall 2003
www.ci.seattle.wa.us/police/OPA/Docs/OPA_AR_03.pdf

In another example, the Charlotte-Mecklenburg police rely on their *Internal Affairs 2004 Annual Report* to inform the public about trends in civilian complaints against department employees. Below are just two of the many illustrations included in that report.

Complaints Events Received/Sustained			
	2003	2004	Change
Citizens Complaint Events Sustained Portion and % of Total	144 39 (27%)	162 30 (18%)	11% -9%
Department Complaint Events Sustained Portion and % of Total	237 200 (84%)	243 297 (81%)	2.5% -3%
Total Complaint Events Sustained Portion and % of Total	381 239 (53%)	405 227 (55%)	5.9% -7%

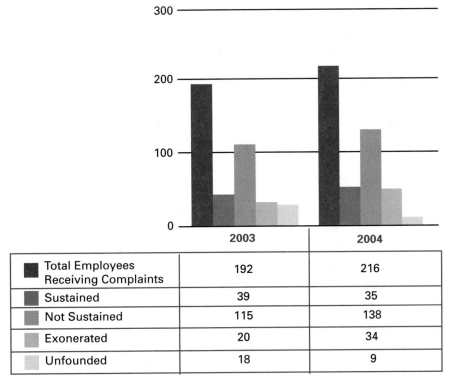

	2003	2004
Total Employees Receiving Complaints	192	216
Sustained	39	35
Not Sustained	115	138
Exonerated	20	34
Unfounded	18	9

Source: Charlotte-Mecklenburg Police Department Internal Affairs
2004 Annual Report
www.charmeck.org/Departments/Police/Home.htm

Recommendations

On the basis of its assessment of federal consent decrees and MOAs as well as the preceding discussion, the IACP offers the following recommendations. The IACP reminds readers that the complaint process may be affected by the local laws and collective bargaining agreements under which a department operates.

The recommendations correspond sequentially with the goals of establishing a civilian complaint process, implementing the process, and remaining accountable to the community served and officers within the department.

Establishing a Clear Policy and Process

1. Establish clear policies and procedures for addressing civilian and internal complaints about officer misconduct.

These policies and procedures for handling civilian and internal complaints may be treated as a standalone section of the department's policy manual or may be embedded within other appropriate policy sections (e.g., internal affairs unit policy).

2. Establish, through policies and procedures, a clear central authority or authorities responsible for the investigation and resolution of misconduct allegations.

Depending on the size of the department, authority to investigate and resolve a complaint may be vested in an individual such as the chief, in the normal chain of command, in a specialized unit such as the internal affairs unit, or in some combination of the above. Depending on the size and organizational capacities of the department, different authorities and investigator processes may be in order for different classes of complaints. This authority or authorities should be clearly articulated in policy.

3. Classify complaints into different categories to ensure appropriate investigatory procedures.

Departments must clearly define the behaviors that constitute misconduct and must categorize these behaviors according to severity to ensure that an appropriate investigation of alleged misconduct occurs.

4. Establish open and accessible complaint filing processes.

Departments' complaint filing processes should not be so burdensome or complicated as to make civilians reluctant to file complaints. Departments should establish multiple means for filing complaints. These might include filing complaints in person, by phone, by fax, by mail, by e-mail, and via the Internet. Instructions and forms should be available in a clear format and in languages commonly in use by the population served.

5. Accept all allegations of misconduct by police officers from all available sources.

Although most allegations of officer misconduct will arise through civilian or internal complaints, departments should actively seek out and require reporting of information about officer misconduct from other sources including arrests of officers (particularly those that occur in other jurisdictions); criminal proceedings against officers; and private civil actions related to official conduct, whether on or off-duty. Officers should be required to report such information about themselves. Departments should establish agreements with local prosecutors and state attorneys who may provide notification of such proceedings. Departments should also be prepared to respond to misconduct allegations brought to light exclusively through the media.

Investigative Processes

6. Establish fair, thorough, and transparent investigatory processes.

Departments must establish processes that ensure a thorough, rigorous, unbiased, and timely investigation of every complaint. To implement such investigations, departments must devote adequate resources to the complaint process and specify reporting protocols and dispositional outcomes to be used at the conclusion of investigations.

7. Select and train investigators based on specific knowledge and skills that are necessary to conduct misconduct investigations.

Departments should not assume that persons who are skilled and experienced in criminal investigations are automatically qualified to conduct misconduct investigations. Although some skills may be transferable, other skills are unique to the misconduct investigation process. Officers investigating civilian complaints should be selected and trained based on skills and knowledge relevant to the specific duties associated with complaint investigations.

8. Policies and investigative practices should stress fairness and balance, both ensuring public confidence in thorough, unbiased investigations and a commitment to protecting officers against false complaints.

To maintain the trust and confidence of both the public department and personnel, investigations must be rigorous yet must protect their officers against false or fabricated allegations. Departments must take great care in distinguishing between fabricated allegations and those that could arise out of confusion or misunderstanding by the complainant. At a minimum, false accusations should be stricken from an officer's record and deleted from any early intervention or personnel assessment management system.

Accountability

9. Track and analyze complaints for the purposes of assessing overall performance and improving policies, procedures, and training.

Departments should fully integrate complaint data into a comprehensive data management strategy. For purposes of assessment, departments should consider complaint data, alongside citizen satisfaction surveys, community group meeting feedback, and ongoing dialogue with a wide cross-section of community leaders, as an indicator of citizen satisfaction with the department. Civilian complaint data must always be analyzed in context. For instance, departments might expect and even welcome a spike in complaints when policies or procedures are changed in order to make the complaint process more open and accessible to civilians. When comparing the number and type of complaints generated across units and across time, police managers must acknowledge and factor in such policy changes. Analyses of complaint data should continually inform department policies and community outreach efforts.

10. Make summary reports available to the public of complaint data analyzed by type, by disposition, and by time period.

By making such information available on web sites and/or through annual reports, departments will demonstrate the transparency of the civilian complaint process to their communities.

Conclusion

Given the nature of law enforcement interactions, complaints by civilians in the communities they serve and internal complaints raised by personnel within the department are a familiar occurrence in all agencies. Law enforcement leaders have a critical choice to make on how best to handle complaints. They may treat them as isolated events which need to be adjudicated. They may also assess complaint data from a broader problem-solving perspective by using complaint data to assess individual performance, unit performance, and as a barometer of the department's success in carrying out its customer-oriented mission. Sweeping complaints under the rug is not only an unethical practice; it also deprives managers of potentially useful information.

Many departments are incorporating complaint data into early intervention strategies or as part of a broader personnel management system. While paying careful attention to providing individuals unfettered access to the complaint process, departments must also ensure that they provide a process by which civilians can file formal commendations about police officers. Data on both complaints and commendations should be used for assessment purposes.

Suggestions for Further Reading

Law enforcement agencies respond to and process civilian and internally generated complaints in a wide variety of ways. The breadth and complexity of this issue extends beyond the issues addressed in this chapter. The following publications are recommended for further reading.

Bobb, Merrick. "Internal and External Police Oversight in the United States." Presentation from an international conference of police oversight at The Hague in October 2005. Police Assessment Resource Center, Los Angeles. www.parc.info/pubs/index.html#issues

International Association of Chiefs of Police. Police Accountability and Citizen Review: A Leadership Opportunity for Police Chiefs. Alexandria (Virginia): 2000. www.theiacp.org/documents/pdfs/Publications/policeaccountability.pdf

Walker, Samuel, Carol Archbold, and Leigh Herbst. Mediating Citizen Complaints Against Police Officers: A Guide for Police and Community Leaders. Police Executive Research Forum, Washington, DC; 2002. www.cops.usdoj.gov/mime/open.pdf?Item=452

Walker Samuel. The New World of Police Accountability. Sage Publications Inc., Thousand Oaks (California): 2005

Endnotes

[1] Thurnauer, Beau. "Best Practices Guide for Internal Affairs: A Strategy for Smaller Departments." Big Ideas for Smaller Departments. Winter 2004. Chief Thurnauer, a 22-year veteran of the Manchester, Connecticut, Police Department, retired with the rank of captain in 1998. He currently serves as the chief of police in Coventry, Connecticut with a staff of 13 sworn officers.

[2] For the purposes of this chapter, discussion of law enforcement employment discrimination allegations are excluded. This should not be interpreted to mean that equal employment opportunity is not an important civil rights issue. Having personnel who are representative of the community they serve is a critical consideration addressed in Chapter 7 of this guide. This topic is omitted because it is an internal civil rights issue and not within the main purview of this document, protecting civil rights of community members.

[3] Memorandum of Agreement Between the United States Department of Justice and the City of Cincinnati, Ohio and Cincinnati Police Department. (4/12/02). www.usdoj.gov/crt/split/Cincmoafinal.htm.

[4] Commission on Accreditation for Law Enforcement Agencies (CALEA) standard 52.1.1.

[5] The 2003 LEMAS survey did not break out university police, railroad police, and other special jurisdictional police as distinct types. Of the tribal police agencies included in the survey, 12 of 15 indicated that they did have a policy directive of citizen complaints, but the sample size for tribal police is not large enough to make reliable projections to all tribal police agencies or to compare across agency size.

[6] *United States* v. *City of Pittsburgh* Consent Decree. (02/26/97). www.usdoj.gov/crt/split/documents/pittscomp.htm.

[7] Agreement Between the United States Department of Justice and Buffalo City Police Department, the Police Benevolent Association, Inc., and the American Federation of State, County, and Municipal Employees Local 264 (9/19/02). www.usdoj.gov/crt/split/documents/buffalo_police_agreement.htm.

[8] *United States* v. *City of Los Angeles* (6/15/2001). Available on the Web at www.usdoj.gov/crt/split/documents/laconsent.htm.

[9] International Association of Chiefs of Police Model Policies. Standards of Conduct, August 1997.

[10] Memorandum of Agreement Between the United States Department of Justice and the District of Columbia and the District of Columbia Metropolitan Police Department (06/13/2000). www.usdoj.gov/crt/split/documents/dcmoa.htm.

[11] Commission on Accreditation for Law Enforcement Agencies (CALEA) standard 52.1.5

[12] International Association of Chiefs of Police. Police Accountability and Citizen Review: A Leadership Opportunity for Police Chiefs. Alexandria (Virginia): 2000. www.theiacp.org/documents/pdfs/Publications/policeaccountability.pdf.

[13] International Association of Chiefs of Police. Police Accountability and Citizen Review: A Leadership Opportunity for Police Chiefs. Alexandria (Virginia): 2000. www.theiacp.org/profassist/ethics/police_accountability.htm.

[14] *United States* v. *City of Los Angeles* Consent Decree. (6/15/2001). www.usdoj.gov/crt/split/documents/laconsent.htm.

[15] International Association of Chiefs of Police. Police Accountability and Citizen Review: A Leadership Opportunity for Police Chiefs. Alexandria (Virginia): 2000. Boise Police Department reference available at www.theiacp.org/profassist/ethics/police_accountability.htm.

[16] Missouri City (Texas) Police Department, Professional Standards. Last updated on 08/06/2002 Retrieved from www.iacpnet.com.

[17] www.co.pg.md.us/Government/BoardsCommissions/pdfs/CCOP_2003-FY2004_Report.pdf

[18] *United States* v. *City of Los Angeles* Consent Decree (6/15/2001). www.usdoj.gov/crt/split/documents/laconsent.htm.

[19] *United States* v. *City of Pittsburgh* Consent Decree (02/26/97). www.usdoj.gov/crt/split/documents/pittscomp.htm.

V. Managing Use of Force

MANAGING USE OF FORCE

> Police departments everywhere have no greater responsibility than to ensure that our officers, who are entrusted by the public to use force in the performance of their duties, use that force prudently and appropriately. In addition, when deadly force is used, police departments have a solemn obligation—to the public and to the officers involved—to investigate these cases thoroughly, accurately and expeditiously.[1]
>
> **Chief Charles Ramsey, Washington, DC Metropolitan Police Department**

Introduction

Occasionally, a use-of-force incident can catapult an individual officer, a whole department, or the entire law enforcement profession into headline news. The mere mention of Rodney King, Amadou Diallo, or Abner Louima, for instance, illustrates the serious concerns that these events can raise in the public forum. Highly visible incidents such as these have an enormous impact not only on the individuals involved, but also on their departments and on law enforcement in general. The unjustified use of force or the use of force that fails to comply with established policy standards damages lives, erodes confidence in the police, destroys careers, and exposes individual officers, departments, and municipalities to substantial civil liability. Individual officers also may be held criminally liable. If excessive force appears to be systemic, it may expose the department to a federal *pattern or practice* investigation.

The law enforcement profession may feel confident, however, in the fact that the use of force—let alone the misuse of force—among police officers is a remarkably rare occurrence. Two large-scale prevalence studies—one based on voluntary submission of police data[2] and one based on a representative national sample survey of the public[3]—found that the use of physical force on the part of officers occurred in less than 1 percent of police and citizen encounters.

Given the fact that most routine police encounters are not confrontational, some suggest that the ratio of use of force to arrests is a more appropriate and revealing standard. A study examining 7 years of data from the Montgomery County (Maryland) police departments found a rate of 6.4 force incidents per 100 adult custody arrests, which, as the authors note, is infrequent considering the context.[4,5]

In his review of research on use of force, University of Central Florida Professor Kenneth Adams observes, "whether measured by use-of-force reports, citizen complaints, victim surveys, or observational methods, the data consistently indicates that only a small percentage of police-public interactions involve the use of force."[6] Thus, data collected by police departments and backed by scholarly research make clear that the overwhelming majority of police-citizen contacts are carried out routinely with no use of physical force.

Still, police executives have the responsibility—both to their communities and to their officers—to effectively handle the small, but serious number of instances in which force is misused. A small percentage of police encounters with the public involve excessive use of force or force without cause. Some officers occasionally stumble into a misuse of force. A small number of officers repeatedly exercise poor judgment or willful disregard for use-of-force policies. Police executives must work to limit such incidents. They must ensure that use of force is kept to a minimum, that excessive force is not tolerated, and that any allegation of excessive or unlawful force is thoroughly investigated.

To this end, a police executive's ability to manage use of force through clear polices, effective training, and sound management is of paramount importance. Through these tools, police executives must require officers to limit their use of force to that which is reasonably necessary for effective law enforcement and for the protection of officers and civilians. As a result, the public should be able to expect that police officers will use force only to the extent necessary to achieve lawful law enforcement objectives and never as a method of retaliation or as an outlet for frustration. Police executives are also responsible for assuring that proper accountability mechanisms are in place. Police executives, appropriately, should track agency patterns in use of force and offer proper intervention or disciplinary action for officers found to have engaged in unlawful use of force.

Finally, police executives must be prepared to respond in highly visible moments when officers have been accused of excessive use of force or force without cause. What police leaders say and do in these moments has a tremendous effect on the public's response as well as on the morale of rank-and-file police officers. In response to any incident involving an excessive use-of-force allegation, a police executive must balance concern for the public with concern for officers. The chief must ensure that the incident will be investigated thoroughly and fairly while avoiding pressure from either side to rush to judgment. Only in this way will the chief sustain the confidence of the department and the community that the department serves.

Chapter Overview and Objectives

This chapter addresses law enforcement leaders' management of the use of force within their departments. Although teaching officers to use force to ensure their own and others' safety and to respond to resistance is an ongoing and critical responsibility, this chapter is not meant to be a primer on use-of-force techniques. Instead, it focuses on the tremendous responsibility that law enforcement officers bear as a result of their authority to use force. Law enforcement leaders must remain vigilant in assisting officers to manage this awesome responsibility if citizens' civil rights are to be protected.

Accordingly, this chapter begins with an investigation of the way in which force is discussed and defined in law enforcement agencies. It explores various levels of force—from the implied force of an officer's presence to deadly force—as well as the reliance on use-of-force continuums to aid officers in their efforts to know when and with what level of force to respond to any given circumstance.

The chapter proceeds from this groundwork to explore four core components of effective use-of-force management. The chapter asserts that every law enforcement leader must design a clear and comprehensive use-of-force policy, implement training that both hones officers' skills in using force and offers them alternatives to this use, maintain accountability mechanisms to ensure that excessive force or force without cause is not tolerated, and establish media and public relations outreach strategies before any critical use-of-force incident threatens to distance the department from the community it is sworn to serve. By combining proper use-of-force policies, training, accountability mechanisms, community outreach, and public relations strategies, law enforcement leaders can effectively limit individual, departmental, and municipal liability while promoting confidence and trust among their own rank-and-file officers and community members. To promote these ends, the chapter concludes with a series of recommendations.

Issues in Defining Use of Force

Discussions of the use and misuse of force revolve around common phrases that are consistently used but not always uniformly defined. The following discussion is intended to clarify these terms for the purposes of this guide.

Use-of-Force Definitions in Context

While use of force is a common phrase in law enforcement and in scholarly research such as the studies mentioned in the chapter introduction, the meaning of the term can be ambiguous. It is best understood in the particular contexts in which it is used.

In the context of departmental policy directives, use of force as a general term is rarely defined. Instead, these policies define at least two classes of force: deadly force (often referred to as lethal force) and nondeadly force (sometimes called nonlethal or less-lethal force). These policies then stipulate the use of various weapons, equipment, and techniques that fall under these two general headings.

In the context of training, departments often do define use of force; generally, they define the phrase rather broadly. Many departments expressly stipulate that all police encounters or at least involuntary police contacts such as traffic stops, pedestrian stops, and arrests imply some sense of force. Under this broad conceptualization of the issue for purposes of training, use of force is seen as a graduated continuum that ranges from the mere presence of an officer—implied force—to the use of deadly force options. This use-of-force continuum as a training tool will be discussed in greater detail below.

Outside the training room, however, the use of force generally is defined more narrowly to refer to specific actions that are over and above an agency defined threshold and excludes the type of routine activities that occur during arrest and other encounters. In this sense, force is seen as a response to subject resistance. The following excerpt from the memorandum of agreement between the Department of Justice and the Detroit Police Department provides a summary of the term as it commonly is understood from an operational law enforcement perspective:

> The term "force" means the following actions by an officer: any physical strike or instrumental contact with a person; any intentional attempted physical strike or instrumental contact that does not take effect; or any significant physical contact that restricts the movement of a person. The term includes the discharge of firearms; the use of chemical spray, choke holds, or hard hands; the taking of a subject to the ground; or the deployment of a canine. The term does not include escorting or handcuffing a person with no or minimal resistance. Use of force is lawful if it is objectively reasonable under the circumstances and the minimum amount of force necessary to effect an arrest or protect the officer or other person.[7]

Deadly and Nondeadly Force

Virtually all policy directives focused on the use of force draw distinctions between deadly and other types force. Deadly—or lethal—force generally is construed as any action that is readily capable of causing death or serious physical injury. According to a federal memorandum of agreement in effect in Washington, D.C., "the term 'deadly force' means any use of force likely to cause death or serious physical injury, including but not limited to the use of a firearm or a strike to the head with a hard object."[8] Other federal agreements use very similar definitions. It is important to note that the implication of many of these definitions is that death or serious injury need not be the intended outcome, just a possible outcome of the force used. For instance, some departments define warning shots and choke holds as deadly force.

By definition, all other uses of force are considered nondeadly—or less-lethal—uses of force. Some departments define nondeadly force by specifying the instruments, weapons, and techniques that fall under this category. These might include specific references to batons, flashlights, chemical agents, conducted energy device (CED) and canine deployments. A CED is sometimes referred to as an electronic control weapon (ECW) or a Taser™, a name of one well-known manufacturer.

Debates regarding distinctions between deadly and nondeadly uses of force certainly exist. Differences of opinion exist on terminology to describe the general types of force, and departments struggle to determine where certain techniques should be placed. The use-of-force continuum is useful in this context. A graphic teaching tool, it can be used to illustrate the distinctions between deadly and nondeadly force options.

> ### A Note on Terminology Used in this Guide
>
> In policies, training, and general discussions, various terminologies are used in distinguishing between two categories of force. Consistent with IACP's model policy on use of force,[9] this guide uses the terms *deadly* and *nondeadly* force, except when using specific terms from quoted or referenced sources. One article suggests this distinction is more consistent with legal standards and less ambiguous than others. "Fourth Amendment law speaks of two categories of force: deadly and nondeadly. The term 'less-lethal' potentially confuses the fact that electronic control weapons, appropriately used, are by definition nondeadly force devices. It also suggests that the use of electronic control weapons is questionable in anything but deadly force situations."[10]
>
> The term "Taser" refers to one particular manufacturer. Besides Taser, however, there are other manufactures such as Stinger™. Although generic terms are being used in lieu of common brand names, these have varied and perhaps add to the confusion. Generic terms include conducted energy devices (CEDs), electro-muscular-disruption-technology (EMDT), and occasionally stun guns. Taking the lead from a recent publication of training guidelines that were developed by the Police Executive Research Forum (PERF) in consultation with law enforcement professionals this guide uses the term conducted energy device or CED.[11] Other terms are used when directly referencing or quoting terms used by other sources.

Reasonableness of Force

In general, legitimate force is described as those "reasonable" actions that are necessary to protect persons or property from illegal harm or to bring about obedience to a valid police order. Stemming from the Fourth Amendment, reasonableness is the legal standard that must guide the decision to use force and the amount of force used. This standard of reasonableness has several implications. One is that an officer is permitted to use the amount of force necessary only to overcome the resistance or aggression that is presented by the subject. In addition, when the resistance or the aggression of the subject is reduced, the officer(s) must reduce his or her force correspondingly. The consent judgment between the Department of Justice and the Detroit Police Department invokes the reasonable-force standard in describing legitimate uses of force: "Use of force is lawful if it is objectively reasonable under the circumstances and the minimum amount of force necessary to effect an arrest or protect the officer or other person."[12]

Understanding two additional legal inferences about the standard of reasonable force is important. First, reasonableness is not assessed from hindsight, but is based on "careful attention to the facts and circumstances of each particular case" and as would be seen from the perspective of a reasonable officer responding to the particular case.[13] Second, in assessing reasonableness, courts have been deferential to the reality that officers are making split-second decisions under difficult circumstances.[14]

Excessive Force

In general, excessive force is defined as being unlawful force or force that exceeds the appropriate thresholds defined by a department's policy directives. The standard for distinguishing excessive force from allowable force is, as discussed above, the standard of reasonableness. Policy directives generally note that the standard of reasonableness is based on the perspective of the officer on the scene at the time the force decision is being made. The following excerpt from a sample policy from the Virginia Department of Criminal Justice Services is representative of an excessive-force definition based on this legal standard and helps ground the legal terminology in a clear operational context.

> Force is excessive when its application is inappropriate to the circumstances, resulting in serious physical injury or death to a suspect. In determining whether force has been excessively applied, the primary concern is whether the on-scene officer reasonably believes that its application was necessary and appropriate. Based on the reasonableness standard, excessive force may be determined based on:
>
> 1. The severity of the crime.
> 2. The nature and extent of the threat posed by the suspect.
> 3. The degree to which the suspect resists arrest or detention.
> 4. Any attempts by the suspect to evade arrest by flight or fight.
>
> In evaluating the reasonable application of force, officers must consider their own age, size, strength, skill level with department weapons, state of health, and the number of officers relative to the number of suspects.

This and other similar directives are necessary for providing context and establishing parameters for proper conduct. It would be impractical, however, for officers to perform the detailed mental checklist suggested in the language when dealing with exigent circumstances in the field. The use-of-force continuum is offered in many departments as a practical way to train officers to assess situations and from which to make force decisions in the field.[15]

Managing Use of Force

Use-of-Force Continuum

In their day-to-day work, police officers must make difficult, split-second decisions about whether to use force and what level of force to use. These decisions must be consistent with departmental policy and legal standards. Written departmental policies taken by themselves can be vague and difficult for officers to apply in the field. As a result, many departments have used a use-of-force continuum—a tool that helps officers visualize variations in levels of force—as a means of clarifying written policies. Indeed, most departments use a use-of-force continuum in training, and many departments now explicitly incorporate a use-of-force continuum into their departmental policy.

Several examples of use-of-force continuums/matrices are presented below:

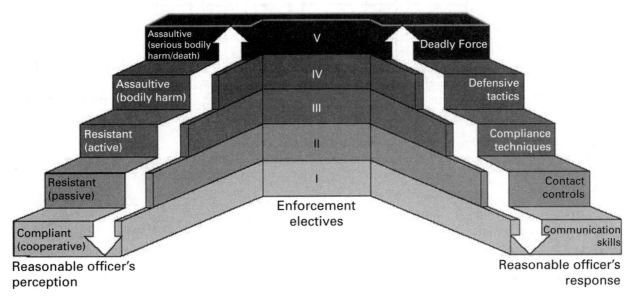

Level of Threat	Corresponding Force
(1) Compliant (blue level)	Communication, such as verbal commands
(2) Passive resistance (green level)	Low-level physical tactics, such as grabbing a suspect's arm
(3) Active resistance (yellow level)	Use of come-along holds, pressure points, and chemical sprays
(4) Assaultive with the potential for bodily harm (orange level)	Defensive tactics, such as striking maneuvers with the hands or a baton
(5) Assaultive with the potential for serious bodily harm or death (red level)	Deadly force

Image of Federal Law Enforcement Training Center (FLETC) Use-of-Force Model.
From GAO/GGD=96-17 ATF Use of Force, page 39

Managing Use of Force

RECOMMENDED RESPONSE TO RESISTANCE MATRIX

RESISTANCE LEVELS

Resistance Level	Arrival	Interview Stance	Dialogue	Verbal Direction	Touch	Restraint Devices	Transporters	Take Downs	Pain Compliance	Counter Moves	Intermediate Weapons	Incapacitation	Deadly Force
6 Aggressive Physical	√	√	√	√	√	√	√	√	√	√	√	√	√
5 Aggressive Physical	√	√	√	√	√	√	√	√	√	√	√	√	
4 Active Physical	√	√	√	√	√	√	√	√	√		√		
3 Passive Physical	√	√	√	√	√	√	√	√	√				
2 Verbal	√	√	√	√	√	√							
1 Presence	√	√	√	√	√	√							

Officer Presence	Communication	Physical Control	Intermediate Weapons	Incapacitating Control	Deadly Force
1	2	3	4	5	6

RESPONSE LEVELS

Checked areas represent authorized, acceptable beginning response levels. Any response in an unchecked area requires explanation. Refer to definitions for each level of resistance and response.

Image from the Florida Department of Law Enforcement, Criminal Justice Professionalism Program, Criminal Justice Standards and Training Commission Defensive Tactics Curriculum, Legal and Medical Risk Summary June 2002, Page 4 (supplied by the Tallahassee Police Department).

DPSST Force Continuum

	Level of Force	Method of Force		Level of Resistance	Threat
VI	Deadly	Any force readily capable of causing death or serious physical injury		Lethal	R E S I S T I V E
V	Serious Physical Control	Neck Restraint Impact Weapon Focused Blows Mace (CN/CS)	O C R E S T R A I N T S	Ominous	
IV	Physical Control	Hair Takedown Joint Takedown Digital Control Joint Come–along Pressure Points Electronic Stun Device Temp. Restraints		Active Static	
III	Physical Contact	Escort Position Directional Contact		Verbal	Undecided
II	Verbal Communication	Direct Order Questioning Persuasion			
I	Presence	Display of Force Option Body Language/Demeanor Identification of Authority		None	Complying

Image from the Oregon Department of Public Safety and Training Standard (DPSST).
Obtained from Portland State University Public Safety Office web site
www.cpso.pdx.edu/html/forcepolicy.htm

Origins and Evolution of Use-of-Force Continuums

The use-of-force continuum originated in the early 1980s. The first continuum was a line with officer presence or verbal commands at one end and deadly force at the other. The continuum has now seen countless revisions and adaptations. While no single use-of-force continuum has been universally accepted, some states such as Florida and Oregon have either adopted or recommended a continuum for statewide use. This tool is not without its detractors, but while its effectiveness in various forms has been debated, and will continue to be debated, it is a widely used training tool and the foundation of many—if not most—departments' use-of-force policies.

Several Department of Justice investigations, consent decrees, and memorandums of agreement (MOA) address the use-of-force continuum. The federal MOA for the Washington, D.C., police, for instance, requires that that department continue to use its continuum and incorporate it as part of its academy and annual training. In its consent decree, the Detroit Police Department is required to revise its use-of-force policy and continuum to meet the following stipulations:

> **The use-of-force policy shall incorporate a use-of-force continuum that:**
>
> a. identifies when and in what manner the use of lethal and less than lethal force are permitted
> b. relates the force options available to officers to the types of conduct by individuals that would justify the use of such force
> c. states that de-escalation, disengagement, area containment, surveillance, waiting out a subject, summoning reinforcements, or calling in specialized units are often the appropriate response to a situation.[16]

Benefits and Drawbacks of the Use-of-Force Continuum

Proponents of the use-of-force continuum maintain that it is a practical training tool that helps officers make decisions that effectively balance safety considerations with individual rights. Proponents argue that in conjunction with proper training—scenario training and shoot-don't-shoot training—the use-of-force continuum enables officers to make sound decisions quickly. They also argue that the use-of-force continuum is a useful tool during post-incident reviews and investigatory interviews where it can help the officer and investigators articulate what level of force was used and why that level of force was necessary under the circumstances. Proponents also note that the continuum has proven to be a useful tool in court where it can help juries understand the standards by which officers operate in making use-of-force decisions.

While many feel that the continuum's advantages are clear and obvious, others have questioned its usefulness in real-life situations. Some have voiced concerns, for instance, that training and responses based on a rigid matrix, in which lower level force options must be ruled out before higher level options can be used, are unrealistic.[17] These critics contend that in real-life encounters where serious threats or levels of resistance must be met with suitable force in a timely manner, the use-of-force continuum can cause officers to hesitate and thus put the officer, fellow officers, and by-standers in jeopardy. Critics also contend that real-life encounters are far more complex than the continuum implies and that use-of-force continuums too often fail to incorporate adequately important issues such as disengagement, de-escalation, or other cooling-off strategies.

An alternative to the use-of-force continuum is the circular situation force model that is common in the United Kingdom and Canada, and gaining popularity in the United States. In a glossary included in a publication on policy and training guidelines relevant to conductive energy device guidelines by the PERF Center on Force and Accountability, this model is described as follows:

> A circular force training model that promotes continuous critical assessment and evaluation of a force incident in which the level of response is based upon the situation encountered and level of resistance offered by a subject. The situational assessment helps officers determine the appropriate force option, ranging from physical presence to deadly force.[18]

Selecting a Use-of-Force Continuum

With so many use-of-force continuums—ranging from the very simple to the complex—available for adoption or modification, law enforcement executives must make careful and deliberate decisions. While law enforcement leaders may find it tempting to simply adopt another agency's continuum or a model continuum, they must take the steps to ensure that the selected use-of-force continuum is tailored to their agency. In the process of developing a continuum or adopting and then tailoring a continuum to their own needs, several considerations are especially important from a civil rights perspective.

- The use-of-force continuum should match the department's actual use-of-force options. It should include all techniques, nondeadly weapons, and deadly weapons available to department personnel. It should include standard-issue weapons that are made available to all officers, as well as weapons that are made available only to specialized units like the SWAT team.
- The use-of-force continuum should clearly demonstrate where each weapon and technique fits onto the continuum's graduated scale and match this scale to levels of subject resistance and actions.
- If an agency uses canines in any effort to control or apprehend suspects or other subjects, that canine deployment should be placed on the continuum. Distinctions should be made about whether a department uses a "find-and-bark" strategy, a "find-and-bite" strategy, or both. Such distinctions may be important in accurately placing the use of canines on the use-of-force continuum.

- As departments adopt CEDs, beanbag guns, and other weapons being developed at a rapid pace and marketed as nondeadly options by vendors, they must make careful and deliberate decisions regarding where to place these technologies on their use-of-force continuums. Placement must depend on the particular manner in which a tool will be deployed within the particular department. For instance, some departments have opted to allow CEDs to be used only when other forms of deadly force would be justified while other departments' policies stipulate that CEDs can be used as a nondeadly option, at a level similar to pepper spray.

CEDs: Decisions Regarding Deployment

The deployment of Conductive Energy Devices (CEDs) has become one of the most hotly debated topics in law enforcement. News regarding sudden and unexpected deaths following CED deployments has brought the issue to the public's attention.

The safety and viability of CEDs as a use-of-force option is fiercely contested. In a recent study, Amnesty International reported that 74 in-custody deaths have occurred since 2001 as a result of CED-related incidents (November 2004). That study recommended suspending the use of these devices until more information is provided on safety, standards, training, and medical protocols. On the other hand, many of the more than 5,000 police departments that have deployed CEDs have documented substantial drops in officer and subject injuries, thus reinforcing manufacturer claims that CEDs offer an effective nondeadly use of force when used within the context of proper policies, procedures, and training.

In response to the need for more definitive information on the use and management of these devices, the IACP has published an executive brief, *Electro-Muscular Disruption Technology: A Nine Step Strategy for Effective Deployment*. This brief offers a step-by-step guide to aid law enforcement agencies in selecting, acquiring, and using the technology. The full text of the report is available on IACP web site[19] (www.theiacp.org/research/RCDCuttingEdgeTech.htm).

While the full report provides a comprehensive guide for law enforcement agencies to develop their own strategies for CED deployment, some basic considerations, especially regarding community relations and accountability, are important enough to review here.

The Nine Step Strategy
1. Building a leadership team with members who can address issues relative to acquisition, costs, policies, training, liability, and evaluation.
2. Placing CEDs on the use-of-force continuum.
3. Assessing the costs and benefits of using CEDs.
4. Identifying roles and responsibilities for CED deployment.
5. Engaging in community outreach.
6. Developing policies and procedure for CEDs.
7. Creating a comprehensive training program for CED deployment.
8. Using a phased deployment approach for CEDs.
9. Assessing CED use.

Community Relations

Departments must consider the potential impact on community relations in its cost-benefit analysis. An agency decision to include CEDs as a force option will elicit a reaction in many communities, even if they concur that the devices falls under the category of nondeadly force. If the community believes that a department has a history of using excessive force or is racially biased in its use of force, it would behoove that department to seek input from community stakeholders as part the decision-making process. Proactive outreach on the part of the department and regular meetings with the community can build mutual trust and respect.

Accountability

Departments must consider any CED deployment as a use of force that is both reportable and reviewable by the chain of command. CED use should be documented and assessed as part of the agency's early intervention strategy. CED usage should also be part of a data-driven management strategy in which both the pluses and minuses of the tool and of the manner of deployment are continually evaluated.

Evaluation

Departments evaluating their deployment of conducted energy devices must ask the following key questions:

- Does the deployment of CEDs correspond to decreases in officer and suspect injuries, or the extent of injuries?
- Does deployment result in greater or lesser overall use-of-force incidents within the department? Is there any evidence to suggest the CEDs are being used in instances where no physical use of force would have been used before this tool became available?
- Does deployment result in increases or decrease in use-of-force complaints?

Although answers to these questions are beginning to emerge from analyses within individual departments, no systematic research has yet been conducted. Law enforcement leaders should note that the results of departmental evaluations will depend on the particular policies, strategies, and types of deployments unique to particular departments rather than on the qualities inherent in the CED tool itself. Considering that these tools are relatively new, are controversial in the public forum, and that no consensus yet exits about the best methods of deployment, law enforcement leaders must remain vigilant and continually assess their departments' deployments of CEDs in light of evolving standards.

Near Universal Prevalence of Use-of-Force Policies

The need for use-of-force policies in law enforcement is widely accepted. The Commission on Accreditation for Law Enforcement Agencies (CALEA) has promulgated accreditation standards as part 1.3 of its Law Enforcement Role and Authority Chapter. In 1989, the IACP issued its first model policy and concept paper on use of force. That policy was last updated in February 2005.[20] Other professional agencies and associations, as well as numerous state organizations, also have developed model policies.

Based on 2003 Law Enforcement Management and Administrative Statistics (LEMAS) census data (and reflecting terminology from a data-collection instrument), the vast majority of municipal police departments and sheriffs' offices have policies on the use of *deadly force and less-than-lethal force* (specific terminology from LEMAS questionnaire). Details about LEMAS methodology and data are available in the text box on page 31 in Chapter 2.

As the charts below reveal, although a smaller percentage of municipal departments and sheriffs' offices have "a written policy directive on *less-than-lethal force* than have a policy on *deadly force*, the clear majority of all agencies, regardless of size, have policies for both categories of force. These charts use the terminology for force categories that are used in the LEMAS survey instrument.

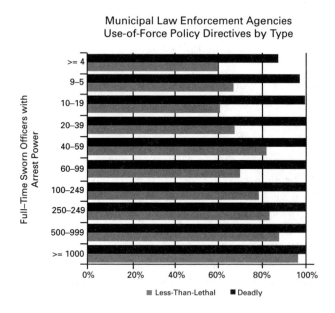
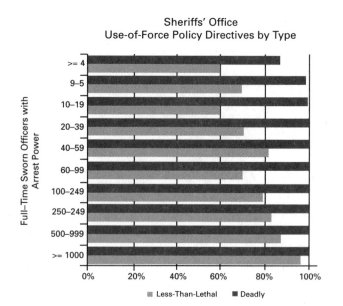

Evolutions in Use-of-Force Policies

While almost universally implemented, specific use-of-force policies still vary by jurisdiction and continue to change over time. As noted above, use-of-force policies evolved to incorporate use-of-force continuums in the 1980s. More recently, federal consent decrees and memorandums of agreement (MOA) have required departments to modify their policies, training, and accountability mechanisms to better ensure the protection of civil rights. Departments have also adjusted use-of-force policies in response to other factors, including civil suits and court settlements. Many departments have adjusted, and continue to adjust, their policies to conform to evolving professional standards or in direct response to particular incidents that have raised legal issues or heightened public concern.

Core Components of Effective Management of Use-of-Force

The authorization to use force is an awesome power that carries with it a tremendous amount of responsibility. For all the variability in the tone and language of use-of-force policies, departments have discovered that certain core components within these policies will result in the effective limitation of use of force, strict accountability, and the effective response to incidents in which force is misused.

As noted above, police officers must use force only when reasonably necessary and must use only the amount of force necessary to overcome resistance or to achieve compliance with the law. As clear as this imperative is, the decision to use force and the judgment of the proper level of force can be difficult and complex. When making use-of-force decisions, officers must simultaneously address their own safety, the safety of surrounding persons, and the well-being and civil rights of the subject.

Of course, the difficult and delicate nature of these decisions makes the need for clear policies, effective training, strong supervision, and strict accountability absolutely paramount. When officers are involved in emotionally charged and potentially violent encounters, the combined influence of policies, training, and accountability are critical. Indeed, assurance must be made that these elements must be integrated and consistent to best ensure that officers respond in a reasoned and disciplined manner.

This chapter asserts that use of force can be managed as a law enforcement strategy, while still protecting civil rights, if law enforcement leaders take care to establish policies and practices (1) that are comprehensive; (2) that carefully consider and alternatives to use of force and consideration of special circumstances and persons; (3) that incorporate strong accountability mechanisms; and (4) that are attentive to public and media relations. The following sections discuss each of these components in more detail and lay out some of the key elements that have been addressed in the consent decrees and MOAs as key issues relating to civil rights.

Component One: Comprehensiveness

To effectively manage the use of force, departments must establish use-of-force policies that clearly address <u>all</u> force techniques and technologies available to their officers. They must also consider the broad range of issues related to those deployments.

Use-of-force policies succeed as they clearly establish their departments' expectations regarding each and every force option available to officers. This is especially critical as departmental policies evolve in response to civil rights concerns. The following paragraphs address several use-of-force options and issues that have direct implication on civil rights concerns. Where relevant, these paragraphs include language from federal consent decrees and MOAs and department policies.

Verbal Warnings

Use-of-force policies increasingly incorporate a discussion of verbal warnings. Encouraging the use of verbal warnings before the deployment of force reinforces the commitment to ensuring that the use of force is no greater than necessary to ensure public and officer safety. Policies generally stipulate that verbal warnings should be issued when appropriate and possible, but should never compromise the safety of officers or of the public. Several federal agreements stipulate the use of verbal warnings prior to the deployment of particular use-of-force options. The MOA with the Cincinnati Police Department requires using a verbal warning, when feasible, before beanbag shotguns or foam rounds are used. This MOA also requires that a "loud and clear announcement" be made before canines are released. The federal agreements with the Cincinnati, District of Columbia, Detroit, and Prince George's County (Maryland) Police Departments require, with limited exceptions, that verbal warnings be issued before the deployment of chemical or Oleoresin Capsicum (OC) spray. The excerpt from the agreement with the District of Columbia's Metropolitan Police Department is illustrative:

> The policy shall require officers to issue a verbal warning to the subject unless a warning would endanger the officer or others. The warning shall advise the subject that OC spray shall be used unless resistance ends. The policy shall require that prior to discharging the OC spray, officers permit a reasonable period of time to allow compliance with the warning, when feasible.[21]

When verbal warnings are issued, it is also imperative that they be appropriate to the circumstances. They must be delivered with clarity and forcefulness. Although these types of warning typically are made during exigent circumstances, officers should maintain their professional demeanor to the extent possible. They should avoid profanity or language that is disrespectful or demeaning to the subject.

Managing Use of Force

Warning Shots
Use-of-force policies also are increasingly addressing warning shots. A search of policies submitted to IACPNet revealed 15 departments that address "warning shots" in their policy directives. All but two of these departments prohibited warning shots under any circumstances. Increasingly, agencies are prohibiting warning shots altogether or narrowly limiting the circumstances in which they are allowed. The policy of the Savannah-Chatham (Georgia) Metropolitan Police Department is illustrative of a narrowly defined exception for allowing the use of warning shots:

> Warning shots are forbidden with the only exception being the Marine Patrol Unit and under the following circumstances:
>
> - Warning shots may be used for mission accomplishment (e.g., to compel a non-compliant vessel to stop as a security measure in Homeland Security defense).
> - Warning shots are a signal to a vessel to stop, for waterway security zone incidents involving terrorist attacks and may be fired only by Marine Patrol personnel who are trained in the use of rifles. The use of warning shots will not endanger any person or property, including persons aboard a suspect vessel and warning shots shall not be fired over land.
>
> Source: Savannah-Chatham (Georgia) Metropolitan Police Department
> Agency Profile: Population 198,000; Officers 575

Choke Holds
Federal agreements and use-of-force policies that address choke holds acknowledge the seriousness of this use-of-force option. The use of choke holds—or similar procedures such as carotid control holds—has long been a topic of debate. The purpose of the technique is to incapacitate an aggressive subject temporarily to gain control of the situation. But because of the risk involved with these techniques—they are intended to restrict the airflow through the windpipe or flow of blood to the brain—some departments have prohibited them outright, while others have narrowly defined the circumstances under which the can be used. Most departments that allow this option classify the choke hold as deadly force. Federal agreements underscore this definition and advocate the restrictive use of choke holds. In relevant consent decrees and MOAs, the Department of Justice states that departments' policies should "explicitly prohibit the use of choke holds and similar carotid holds except where deadly force is authorized."[22] The policy of the Des Moines (Washington) Police Department, for instance, underscores the seriousness of this use-of-force option:

> The choke hold shall be considered deadly force and officers will use this hold only in defense of human life. Anytime this hold is used, an officer's report will be submitted.
>
> Source: Des Moines (Washington) Police Department
> Agency Profile: Population 29,267; Officers 43

Canine Deployments

Use-of-force policies address canine deployments in detail. Some departments use dogs to help establish subject compliance as well as to apprehend dangerous or fleeing suspects or escapees. As with other uses of force, canine deployments must be based on balancing the risks inherent in their use against the risks that arise in the absence of their use. In all instances, canine deployments should be attended by strict selection, training, and accountability measures that apply to both handlers/trainers and dogs. The Manchester (Connecticut) Police Department policy explicitly addresses canine deployments:

Use of Force

1. The use of specially trained police canines for law enforcement responsibilities constitutes a real or implied use of force. The police officer/handler may only use that degree of force that is reasonable to apprehend or secure a suspect, protect him/herself, protect another officer and/or a civilian as governed by General Order 1-6 Use of Force. The police officer/handler shall file the appropriate reports documenting the use of force as required by General Order 1-6 Use of Force.

2. The police officer/handler and other officers shall adhere to the following levels of force when protecting the canine.

   a. The use of Less Lethal Force may be used to protect the canine from an assault or attempted assault.

   b. The use of Lethal Force shall not be used to protect the life of the canine. The canine is a piece of equipment utilized by the police officer/handler.

   c. The police officer/handler may use the canine in preventing the infliction of less lethal and lethal force against him/herself, another officer and/or civilian.

3. Canine warning

   a. The canine warning should consist of the following or similar announcement:

   "This is the Manchester Police Canine team, speak to me now/stop now or I will send the dog."

   b. The police officer/handler shall deliver a series of warnings to ensure that the suspect has had ample warning, that the canine shall be used to apprehend him/her.

   c. A warning allows the suspect time to surrender and shall also alert any innocent persons in the same area of the canine's teams' presence and intention.

d. The canine warning should not be given when, in the opinion of the handler, doing so would cause undue risk to the canine team's presence and intention.

e. At NO time shall the canine team's police officer/handler use his/her canine to affect the arrest of a person(s), who cannot escape or resist the officer, nor to intimidate, coerce or frighten the suspect(s).

Source: Manchester (Connecticut) Police Department
Agency Profile: Pop. 52,500; Officers 119

Discharging Firearms at or from Moving Vehicles

Increasingly, use-of-force policies specifically address the issue of shooting at or from moving vehicles. Most policies prohibit these acts altogether or strictly limit the circumstances in which such shooting is justified. A sample directive from the Virginia Department of Criminal Justice Services addresses this issue:

Firing at a moving vehicle is prohibited except where the officer reasonably believes that:

(1) An occupant of the other vehicle is using, or threatening to use, deadly force by a means other than the vehicle; OR (2) A vehicle is operated in a manner deliberately intended to strike an officer or a citizen and all other reasonable means of defense have been exhausted (or are not present), including moving out of the path of the vehicle, and the safety of innocent persons would not be unduly jeopardized by the officer's action.[23]

Police training must stress that one clear option in response to moving vehicles is for the officer to evade the car. Courts have used the criterion of whether the officer had an opportunity to move out of the way as a factor in determining the reasonableness of force.[24]

Pursuits

Departments have been increasingly careful to consider the advisability of pursuits from a cost-benefit perspective. A variety of broad concerns including public safety, officer safety, fiscal liability, and civil rights, have refined the circumstances in which departments will deploy this use-of-force option. Indeed, pursuit policies and practices have evolved tremendously over the last several decades. Pursuits that would have been initiated years ago based on so-called "contempt of cop" motivations have been significantly curtailed by recent policies and training that stress alternative responses. While curtailing pursuits is often seen as a safety and civil liability issue, the topic raises issues of reasonableness as well as equal protection. Pursuits have been specifically addressed in several of the federal consent decrees and MOAs.

Vehicle Pursuits

The most recent data available from the Bureau of Justice Statistics (BJS) reveals that approximately 95 percent of law enforcement agencies have policies on vehicle pursuits. Law enforcement agencies have long recognized that vehicle pursuits are dangerous, high-liability events. A substantial percentage of police pursuits end in crashes.[25] High-visibility pursuits that end with injuries or property damage can undermine public trust and confidence. Vehicle pursuits also raise considerable risks of fiscal liability. Officers in car chases may experience the phenomena of "adrenaline rush" that clouds their judgment. Additionally, when pursuits within a particular jurisdiction overwhelmingly involve minority drivers, they can also heighten the perception that racial profiling is taking place.

The BJS survey revealed that 59 percent of law enforcement agencies have "restrictive" policies. These policies limit officers from using pursuit unless specific criterions such as seriousness of offense, safety, or fleeing-vehicle speed are met. The following policy except from the Illinois State Police is representative of those that would be described as restrictive in the BJS survey terminology:

> [The Illinois State Police] will initiate a motor vehicle pursuit *only* [emphasis added] when an officer has an articulable reason to believe the occupant(s) of a fleeing vehicle has committed or attempted a forcible felony which involves the infliction or threatened infliction of great bodily harm or is attempting to escape by use of a deadly weapon, or otherwise indicates they will endanger human life or inflict great bodily harm unless apprehended without delay. All officers involved in a pursuit must, at all times, be able to justify their reasons for the pursuit.
>
> Source: Illinois State Police Directives Manual
> Agency Profile: Pop. 12,713,634; Officers 2,089

Other agencies that have not developed restrictive policies are nevertheless increasingly attentive to the need to balance the capture of suspects fleeing in vehicles with the need to protect both the public and police officers from unnecessary risks. The BJS survey cited above revealed that 27 percent of agencies have "judgmental" policies that leave the decision up to the discretion of the officer. In BJS survey terminology, the IACP's model policy would be described as a judgmental or discretionary policy. It explicitly recognizes that vehicle pursuits are inherently dangerous and that the risks of pursuit must be weighed against the risks of not apprehending the subject:

> The decision to initiate pursuit must be based on the pursuing officer's conclusion that the immediate danger to the officer and the public created by the pursuit is less than the immediate or potential danger to the public should the suspect remain at large.[26]

Foot Pursuits

Foot pursuits appear less frequently in use-of-force policies than vehicle pursuits. Although the risk of collateral damage may not be as high, foot pursuits do have attendant risks and civil rights implications. Officers are often injured during foot pursuits and, at the time of capture, can experience the phenomena of "adrenaline rush" which can cloud their judgment and diminish their capacity to react with appropriate restraint. Thus, foot pursuits require careful consideration as a policy and training issue.

As a result of pattern and practice investigations, the Cincinnati Memorandum of Agreement and the Detroit Consent Judgment each enjoined the departments to develop policies specific to foot pursuits. The Cincinnati MOA required the following:

> The CPD will develop and adopt a foot pursuit policy. This policy will require officers to consider particular factors in determining whether a foot pursuit is appropriate. These factors will include, inter alia, the offense committed by the subject, whether the subject is armed, the location (i.e., lighting, officer familiarity), and the ability to apprehend the subject at a later date. The policy will emphasize alternatives to foot pursuits, including area containment, surveillance, and obtaining reinforcements.[27]

Accordingly, the Cincinnati Police Department enacted a specific policy directive on foot pursuits, which includes the following excerpt:

> Whenever an officer decides to engage, or continue to engage, in a foot pursuit a quick risk assessment must take place. They must evaluate the risk involved to themselves, to other officers, the suspect, and the community versus what would be gained from pursuing the suspect.[28]

Component Two: A Focus on Alternatives to Force

To effectively manage the use of force and limit its application to situations in which it is warranted, departments should stress alternatives to force, incorporate these into their policies, and offer specific training in these alternatives in ways that complement traditional training in force techniques.

Policy guidelines, instructional literature, and training programs on the use of force—focused, specifically, on issues such as the proper use of firearms, other weapons, and policing equipment; proper physical restraint and handcuffing techniques; and officer safety—are commonplace. Such instruction often includes detailed information regarding the characteristics of armed persons and officer survival techniques. An officer's use-of-force knowledge base, gained through academy training and subsequent field training, must be continually honed and reinforced through roll-call training and yearly in-service training. It must also be continually tested through qualification tests and simulations.

While this training is absolutely necessary—indeed, vital—to ensuring effective policing as well as the safety of the officers and public, it must be balanced with training that provides viable alternatives to the use of force. Some police executives have expressed concern about the balance of training and instruction directed to "how to use force" as opposed to "how not to use force." As one police chief noted:

> For every hour we spend training our officers in the skills necessary to de-escalate conflict and to avoid the use of force, we spend many more hours teaching officers use-of-force tactics. The message is clear to our officers: use of force is not only appropriate but it is the favored tool for controlling subjects and situations.[29]

Many departments are attempting to achieve more balance by adding training in de-escalation options, as well as training in recognizing and handling situations in which use-of-force decisions may be particularly critical, such as encounters with the mentally ill.

Verbal De-escalation
Acting on the realization that many violent encounters between a police officer and a subject begin as verbal confrontation, departments have adopted verbal de-escalation training to help officers prevent the need for use of force and to enhance officer safety. Verbal judo, one popular form of de-escalation, is also known as tactical communication. Much like physical judo, verbal judo stresses the use of deliberate verbal response rather than reflexive reaction to others' words and deeds. Officers are also instructed in the use of conflict management tactics to check their impulse to respond on the basis of personal feeling. The following excerpt from the Pittsburgh Bureau of Police Consent Decree illustrates the purpose of these techniques:

> The PBP shall train all officers in the use of verbal de-escalation techniques as an alternative to the use of force, and shall incorporate such techniques into all other training that implicates the use of force. Such training shall include specific examples of situations that do not require the use of force, but may be commonly mishandled, resulting in force being used (for example, individuals verbally challenging an officer's authority or asking for an officer's identifying information).[30]

Recognizing and Responding to the Mentally Ill

Many police departments proactively are enacting policies and providing training that equips officers with basic skills for recognizing mental health issues and responding to them appropriately. Police officers are often called into situations where they are required to confront persons with known mental illness or other debilitating conditions. In other cases, a person's mental illness or temporary mental incapacitation may first become apparent during the encounter. Departmental policies and training prepare the officers to handle the situation at hand, to recognize symptoms of mental impairment, and to obtain those services that the subject needs. The policy of the North Royalton (Ohio) Police Department describes the special attention and consideration that a mentally ill subject should receive:

Intervention Approach

1. Incidents dealing with a mentally ill person require tactful, patient responses. To the extent possible an officer should:

    a. Attempt to learn about the person [and] the situation by talking with the mentally ill, his family, friends, [and] witnesses.

    b. Regardless of the person's conduct, respond to them in an objective, non-abusive, non-threatening manner to calm [and] control the person.

    c. Not deceive the mentally ill person. (Deception thwarts the chance for trust. Trust enhances the opportunity for controlling the subject in a non-violent manner.)

2. If it appears a situation involving a mentally ill person requires police action, a minimum of two officers will be dispatched. A lone officer who encounters such a person will request backup [and] wait for it to arrive unless a life threatening circumstance is occurring.

Source: North Royalton (Ohio) Police Department
Agency Profile: Population 28,000; Officers 39

Departments that do not have specific policies for dealing with the mentally impaired should develop these policies. The IACP has two model policies: "Dealing with the Mentally Ill"[31] and "Encounters with the Developmentally Disabled".[32] Also, CALEA recently promulgated new standards for police encounters with persons suffering from mental illness.[33]

A growing number of departments have established designated units, often called crisis intervention teams (CITs) that are specifically trained to respond to mentally ill subjects and to attend to their unique needs. The Department of Justice MOA with the Cincinnati Police Department (CPD) specifies the core elements of such a unit to be developed in that city.

> The CPD will create a cadre of specially trained officers available at all times to respond to incidents involving persons who are mentally ill. These specially trained officers will assume primary responsibility for responding to incidents involving persons who are mentally ill. They will be called to the scene of any incident involving a person who is mentally ill, unless the need for fast action makes this impossible. These officers will respond to any radio run known to involve a person who is mentally ill (including escapes from facilities or institutions). The officers selected for this training should be highly motivated volunteers and should receive high level, multi-disciplinary intervention training, with a particular emphasis on de-escalation strategies. This training will include instruction by mental health practitioners and alcohol and substance abuse counselors. The CPD will develop and implement a plan to form a partnership with mental health care professionals that makes such professionals available to assist the CPD on-site with interactions with persons who are mentally ill.[34]

Component Three: Assuring Accountability in the Use of Force

To effectively manage the use of force, departments must establish strong accountability mechanisms to ensure that use-of-force incidents are reported, reviewed, and, as necessary, investigated, and that the results of these processes are used to enhance department management.

As previously noted, the authorization to use force is an awesome power that carries with it a tremendous amount of responsibility. Departments fulfill this responsibility, in part, by implementing strong supervision and strict accountability mechanisms. Use-of-force policies commonly require systematic reports, reviews, and, as necessary, investigations, of use-of-force incidents involving physical force. The need for these systematic steps cannot be overstated. They are the subject of extensive discussion in federal consent decrees and MOAs.

Use-of-Force Reporting

Although use-of-force policies typically do not require reporting for low levels of force (i.e., when handcuffs are applied in a routine manner or with soft-hands control), these policies increasingly require that use-of-force incidents be reported if the level of force meets or exceeds an agency defined threshold. While this level varies by department, it is most often set at some less-lethal force level (e.g., "anything above soft-hands control"). Typically, these policies specify the format and required elements of use-of-force reports. The following policy of the Colorado Springs (Colorado) Police Department illustrates such reporting requirements:

> NON-LETHAL FORCE [REPORTING]: When a chemical agent, the baton, or any other non-lethal instrument of physical force has been used against any person, the officer(s) involved shall document the incident by inclusion either in a case report or incident report. In all instances, a copy of the report shall be sent through channels to the Division Commander. A cover memorandum containing supplementary or explanatory information may be attached at the officer's discretion or if necessary to complete the required information. Details of the memorandum and/or report shall include:
>
> - Circumstances surrounding the action
> - Type of force used
> - Reasons for the use of force
> - Extent of injury to the officer or other person
> - Medical treatment required
> - The name of the medical facility used
> - Other pertinent information the officer wishes to include.
>
> Source: Colorado Springs (Colorado) Police Department
> Agency Profile: Population 315,000; Officers 501

Reporting Medical Intervention and Follow-up

In addition to requiring reports whenever a use-of-force incident exceeds a certain level of force, policies generally require medical follow-up in the event that a use-of-force incident results in an apparent injury or claim of injury involving the subject, bystanders, or officers. Additionally, policies mandate medical follow-up when certain force options are exercised (e.g., CEDs or chemical sprays) even when injury is not apparent or there is no claim of injury. Typically, all apparent injuries, complaints of injuries, and medical attention must be documented and reported, even when the level of force used was below the agency defined threshold for reporting. The following policies from the Marietta (Georgia) Police Department and the Oregon State Police are representative of such requirements:

> **Medical Care [after use of Oleoresin Capsicum Spray/Foam]**
>
> A. Police officers and Civilian Transport Officers shall notify communications as soon as possible after the use of O.C. spray/foam. Police officers and Civilian Transport Officers shall request fire rescue, an ambulance, and a supervisor. A police officer or Civilian Transport Officer shall accompany the individual to the hospital and shall remain there until properly relieved, or until the individual is released from medical care by hospital personnel.

B. Should the individual resist attempts to decontaminate by medical personnel, the police officer or Civilian Transport Officer will document this refusal to cooperate in the departmental incident report, and monitor the individual closely while at the hospital and during all phases of transport. The police officer or Civilian Transport Officer will then notify detention personnel of the individual's resistance to treatment so the detention personnel can closely monitor the individual.

Source: Marietta (Georgia) Police Department
Agency Profile: Population 45,856; Officers 135

In all use-of-force incidents, including those in which a person is injured, or an employee becomes aware that a person has reported to have sustained an injury during the course of action taken by the sworn employee, a supervisor will be notified as soon as practicable. The supervisor will review the specific circumstances of the respective case and determine if a report to General Headquarters through the chain of command is needed.

Source: Oregon State Police (www.egov.oregon.gov/osp)
Agency Profile: Population 3,480,000; Officers 871

Reviewing Use of Force

Policies often require formal review of use-of-force incidents, generally when such incidents exceed an agency specified level of force. In some departments, the threshold for *reviewable* force is consistent with the threshold for *reportable* force. Typically, reviewable use-of-force incidents include any use of force involving a weapon, whether deadly or nondeadly, and any use of force involving apparent or alleged injury or death. In virtually all departments, the discharge of a firearm must be reviewed.

In many departments, the type of review depends on the level of force used. Some departments draw a distinction between review required with relatively low levels of force and higher levels. Lower level use of force will result in an initial supervisory review that may be followed by reviews up the chain of command. Higher levels of force often result in automatic review by specialized units (e.g., internal affairs or critical incident units) and/or independent bodies (civilian review boards). The following policy of the Des Moines (Washington) Police Department lays out a protocol for reviewing standard use-of-force reports:

Review Of Use Of Force Reports: Team sergeants are responsible for reviewing case reports and the department "Use-of-Force" report form. Sergeants will forward all reports to the Operations Commander for review and submittal to the Chief of Police.

Appropriate reports will be prepared for each incident in which a Use-of-Force Report is necessary by the end of the shift on which the incident occurred. It must include the facts that made the use of force necessary and shall explain in detail the nature and amount of force used. It is the responsibility of the supervisor reviewing the report to insure that thorough and accurate documentation is provided.

Source: Des Moines (Washington) Police Department
Agency Profile: Population 29,267; Officers 43

First-line supervisors should be held accountable for assessing both individual cases and overall use-of-force patterns by their subordinates. Individual officers who show more frequent use of force or a tendency to use higher levels of force when compared to peers in similar assignments should be assessed more closely for possible intervention. Ideally, this function should be integrated into a broader early intervention strategy, as discussed in Chapter 3 of this guide.

Use-of-Force Investigations

Going beyond report reviewing, many departments have recognized the value of thoroughly investigating all serious use-of-force incidents. To limit liability and assure accountability, these departments require thorough, open, and fair investigations by qualified investigators whenever an officer discharges a firearm, deploys other deadly force, or whenever the deployment of force results in death or serious injury. While investigation protocols may differ, the following elements are a vital part of an investigatory process that will ensure accountability within the department and confidence within the community:

- The investigation should include a full chronology of events that occurred before, during, and immediately following the use of force.
- The investigation should be fair, thorough, and conducted with the same rigor as is afforded to major crime investigations. Although many use-of-force investigations will reveal that the use of force is justified, the transparent and rigorous nature of these investigations can shore up public confidence.
- The investigator should be selected and trained specifically to fulfill this task. Efforts should be made by police leaders to identify particular persons who are well suited to this role because not all individuals have the aptitude or commitment to perform these types of investigations. The ability of individual investigators to conduct thorough investigations should be continually assessed. The systematic review of investigatory reports and taped investigatory interviews should be part of the overall assessment.
- The investigation should apply the consequences for willful and blatant use of excessive force clearly and uniformly. They should result in the appropriate level of discipline to re-enforce the message that unlawful force will not be tolerated.

While all investigations share the above-mentioned elements, departments will vary in how the investigatory processes are organized. Large police departments may have sufficient resources to support specific units that investigate incidents of serious nondeadly and deadly force deployment. Smaller agencies, however, may have neither the resources nor the staff to support these units. Indeed, the incidence of deadly force deployments may be so rare in smaller agencies that specific investigatory units may not make sense even if resources could be made available. Many smaller police agencies will turn to outside agencies, often the state police, to conduct these investigations. Other innovative approaches also exist. The investigatory processes identified in the text boxes—one adopted in the Boston (Massachusetts) Police Department and another in Champaign County, Illinois, where several local police agencies have pooled their resources and established the Multi-Jurisdictional Investigation Team—demonstrate two different approaches.

The Boston "Team Model" of Force Investigations

The Boston Police Department has a Firearms Discharge Investigation Team (FDIT) divided into two units, a "red" team and a "blue" team. Despite the name, the FDIT investigates other types of force besides firearms discharges. The red team responds to deaths or major injuries, while the blue team investigates non-lethal discharges, less-lethal, and animal dispatches. The FDIT protocol divides components of investigation, assigning responsibilities to squads that provide distinct and uniform information, without overlap, to the team commander. Investigators are divided into four teams—Crime Scene, Interview, Intelligence, and Organizational—each headed by a team leader. In addition to the teams, an incident coordinator assists the lead investigator/incident commander in procuring personnel and equipment, obtaining logistical support, and keeping a record of who did what and when. Each team has specific responsibilities as outlined in the protocol; for example the responsibilities for the Crime Scene Team include: Securing the scene and setting an access point; obtaining information needed for search warrant application, if applicable; logging all persons and equipment entering the scene; and relevant photography and videotaping at the scene. The scene team is also responsible for obtaining crime scene evidence and seeking out other relevant evidence (e.g., bank surveillance tapes).

Source: Boston (Massachusetts) Police Department, Firearms Discharge Investigation Team
Agency Profile: Population 604,000; Officers 2050

Champaign County Multi-Jurisdictional Team Approach to Investigations :

The Champaign County (Illinois) Serious Use of Force Investigation Team is composed of five agencies (combined sworn 370), representatives from the Illinois State Police and the local district attorney. The team serves as the primary response and investigation unit to an officer-involved shooting in the county (pop. 175,000). Each agency has two response personnel assigned to the team. For any incident the representative for the agency being investigated may not be the lead case investigator, but can serve as a facilitator of information for the lead agent.

The team came about in response to a controversial shooting in mid-1990s and has evolved since. One issue that arose frequently was that officers involved were often unsure of what was going to happen in the investigation, so the team came up with a guide for line officers that delineates the step in the investigation process and the role of the officer being investigated in that process. This guide has proven effective and is now utilized in yearly in-service trainings of all officers in the five agencies. The team recently developed an updated field investigation manual that every investigator has and serves as the guide for conducting the inquiry. The manual includes the county-wide use of force policy and the memorandum of understanding that was used to establish the teams. Administrative forms such as a team-leader assignment sheets, as well as checklists for interview teams, crime scene technicians, and other involved parties. Also included are neighborhood canvass forms and photo evidence forms.

Source: Sgt. Bryant Seraphin, Urbana (Illinois) Police Department Team Coordinator

Managing Use of Force

Concurrent Criminal Investigations
Occasionally, use-of-force investigations will reveal that the officer's actions constitute potential criminal behavior. While internal procedures—including supervisory reviews, internal affairs division reviews, and department-based critical incident team reviews—are suitable for addressing alleged or apparent use-of-force violations, criminal behavior must be addressed through appropriate criminal procedures. Federal agreements are unequivocal on this point. As an excerpt from the MOA with the Metropolitan Police Department in Washington, D.C., makes clear, "[the] MPD shall consult with the USAO [United States Attorney's Office] regarding the investigation of an incident involving deadly force, a serious use of force, or any other force indicating potential criminal misconduct by an officer."[35]

Department policies and practices may vary as to whether the department's internal use-of-force investigation would be ongoing at the same time as the prosecuting attorney's criminal investigation. If investigations are simultaneous, all reasonable attempts should be made by both the department and the prosecutor's office to coordinate efforts. However, there may be certain circumstances under which it might not be advisable to share information or under which the department may need to suspend its investigation, or parts of its investigation, in deference to the prosecutor. As the following excerpt from the MOA with the Metropolitan Police Department in Washington, D.C., states:

> If the USAO [United States Attorney's Office] indicates a desire to proceed criminally based on the on-going consultations with MPD, or MPD requests criminal prosecutions in these incidents, any compelled interview of the subject officers shall be delayed, as described in paragraph 60. However, in order to ensure the collection of all relevant information, all other aspects of the investigation shall proceed. The USAO shall respond to a written request by MPD for charges, declination, or prosecutorial opinion within three business days, by either filing charges, providing a letter of declination, or indicating the USAO's intention to continue further criminal investigation.[36]

Use-of-Force Reports, Reviews, and Investigations as Management Tools
Many departments have found value in using aggregated use-of-force data to assess trends and patterns and to help make informed management decisions. Current policies often require agencies to conduct some form of aggregate analysis to detect patterns and trends in the use of force across the department. Aggregate analyses at the individual or unit level allow for comparisons against normative standards consistent with early intervention management strategies discussed in Chapter 3. For instance, do particular officers or units have inordinately high reportable or reviewable use-of-force incidents relative to similar officers or units? Aggregate analyses at the agency level can serve a critical feedback and accountability function. For instance, does analysis reveal that reportable use-of-force incidents increase when particular force options are introduced, removed, or replaced? Such analyses can

identify the need to change policies, to revisit training, to update a department's use of force options, or to redefine weapon deployment practices. The Pittsburgh Bureau of Police relies on use of force analyses to improve agency management:

> The Pittsburgh Bureau of Police issues what it calls "Subject Resistance Reports" for reportable uses of force.[37] These reports serve the purpose of allowing a mechanism for standardized review of cases and also provide valuable information that can be used in quantitative analyses. Information from these reports is tracked and maintained as part of the Bureau's Personnel Performance System (PARS) and reviewed quarterly at COMPSTAR. Trends and patterns of subject resistance incidents (use of force) are reviewed by managers. Analysis includes comparisons across police sectors; precipitating circumstances (e.g., warrant arrests, prisoner transports, etc); how use-of-force incidents trend alongside monthly calls for service and arrest data. From a managerial perspective, data analysis allows department leaders to spot trends and take effective action to mitigate issues.[38]

Component Four: Maintaining Public and Media Relations

To effectively manage the use of force, departments must handle media and public relations proactively rather than reactively.

Use-of-force incidents that make headline news or appear as the lead story on the local evening news present both a challenge and an opportunity for police executives. In high-profile cases, police executives face the potential challenge of serving two constituencies—the rank-and-file officers and the local residents—who are sometimes at odds regarding use-of-force incidents. Whether holding a press conference or responding to the media on such volatile issues, police executives should maintain a posture of neutrality, fairness, and transparency. In maintaining this posture, police executives may realize opportunities to communicate effectively with the community. The media is the primary vehicle through which agencies communicate with the public. Police executives should establish a media relations strategy that makes proactive use of this outlet for communication rather than dealing solely in a reactive mode during moments of crisis.

Establishing Community Support Prior to Critical Use-of-Force Incidents

Police executives must proactively build relationships of trust with community leaders, community members, and the local media before critical incidents occur. Developing and sustaining such contacts through community meetings, participation in community events, citizen academies, public awareness campaigns, and the department web site is an essential part of any community outreach strategy. Establishing and maintaining strong ties with political, religious, and business leaders within the community will benefit the department. Developing a foundation of trust with the community can be thought of as putting "money in the bank," so that community support can be drawn on when needed. Police executives should be particularly attentive to proactively informing community stakeholders about the department's use-of-force policies, practices, and accountability mechanisms. It is better that the public is informed of these details before a critical use-of-force incident occurs than after.

Departments should avail themselves of the resources that will help them establish good community and public relations and that promote education regarding use-of-force policies and practices. The U.S. Department of Justice Community Relations Service (CRS) provides several resources that can help police establish good relations with key community stakeholders and community members before critical incidents occur as well as guidelines that executives can use to assist in mediation with community members after an incident.

Police executives should consider CRS's practical handbooks including *Principles of Good Policing: Avoiding Violence Between Police and Citizens* (September 2003), *Responding to Incidents Involving Allegations of Excessive Use of Force: A Checklist to Guide Police Executives* (Revised September 2003), *Distant Early Warning Signs (DEWS) System* (November 2001), and *Community Dialogue Guide* (September 2003). These and other publications are available for download at www.usdoj.gov/cr.

Police executives, or designees such as public information officers, are often expected to make statements immediately following critical and often controversial use-of-force incidents. When doing so, police executives must remain objective and neutral. It is never advisable to express premature judgments about incidents before investigations are completed. While initial evidence may seem to point in a certain direction, it is a disservice to the purported victim of excessive force, the community, and the officer(s) involved to make premature statements. The message police executives should strive to convey as soon after a controversial use-of-force incident as possible is that the incident is under investigation and that the investigation will be thorough. Police executives should underscore this message by discouraging any speculation by the media, the public, or other police personnel before the investigation is complete. A police executive may express empathy for the subject who may have been harmed and for the officers involved, as appropriate, but in doing so should avoid any suggestion of bias toward either side.

Sharing Use-of-Force Data with the Public

Many departments elect to share aggregate information about use of force with the public through web sites or annual reports. Using the department web site to publish use-of-force reports sends an important message of accessibility and transparency. In some instances, federal agreements have stipulated providing aggregate use-of-force data to the public. The MOA between the Department of Justice and the Metropolitan Police Department in Washington, D.C., establishes such a requirement:

> MPD shall prepare quarterly public reports that include aggregate statistics of MPD use-of-force incidents broken down by MPD districts covering each of the geographic areas of the City, indicating the race/ethnicity of the subject of force. These aggregate numbers shall include the number of use-of-force incidents broken down by weapon used and enforcement actions taken in connection with the use of force. The report shall include statistical information regarding use-of-force investigations conducted, including the outcome. The report shall also include the total number of complaints of excessive force received, broken down by MPD Districts, and the number of complaints held exonerated, sustained, insufficient facts, and unfounded.[39]

 *Managing Use of Force*

While the Metropolitan Police Department in Washington, D.C, does publish detailed statistical summary reports on a quarterly basis,[40] other agencies report data at the case level, describing them with short synopses. The Iowa City (Iowa) Police Department, for instance, provides monthly reports with brief narrative descriptions on its web site.[41] A portion of the web site is depicted below:

IOWA CITY POLICE DEPARTMENT
USE OF FORCE REPORT
October 2005

OFFICER	DATE	INC#	INCIDENT	FORCE USED
20,44	100105	49648	Open Container	Subject was placed under arrest and resisted handcuffing efforts. Officers attempts to use control techniques were unsuccessful. Officers than exposed the subject to a chemical irritant and used control techniques to place handcuffs on the subject.
95,09	100205	49892	Public Intoxication	Subject was placed under arrest and resisted handcuffing efforts. Officers used control techniques to place handcuffs on the subject.
31	100305	50091	Vehicle Pursuits	Officers attempted to stop a vehicle reference a welfare check on the driver. The driver failed to yield and a pursuit began. After a short distance the pursuit was discontinued.
36	100605	50573	OWI	Subject to assault officers. Officers used control techniques to place handcuffs on the subject.

In many departments, internal policies or collective bargaining agreements with police unions may affect the type of information that can be publicly posted. If information is posted at the incident level, data must be "sanitized" to not to allow any civilian subject or officer to be personally identified.

Recommendations

On the basis of its assessment of federal consent decrees and MOAs as well as the preceding discussion, the IACP offers the following recommendations on use-of-force policies and practices. Because use-of-force options—techniques and technologies—continue to evolve, these recommendations should not be considered static. The recommendations below correspond sequentially to the goals of creating clear and comprehensive use-of-force policies, effective use-of-force training, robust accountability mechanisms, and fair and transparent media and public relations.

1. Implement a clear use-of-force policy that specifically addresses both deadly and nondeadly use of force and that is consistent with all legal and professional standards.

Regardless of size or function, all agencies should have a use-of-force policy with directives on deadly and nondeadly force. These policies, which must be clear and easy to interpret, should not be less restrictive than applicable state laws or professional standards.

2. Implement a comprehensive use-of-force policy that addresses all available use-of-force options, clearly places these options within a force continuum or a force model, and associates these options with corresponding levels of subject resistance.

Special care should be taken to assure that the department's use-of-force policy is comprehensive. The policy must cover all use-of-force deployment options—techniques and technologies—authorized within the department. It should include the use-of-force options available to all sworn officers as well as options available only to specialized units (e.g., canine units or SWAT teams). The following two recommendations provide more detail that may be applicable to certain departments.

3. Address canine deployment as a use-of-force option in policies and develop detailed directives regarding its use.

Departments should make clear that canine deployment for pursuit purposes or to establish subject compliance is a use-of-force option. Use-of-force policies should articulate whether a department relies on a "find-and-bark" and/or "find-and-bite" strategy. Policies should require that, whenever feasible, a clear verbal warning be issued and a reasonable allowance of time made for subjects to comply before canines are released.

4. Address CEDs (conducted energy devices)—often referred to by the brand name Taser™—as a use-of-force option in policies and develop detailed directives regarding its use.

Although no clear consensus yet exists regarding the relative benefits and risks of CEDs, these devises are clearly a use-of-force option and must be included on the use-of-force continuum in every department where they are in use. Determining where CEDs should appear in the use-of-force continuum should depend on the specific manner of deployment allowed by the agency's policy directive. The consensus opinion of advisors to this project is that CEDs should be placed no lower than irritant spray. Regarding Tasers™, the Police Executive Research Forum recently announced its recommendation that these weapons should be used only on people who are aggressively resisting arrest.[42]

Policies should require that, whenever feasible, a clear verbal warning be issued and a reasonable allowance of time made for subjects to comply before a CED is deployed. Agencies should also carefully consider including provisions, special-risk considerations, or restrictions regarding the use of CEDs on particular subjects including the young, the elderly, the mentally disturbed, persons with known medical conditions, and persons on drugs. Finally, a department's CED policy should address the duration of electrical charges and the number of charges that may be applied to a subject. These types of limitations on CED deployment are likely to evolve as more departments consider their use, fine-tune their policies and training, and as more data become available about potential risks of this technology

5. Review and update use-of-force policies to reflect changes in use-of-force options, laws, and standards.

Whenever techniques or technologies that are used as use-of-force options are acquired or upgraded, relevant policies should be reviewed and updated as necessary. In addition to monitoring the development of new techniques and technologies that may affect use-of-force options, department personnel should monitor relevant legal cases, medical research, and professional research that may necessitate use-of-force policy revisions.

6. Provide specialized and comprehensive training and testing for the department's full range of use-of-force options.

Departments should provide training to ensure competency in all use-of-force options used within the department. Specific performance and competency testing criteria should be used and requalification should occur on a regular basis. The steps that officers who fail to requalify must take should be fully articulated. Training and competency testing should be kept current with changes in the use-of-force options available within the department or as officers are assigned to specialized assignments or units with access to different force options.

7. Provide specialized training on verbal de-escalation techniques and other appropriate alternatives to the use of force.

To minimize use of force by preventing escalation, use-of-force policies should expressly encourage verbal de-escalation techniques and provide the necessary training. Training should be of the highest standards and officers should receive periodic refresher courses.

8. Specify the circumstances under which supervising officers, or specialized units such as force investigation teams (FIT), must report to the scene of a use-of-force incident.

Use-of-force policies must define what is meant by a "serious" use-of-force incident and must require supervisors to report to the scene of all serious use of force incidents, including all incidents in which deadly force is deployed and all incidents resulting in serious injury to or death of an officer, subject, or bystander. Use-of-force policies should also, to the extent practical, require supervisors or FITs to report to the scene of any incident in which excessive force is alleged. The presence of supervisors or FITs provides support to officers at the scene and enhances accountability.

9. Clearly stipulate the level of force at which a written use-of-force report is required.

Use-of-force policies should clearly stipulate the level of force at which written use-of-force report is required. The consensus recommendation of the advisors to this project is that any instance of force above "soft-hand control" should be considered a reportable use of force. If the department does not use a use-of-force continuum, then the force options, the circumstances of deployment, and the outcomes that result in a reportable use of force must be explicitly articulated. Policies should require a use-of-force report any time there is an apparent injury or a complaint of injury, even if the force used otherwise would have been below the reportable force threshold. Policies should require a use-of-force report any time there is a complaint about the level of force deployed. These reports must be initiated whether the complaint is filed by the subject or by a third party who witnessed the use of force. Reports aid supervisors and investigators in resolving such complaints.

10. Clearly stipulate the level of force at which a use-of-force review is required.

Use-of-force policies should clearly stipulate the level of force at which use-of-force review is required. The consensus recommendation of the advisors to this project was that, as with reportable force, any instance of force above "soft-hands control" should be considered a reviewable use of force.

11. Ensure that accountability mechanisms including use-of-force investigations for allegations of excessive force or force without cause are fair, thorough, rigorous, and transparent.

Unlawful or excessive use of force is contrary to the ethics of policing, creates tremendous liabilities, and undermines the credibility of the department in the eyes of the public and the department members themselves. In response, law enforcement leaders must hold themselves, their supervisors, and their officers to the highest levels of accountability. Investigatory processes must be fair, thorough, rigorous, and transparent. They must be staffed with investigators who are appropriately motivated, skilled, and trained for these duties. Disciplinary actions should be fair, while making it explicit that no unlawful or willfully excessive force will be tolerated.

12. Collect and analyze use-of-force data for organizational management and assessment purposes.

Departments should collect data that will allow them to analyze the frequency of use-of-force incidents over time and across units. Data collection should be frequent enough to enable analysis on a monthly or quarterly basis. Analyses should assess the impact of changes in policy, training, or force options. Analyses should assess trends in use-of-force complaints and use-of-force-related injuries to officers and subjects. Use-of-force data should be routinely reviewed by supervisors and, ideally, incorporated into the data-management system as part of early intervention. Ultimately, police executives should assess whether they are moving in the right direction with use of force, whether use-of-force standards are equally applied across the department (with appropriate consideration of difference in risk across units and assignments), and whether the trends reflect professional standards and a commitment to the community and civil rights.

13. Establish proactive media and public relations strategies regarding department use-of-force policies and practices.

Departments should not wait for a critical use-of-force incident to occur before beginning to educate the media, public officials, and the general public regarding use-of-force policies and practices. Establishing community outreach strategies will build the social capital on which departments may draw in the event of a critical use-of-force incident.

Conclusion

The use force in police-citizen encounters is one of the most complex and emotionally charged issues in law enforcement. Officers must make decisions that are compliant with applicable laws, professional standards, and departmental policies, often in the context of split-second life-or-death circumstances. While the safety of officers and civilians remain a paramount concern, law enforcement leaders must create accountability mechanisms to ensure that the application of force remain within legal strictures or "reasonableness." As force tools and techniques continually evolve, departments must carefully consider their use-of-force options. Maintaining public relations and respect for civil rights must continually be part of the decision-making equation.

Suggestions for Further Reading

Because use of force—and the proper deployment of associated weapons and techniques—remain a complex and often debated issue, much has been written on the topic, particularly from an operational and legal perspective. As can be seen from the forgoing discussion, use of force raises civil rights and community outreach implication as well. Recent publications on use of force that address these issues include the following.

Alpert, Geoffrey P., and Roger G. Dunham. *Understanding Police Use of Force: Officers, Suspects, and Reciprocity*. Cambridge University Press, New York; 2004.

U.S. Department of Justice Community Relations Service. *Police Use of Force: Addressing Community Racial Tensions*. August 2002. www.usdoj.gov/crs/pubs/pubbullpoliceuseofforcedraftrevision72002.htm

Walker Samuel. *The New World of Police Accountability*. Sage Publications Inc., Thousand Oaks (California); 2005.

Peters, John G. "Force Continuums: Three Questions." *The Police Chief*. January 2006.

Endnotes

1. Ramsey, Charles H. in a letter to Deputy Attorney General of the United States Available on January 6, 1999. Available on the web at www.dcwatch.com/police/990106.htm.
2. Police Use of Force in America. Alexandria (Virginia): International Association of Chiefs of Police, 2001.
3. Langan, Patrick A., Lawrence Greenfeld, Steven K. Smith, Matthew R. Durose, and David J. Leven. *Contacts between Police and the Public—Findings from the 1999 National Survey*. United States Department of Justice, Bureau of Justice Statistics (February 2001) NCJ-184957.
4. Hickey, Edward R.; Garner, Joel H., *The Rate of Force Used by the Police in Montgomery County, Maryland, Executive Summary [and Final Report]: A Report to the Montgomery County Department of the Police and the National Institute of Justice*. Washington, D.C.: United States Department of Justice, National Institute of Justice (March 2002) NCJ-199877.
5. It is also relevant to note, that departments with expansive early intervention systems, such as Pittsburgh and Phoenix discussed in Chapter 3, collect the basic data (reportable use of force and arrest data) that allow for routine calculation of rates per arrest.
6. Adams, K. (1996). Measuring the Prevalence of Police Abuse of Force. In W. A. Geller, and Toch, H. (Eds.), *Police Violence: Understanding and Controlling Police Abuse of Force* (pp. 52-93). New Haven (Connecticut): Yale University Press. Adams maintains that the proportion of encounters that involve use of force can vary as definitions of "use of force" vary. In the cited studies, for instance, the routine application of handcuffs was not considered a use of force. Defining routine handcuffing as use of force would certainly drive the rate of using force much higher. The rate of use of force is also influenced by the types of police citizen contact that are examined. Studies that focus on exclusively on arrests rather than traffic stops tend to identify considerably higher rates of use of force since arrests are more likely to involve resistance, confrontation, and retaliation than traffic stops. Still, even considering these measurement issues, the use of force remains a rare event.
7. *United States* v. *City of Detroit, Michigan, and the Detroit Police Department*, Consent Judgment. (June, 12, 2003) Available on web at www.usdoj.gov/crt/split/documents/dpd/detroitpd_uofwdcd_613.pdf.
8. United States Department of Justice and the Metropolitan Police Department of the District of Columbia. (June 13, 2001) Available on web at www.usdoj.gov/crt/split/documents/dcmoa.htm.
9. International Association of Chiefs of Police Model Policies. Use of Force. February 2005.
10. Means, Randy, and Eric Edwards. "Chief's Counsel: Electronic Control Weapons: Liability Issues." *The Police Chief*, November 2005: 10-11.
11. See Police Executive Research Forum, Center on Force & Accountability. *PERF Conducted Energy Device Policy and Training Guidelines for Consideration* and the associated document Conducted Energy Device (CED) Glossary of Terms. October 2005.
12. *United States* v. *City of Detroit, Michigan and the Detroit Police Department* Consent Judgment (06/12/03). Available on the web at www.usdoj.gov/crt/split/documents/dpd/detroitpd_uofwdcd_613.pdf.
13. *Bell* v. *Wolfish*, 441 U.S. 520 (1979).
14. *Graham* v. *Connor*, 490 U.S. 386 (1989)

15. "Sample Directives for Virginia Law Enforcement Agencies." Use of Force Directive. Effective Date: July 1, 1999. Virginia Division of Criminal Justice Services. Available on web at www.dcjs.virginia.gov/cple/sampleDirectives/manual/pdf/2-6.pdf.
16. *United States of America* v. *City of Detroit, Michigan and the Detroit Police Department* Consent Decree (06/12/03). Available on web at www.usdoj.gov/crt/split/documents/dpd/detroitpd_uofwdcd_613.pdf.
17. Petrowski, Thomas D. "Use-of-force Policies and Training: a Reasoned Approach - Legal Digest" *The FBI Law Enforcement Bulletin,* October 2002. Available on the web at www.fbi.gov/publications/leb/2002/oct02leb.pdf.
18. Police Executive Research Forum, Center on Force & Accountability. *Conducted Energy Device (CED) Glossary of Terms.* October 2005
19. Electro-Muscular Disruption Technology 'A Nine-Step Strategy for Effective Deployment'. Alexandria (Virginia): International Association of Chiefs of Police, 2005. Available on the web at www.theiacp.org/research/RCDCuttingEdgeTech.htm.
20. International Association of Chiefs of Police Model Policies. Use of Force. February 2005.
21. Memorandum of Agreement Between the United States Department of Justice and the District of Columbia and the District of Columbia Metropolitan Police Department. (06/13/2001) Available on the web at www.usdoj.gov/crt/split/documents/dcmoa.htm.
22. Memorandum of Agreement Between the United States Department of Justice and the City of Cincinnati, Ohio and Cincinnati Police Department. (4/12/2002) Available on the web at www.usdoj.gov/crt/split/Cincmoafinal.htm.
23. *Sample Directives for Virginia Law Enforcement Agencies.* Use of Force Directive. Effective Date: 1 July 1999. Virginia Division of Criminal Justice Services. 17 Nov. 2005 Available on the web at www.dcjs.virginia.gov/cple/sampleDirectives/manual/pdf/2-6.pdf.
24. *Acosta* v. *City and County of San Francisco* 83 F.3d 1143, 1147 (9th Cir. 1996)
25. Alpert, Geoffrey, Dennis Kenney, Roger Dunham, William Smith and Michael Cosgrove. "Police Pursuit and the Use of Force, Final Report." Washington, D.C.: U.S. Department of Justice, National Institute of Justice, 1996, NCJ-64833.
26. International Association of Chiefs of Police Model Policies. Use of Force. February 2005.
27. Memorandum of Agreement Between the United States Department of Justice and the City of Cincinnati, Ohio and Cincinnati Police Department. (4/12/02). Available on the web at www.usdoj.gov/crt/split/Cincmoafinal.htm.
28. Streicher, Thomas H. "Staff Notes." May, 20 2003. Cincinnati Police Department. Available on 10 October. 2005 from www.cincinnati-oh.gov/police/downloads/police_pdf5988.pdf.
29. Gruber, Charles. "A Chief's Role in Prioritizing Civil Rights." *The Police Chief International Association of Chiefs of Police.* November 2004. Available on the web at www.policechiefmagazine.org/magazine select "Archive."
30. *United States* v. *City of Pittsburgh* Consent Decree. (02/26/97) Available on web at www.usdoj.gov/crt/split/documents/pittscomp.htm.
31. International Association of Chiefs of Police Model Policies. *Dealing with the Mentally Ill.* February 2005.
32. International Association of Chiefs of Police. Model Policies. *Encounters with the Developmentally Disabled.* March 2003.
33. Commission on Accreditation for Law Enforcement Agencies (CALEA) standard 41.2.8.

[34] Memorandum of Agreement Between the United States Department of Justice and the City of Cincinnati, Ohio and Cincinnati Police Department. (4/12/2002) Available on the web at www.usdoj.gov/crt/split/Cincmoafinal.htm.

[35] Memorandum of Agreement Between the United States Department of Justice and the District of Columbia and the District of Columbia Metropolitan Police Department. (06/13/2003) www.usdoj.gov/crt/split/documents/dcmoa.htm. Note: Operating in a federal jurisdiction, the U.S. Attorney's Office (USAO) in the District of Columbia holds the same responsibilities that local prosecutors hold in other jurisdictions.

[36] Memorandum of Agreement Between the United States Department of Justice and the District of Columbia and the District of Columbia Metropolitan Police Department. (06/13/2003) www.usdoj.gov/crt/split/documents/dcmoa.htm.

[37] By policy, the Pittsburgh Police Bureau Subject Resistance Report From **must** be completed for any use of force with the exception of: (1) mere presence of police officers and canines, (2) verbal commands, (3) handcuffing with no or minimal resistance when transporting, (4) come along holds, (5) physical removal of peacefully resisting demonstrators, and (6) displaying or unholstering of a firearm.

[38] Davis, Robert C., Christopher W. Ortiz, Nicole J. Henderson, Joel Miller, and Michelle K. Massie. *Turning Necessity into Virtue: Pittsburgh's Experience with a Federal Consent Decree*. New York: Vera Institute of Justice, 2002.

[39] Memorandum of Agreement Between the United States Department of Justice and the District of Columbia and the District of Columbia Metropolitan Police Department. (06/13/2003) www.usdoj.gov/crt/split/documents/dcmoa.htm.

[40] *Metropolitan Police Department Use of Force Statistics 2005* (Quarter 2). Force Investigation Team. September 29, 2005. Available on the web at: www.mpdc.dc.gov/mpdc/frames.asp?doc=/mpdc/lib/mpdc/publications/useofforce/FIT_2005_Q1.pdf.

[41] *Use of Force Report: October 2005*. Iowa City Police Department. Available on web at www.icgov.org/police/useofforce.asp.

[42] Crowe, Robert. "Police Think Tank Urges Rules for Taser Use." *Houston Chronicle*. October 20 2005 (Internet). See also: Police Executive Research Forum, Center on Force & Accountability. PERF Conducted Energy Device Policy and Training Guidelines for Consideration. October 2005.

VI. Addressing Racial Profiling: Creating a Comprehensive Commitment to Bias-Free Policing

ADDRESSING RACIAL PROFILING: CREATING A COMPREHENSIVE COMMITMENT TO BIAS-FREE POLICING

> The practice of racial profiling has no place in law enforcement. It is an activity that undermines the public trust vital for an effective community policing organization. Police must be perceived as both providers of public safety and deferential to the civil liberties of those they have sworn to protect and serve. While the majority of police officers serve their communities in a professional and ethical manner, the debate over the reality of racial profiling as a practice in law enforcement is loudest on the side of its existence on a national level.[1]
>
> **Chief Russ Leach, Riverside (California) Police Department**

Introduction

Questions regarding the existence of and the extent to which racial profiling is practiced among police officers are subject to fervent debate in the media, in academia, and in law enforcement agencies themselves. In this debate, perspectives vary broadly. Some observers suggest that the extent of racial profiling is wildly exaggerated and go so far as to call racial profiling a myth. Others consider racial profiling to be a widespread and systematic problem in law enforcement agencies across the country. Still others, however, fall in between these views. Some of these latter observers feel that racial profiling may be endemic to particular departments or particular units within departments, but not generally widespread. Others acknowledge the existence of racial profiling and express their grave concerns but assert that it is a rare practice invoked by only a few officers. In his 2001 address before a Joint Session of Congress, President George W. Bush put the problem of racial profiling in the following context:

> "[Racial profiling] is wrong, and we will end it in America. In so doing, we will not hinder the work of our Nation's brave police officers. They protect us every day, often at great risk. But by stopping the abuses of a few, we will add to the public confidence our police officers earn and deserve."[2]

Public opinion polls reveal that racial profiling is a concern to a clear majority of Americans. A recent Gallup Poll found that 81 percent of Americans thought racial profiling to be wrong and that 59 percent felt that racial profiling was widespread.[3] While the poll revealed expected differences between the perceptions of Whites and African-Americans, a solid majority of White (56 percent), and more than three out of four African-American (77 percent) survey respondents indicated they believed the practice was widespread. However prevalent racial profiling actually is, public perceptions implore police executives to address it.

Many law enforcement executives deserve credit for their proactive approaches to bias free policing. Their earnest attempts at preventing racial profiling—through issuing strong policy directives, providing comprehensive training, requiring supervisory review and accountability, and collecting and reviewing stop and search data—are impressive. These efforts are especially remarkable because they are often complex, resource intensive, and politically thorny. Data collection, in particular, is a complicated undertaking. Currently, civil rights groups, the media, and state and federal government officials are making increased demands for racial profiling data collection. Many agencies are required to collect data on racial profiling as part of their mandated statewide data collection or as a result of legal decisions or settlements including federal consent decrees and memorandums of understanding. No law enforcement agency— including an agency that has not been singled out for engaging in racial profiling or that has a racially or ethnically homogeneous population—is immune to the potential of confronting the complexities of racial profiling data collection. Indeed, as more agencies collect data—whether mandated or voluntarily—it may become increasingly difficult for other agencies to withstand the pressure to do so. As a result, enforcement leaders are increasingly looking for guidance regarding this multifaceted and volatile issue.

Chapter Overview and Objectives

Racial profiling is a remarkably complex topic. Beginning with an in-depth consideration of the various and differing definitions of racial profiling, this chapter acknowledges that complexity. It still strives, however, to offer law enforcement leaders clear and compelling directives on steps they can take to address and prevent problems within their individual agencies. To this end, the chapter explores the five core responsibilities that every department has (1) to design policies prohibiting the practice of racial profiling, (2) to implement a sound training regimen that reinforces departmental policies, (3) to sustain accountability mechanisms that measure adherence to professional, legal, and ethical standards as well as the specific effectiveness of training, (4) to communicate with the community, and (5) to establish consistency and continuity in the pursuit of all of these efforts.

Having offered these directives, the chapter turns to the consideration of racial profiling data collection and analysis. While this practice appears to be increasingly prevalent, the standards guiding it are still evolving. Law enforcement leaders struggle with questions ranging from whether to collect data, to what data to collect, to how that data should be analyzed to yield definitive conclusions. This chapter does not recommend that every department pursue racial profiling data collection and analysis. Instead, it is intended to help police make informed decisions and navigate the complex statistical, political, and public relations issues related to this practice.

The chapter concludes with a series of recommendations for law enforcement leaders working to prevent racial profiling within their departments. Still, the chapter is not intended to provide exhaustive coverage or even definitive conclusions regarding all facets of racial profiling. Readers interested in exploring the issues surrounding racial profiling in greater detail should reference the documents listed under Suggestions for Further Reading at the end of this chapter.

Differing Definitions of Racial Profiling

As law enforcement agencies work to address perceptions of racial profiling in the community and to self-assess agency performance in this area, it is vital that they understand what racial profiling is. Regrettably, no single, standard definition of racial profiling exists. Differing definitions reflect the differing perspectives of attorneys, police officers, civil rights activists, and researchers. Although few among them would condone racial profiling as a legitimate law enforcement technique, there is only limited consensus on what particular behaviors actually constitute racial profiling. Police leaders must concern themselves not just with their own departments' definitions of racial profiling; they must be able to articulate and explain these definitions in operational terms to representatives from media and the public who may have entirely different perspectives on what constitutes racial profiling and how the term is defined.

An Evolving and Broadening Concept

What is clear to all observers, however, is that the issue of racial profiling has expanded in the public consciousness and that the categories of persons who may be "racially profiled" have expanded beyond those that existed when the term first became popular. Racial profiling initially emerged out of concerns that African-Americans and Hispanics were more likely to be stopped by police and were being treated differently by police during those stops than other citizens. In the 1980s, some drug interdiction efforts targeted African-American and Hispanic drivers on the presumption that they were more likely to be involved in drug trafficking. Thus, the terms "driving while black" and "driving while brown" were among the earliest expressions of racial profiling.

Now, however, some observers more broadly construe racial profiling to include any police action—not merely traffic stops—that targets an individual based on a variety of group statuses other than race. Concerns over racial profiling extend beyond the African-American and Hispanic race categories. For instance, "flying while Arab" and "flying while Muslim" are now considered part of the racial profiling lexicon. In fact, the focus on "racial" profiling actually extends well beyond race. In addition to considering the race, ethnicity, color, national origin, or ancestry of an individual that is subject to police action, the term is often extended to address groups of individuals defined by gender, sexual orientation, religion, age, occupational status, socioeconomic status, immigrant status, or ability to speak English.

Although alternative terms such as "bias policing" have been used to convey this broader focus, for the purposes of this chapter we will continue to use the term "racial profiling" with the understanding that it applies to broadly defined police actions on the basis of broadly defined group statuses. Through constant attention by the media, the term "racial profiling" has become a household word that, as most people understand, addresses a spectrum of groups beyond just those defined by race.

Sorting Through Definitions

Given this broader understanding, it is critical to consider the more common definitions of racial profiling and briefly assess the implications of each. In general terms, definitions often vary in the degree to which they allow for race—or another group status—to be a factor in police action. Differing definitions of racial profiling hold that race should:

- Not be considered the **sole** factor in a police action.
- Not be the **primary** or **motivating** factor in a police action.
- Not be a factor in a police action **except** in the manner that hair color, weight, or other physical descriptors are used in instances of identifying a suspect for a specific crime. Commonly referred to as the "be on the lookout" or BOLO exception, this definition is often used in combination with or as an elaboration of the above definitions.
- Not be a factor in a police action under any circumstances.

Factor-Based Definitions

The basic difference in racial profiling definitions is how much of a role race can, or should, play as a factor in those decisions. These definitions consider the circumstances under which race may be considered in deciding whom to target as well as how restrictive those circumstances must be. As evidence of the existence of various definitions of racial profiling, consider the following passages, drawn from a variety of sources including police policy directives, that carry different implications about the degree to which race, ethnicity, national origin, or other group status can be used in police decisions.

The Texas American Civil Liberties Union (ACLU) report cited, but did not endorse, the following definition of racial profiling as common in a number of Texas law enforcement agencies:

> Acts initiating law enforcement action, such as a traffic stop, a detention, a search, issuance of a citation, or an arrest based solely upon an individual's race, ethnicity, or national origin or on the basis of racial or ethnic stereotypes rather than upon the individual's behavior.[4]

The following definition, published on the Fairborn (Ohio) Police Department web site, prohibits police actions that rely on race as a primary or motivating factor:

> Except as provided in this policy, race/ethnicity/human diversity shall not be *motivating factors* in making law enforcement decisions.[5] (Emphasis added.)
>
> Source: Fairborn (Ohio) Police Department
> Agency Profile: Population 33,000; Officers 45

The following definition, an excerpt from a U.S. District Court case, prohibits police actions other than the BOLO exception:

> The term 'racial profiling' means the consideration by an officer in any fashion or to any degree, of the race or ethnicity of any civilian in deciding whether to surveil, stop, detain, interrogate, request consent to search, or search any civilian; except when officers are seeking to detain, apprehend or otherwise *be on the lookout* for a specific suspect sought in connection with a specific crime who has been identified or described, in part, by race or ethnicity and the officer relies, in part, on race or ethnicity in determining whether reasonable suspicion exists that a given individual is the person being sought.[6] (Emphasis added.)

These directives, which capture the sole factor, primary or motivating factor, and BOLO exception prohibitions regarding racial profiling, are representative of those definitions that most commonly appear in police policy directives and training curriculum. As is evident, in order of presentation, the definitions range from narrow prohibitions to broad prohibitions of using race (or other status) as a basis for police action. None of the definitions prohibit the consideration of race altogether.

Few individuals inside or outside of law enforcement would argue that race should never be used as a factor in police action. Within the context of all of the above examples, race can and should be considered a factor when police are responding to the description of a suspect for a particular crime. In such a context, race is merely a descriptor of the suspect in the same sense as hair color, weight, age, and gender. Indeed, many agency policies stipulate that the BOLO exception is the only exception under which race may be used in police decisions to stop or search a person.

Clarification of the Term Profiling

The term *profiling* has a long history in law enforcement. It is important to distinguish the practice of *racial profiling*, which is unlawful, from other types of profiling—such as *criminal*, *psychological*, and *geographic profiling*—that have useful and lawful roles in policing. Criminal profiling, for instance, is used to discern investigative leads when suspect information is sketchy, such as was the case in the Washington, D.C.-area sniper case in 2002. Criminal profiling involves using evidence gathered from crime scenes, coupled with information about subject modus operandi and suspect behavior obtained from victims and witnesses, to develop an offender description based on psychological and other scientific principles. The goal of criminal profiling is to provide a description of the probable suspect or suspects based on scientific principles. The suspect description often comprises psychological traits—behavioral tendencies, personality traits, or psychopathologies—and demographic descriptors such as expected gender, age, race, or geographic location.

Race-based versus Behavior-based Definitions

The above definitions addressed how much of a role race could play as a factor in police decisions. An alternative approach stresses that behavior rather than race should be the operative factor. The definition below from the U.S. Department of Justice publication, "A Resource Guide on Racial Profiling Data Collection Systems: Promising Practices and Lessons Learned," defines the prohibited act of racial profiling as based on the person rather than behavior.

> Any police-initiated action that relies on the race, ethnicity or national origin rather than the behavior of an individual or information that leads the police to a particular individual who has been identified as being, or having been, engaged in criminal activity.[7]

Another approach is illustrated in the definition from the U.S. Department of Justice's "Guidance Regarding the Use of Race by Federal Law Enforcement Agencies," dated June 2003, which describes the unlawful practice in the following terms:

> "Racial profiling" at its core concerns the invidious use of race or ethnicity as a criterion in conducting stops, searches and other law enforcement investigative procedures. It is premised on the erroneous assumption that any particular individual of one race or ethnicity is more likely to engage in misconduct than any particular individual of another race or ethnicity.

Criticism of Sole-Factor Definitions

Sole-factor definitions of racial profiling attract frequent criticism because they are perceived as too narrow with regard to the behavior they prohibit. Critics believe that the sole-factor definition of racial profiling is operationally too easily exploited. Specifically, critics contend that if an officer can articulate any reason for his or her action other than race or other group status, then the real underlying reason is masked and the legal onus of racial profiling is lifted.

This argument is sometimes broached by referring to the term 'pretext stops.' Although the precise meaning of the term may be debated, pretext stops are those in which an officer can cite a reason or reasons for the stop other than the actual reason. As the Supreme Court has stated, pretext stops are generally legal and permissible.

> The decision in *Whren* v. *U.S* provides the legal precedent that most observers agree effectively permits pretext stops. In this case, Washington, D.C. Metropolitan police officers who had identified a suspicious vehicle in a known drug area used the violation of traffic laws as the stated basis of the stop. Drugs were found as a result of the stop and the officers did not deny that the traffic violation was a pretext for general drug related suspicion. In its decision, the U.S. Supreme Court ruled that "subjective intentions" were not relevant to establishing probable cause. In other words, the fact that the suspects were stopped on the "pretext" of a traffic violation was determined by the court not to matter. In the language of the federal appeals court ruling, which was upheld by the U.S. Supreme Court, "a traffic stop is permissible as long as a reasonable officer in the same circumstances *could have* stopped the car for the suspected traffic violation." [emphasis added][8]

However, as critics of the sole factor definition contend, pretext stops are problematic if the real reason for the stop is race. Under the sole factor definition, a police officer intent on stopping someone on the basis of race merely needs to wait for some violation to occur to use it as the stated reason for the stop. Even if the officer concedes that race played a role in the stop, it isn't the sole reason for the stop.

In short, critics argue that under the sole-factor definition, a hypothetical officer who routinely stops African-Americans for rolling stops or obscured license plates but does not stop Whites for the same infractions is not technically engaging in racial profiling because a reason other than race can be used to justify the stops. Critics of the sole-factor definition argue that the real question should be whether race influenced the officer's decision to stop the individual.

Through the efforts both within and outside of law enforcement—including local chapters of the ACLU, civilian review boards, as well as organizations like the National Organization of Black Law Enforcement Executives and the National Latino Peace Officers Association—so-called sole-factor definitions are increasingly being abandoned in favor of definitions which are seen as clearer and broader in their definitions of unlawful stop activity, and more effective in protecting civil rights.

The Prevalence of Efforts to Address Racial Profiling

Whether racial profiling is perceived as an isolated practice or a widespread problem, every agency must work toward the goal of bias-free policing. To this end, many agencies have already begun to address racial profiling through developing sound policies, training, and adequate supervision and accountability mechanisms.

Prevalence of Policies

Policies on racial profiling and bias-free policing are now commonplace in most law enforcement agencies, particularly larger agencies. Results from the 2003 Sample Survey of Law Enforcement Agencies (LEMAS), conducted by BJS, reveals that 43 of 48 (90 percent) state police agencies responding to the survey reported having policy directives on racial profiling. Based on the survey, 62 percent of municipal police departments and 63 percent of sheriffs' offices reported having racial profiling policies. As is evident in the graphs below, the prevalence of racial profiling policy directives generally increases with department size. Details about LEMAS methodology and data are available in the text box on page 31 in Chapter 2.

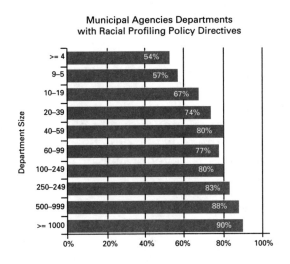
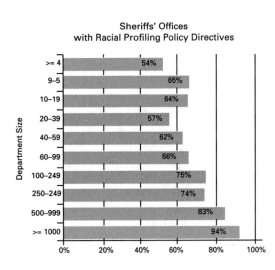

Prevalence of Racial Profiling Training and Accountability

The LEMAS survey did not address the presence of training or accountability with respect to racial profiling. No national data was available to address this issue. As we have discussed in other chapters, however, the collection of racial and ethnic data is central to many accountability strategies now being used in police departments. For instance, to help ensure accountability, agencies are increasingly relying on their existing early intervention systems (see Chapter 3) and incorporating traffic stop data as a way to assess the performance of individual officers. Through the reliance on citizen complaint processes and related data analysis (see Chapter 4), law enforcement leaders and supervisors can assess which communities are experiencing problems with the department, including complaints that specify biased treatment. In addition to these efforts, many agencies have begun to collect and analyze racial profiling data either voluntarily or by mandate as a result of state regulation or individual lawsuits. This chapter will address the prevalence of data collection in a later section.

Multiple Motivations for Addressing Racial Profiling

Law enforcement leaders must make every effort to prevent acts of racial profiling. The foremost reason to take an unequivocal position against the practice and deal with the issues in a forthright manner is because it is the right thing to do. Racial profiling is unlawful and unconstitutional. The use of race by law enforcement agencies is strictly limited by the Equal Protection Clause of the 14th Amendment and Title VI of the Civil Rights Act of 1964 which prohibits agencies that receive federal funding from engaging in racially discriminatory practices. Increasingly, through legislation or executive orders, states have mandated that law enforcement agencies establish policies banning racial profiling.

Other motivations for taking steps to prevent racial profiling, and proactively addressing community perceptions of racial profiling, include the following:

- **Sustaining the equality that is fundamental to ethical policing in a democratic society:** The fundamental focus on equal protection under the law is an established hallmark of policing in democratic societies. During the last 2 decades, growing commitments to community policing and service-oriented approaches in the United States has served to extend the concept of equal protection to one of equal service. All consumers of police services—whether they are living, working, or visiting the jurisdiction—expect and deserve both equal protection and equal service under the law. Bias policing, in any form, undermines this fundamental right.

- **Enhancing trust and confidence in the police:** To the extent that racial profiling is allowed to exist or that perceptions of racial profiling persist, the legitimacy of police authority is diminished. This may be felt most strongly among historically disadvantaged and disenfranchised communities that ironically are often most dependent on police services for public safety. A community's trust and confidence in the police is directly related to the extent to which a department takes a proactive approach to prevent racial profiling and address alleged racial profiling in a forthright manner.

- **Enhancing the philosophy and practices of community policing:** Racial profiling reinforces a negative us-versus-them mentality within communities and law enforcement agencies. Communities that feel they are racially profiled are less likely to report crime, less likely to cooperate as witnesses, and less willing to form constructive problem-solving partnerships with police. Members of these communities who come into contact with the police may act with more hostility because of real or perceived biased treatment. As Lorie Fridell (2005) suggests in a publication issued by the Police Executive Research Forum, "Decades of profound reform reflected in community policing are threatened by perceptions of racially biased policing and its practice."[9] By addressing the communities' concerns about racial profiling, law enforcement agencies realize the full benefits of community policing.

- **Building capacity to recruit minorities and other qualified individuals to work in law enforcement:** Many agencies work toward the ideal of mirroring the demographic composition of the jurisdictions they serve. Real or perceived racial profiling directly undermines efforts to recruit minorities and other qualified individuals who may perceive an agency—or the entire law enforcement profession—as being fundamentally biased against certain groups. This is a particularly pressing concern for departments that struggle with shortages of recruits. Meaningful efforts to address racial profiling can reduce feelings of disenfranchisement and make law enforcement careers more desirable. Moreover, a proactive approach to addressing racial profiling will help draw candidates of all backgrounds who share a commitment to bias-free policing and are motivated by public service ideals.

- **Limiting financial liability:** Allegations of racial profiling may result directly in payouts associated with civil lawsuits and settlements. An ounce of prevention may be worth a pound of cure. Agencies that take proactive steps to prevent racial profiling can reduce the costs associated with these payouts.

Core Components for Addressing and Preventing Racial Profiling

Police departments benefit as they succeed in addressing and preventing the perception, as well as the actual occurrence, of racial profiling. Although departments' efforts to address and prevent racial profiling may differ according to management priorities and legal mandates, the enactment of five core components will offer all departments the best possibility of success.

Component One: Clear and Compelling Policies

To address and prevent racial profiling, departments must establish clear and comprehensive policies against it and agency missions that promote equal protection and equal service to all.

The first step in preventing racial profiling is the development of a clear departmental policy banning the practice. This policy directive must unambiguously define and denounce racial profiling. Ambiguous policy definitions and directives are of no assistance to officers on the street and have no value for developing relationships of trust between the department and the community.

Departmental policies should clearly convey that behavior and evidentiary standards—not race—should guide police stop-and-search decisions. To this end, departmental policies should specify that race should play no role in decisions of whom to stop or search except under very narrow circumstances where race descriptors are linked to a suspect for a particular crime (the BOLO exception). Finally, departmental polices should reinforce the legal standards for stops, searches, and other police actions. These policies should deter officers from making racially discriminatory pretext stops by stipulating that officers must be able to articulate how they established reasonable suspicion or probable cause for every stop or search.

Departmental policies to address and prevent racial profiling should move beyond a focus only on equal protection. In most departments, the majority of police activity revolves around service rather than enforcement of the law. Departments' commitment to fair and equitable policing and to the tenets of community policing should ensure that all persons, groups, and communities within a jurisdiction are afforded equal service.

Many such policies are already in place and successfully allow departments to address and prevent racial profiling. The policy of the Dearborn Heights (Michigan) Police Department, for example, addresses racial profiling and unequivocally prohibits the practice, yet contains language that does not compromise on aggressive enforcement:

I. PURPOSE

The purpose of this policy is to explicitly state that racial and ethnic profiling in law enforcement are totally unacceptable; to provide guidelines for officers to prevent such occurrences; and to protect our officers from unwarranted accusation when they act within the directives of the law and policy.

II. POLICY

It is the policy of the Dearborn Heights Police Department to patrol in a proactive manner, to aggressively investigate suspicious persons and circumstances, and to actively enforce the motor vehicle laws, while insisting that citizens will only be stopped or detained when there exists reasonable suspicion to believe they have committed or are committing an infraction of the law.

Discussion

A fundamental right that is guaranteed by the Constitution of the United States to all who live in this nation is the equal protection under the law. Along with this right to equal protection is the fundamental right to be free from unreasonable searches and seizures by governmental agents. Citizens are free to walk and drive our streets, highways and other public places without police interference so long as they obey the law. They also are entitled to be free from crime and from the depredations of criminals, and to drive and walk our public ways safe from the actions of reckless and careless drivers.

The Dearborn Heights Police Department is charged with protecting these rights for all, regardless of race, color, ethnicity, sex, sexual orientation, physical handicap, religion or other belief system.

Because of the nature of our business, police officers are required to be observant, to identify unusual occurrences and law violations and to act upon them. It is this proactive enforcement that keeps our citizens free from crime, our streets and highways safe to drive upon, and detects and apprehends criminals.

This policy is intended to assist our police officers in accomplishing this total mission in a way that respects the dignity of all persons and yet sends a strong deterrent message to actual and potential lawbreakers that if they break the law, they are likely to encounter the police. This policy is to address the agency accepted protocols for conducting all motor vehicle stops with the exception of "high risk" stops.

Source: Dearborn Heights (Michigan) Police Department[10]
Agency Profile: Population 60,000; Officers 88

Departments that successfully establish clear and comprehensive policies denouncing racial profiling and expressing a commitment to equal protection should underscore this message in their mission statement. Below are several examples of the countless law enforcement agency mission statements that embrace these ideals.

Our mission, collectively as a department and as individual officers, is to provide an exemplary level of service and protection to the residents and businesses of the City of Town & Country and to all those who may visit, work in, or travel through our community.

We will serve the community through professional conduct at all times and the enforcement of criminal and traffic laws without prejudice or bias, with respect for the rights of all people, to assure a safe and secure environment for all.

Source: Town and Country (Missouri) Police Department
Agency Profile: Population 10,894; Officers 34

It is the mission of the Hamden Department of Police Services to protect the rights and integrity of all persons without prejudice or bias against race, religion, ethnic and national origin or sexual orientation within its jurisdiction; to safeguard the diversities of our communities and its citizens, to be free from criminal attack, threats of violence and persecution, secure in their possessions, and vigilant that together we can enjoy peace and harmony.

Source: Hamden (Connecticut) Police Department web site
Agency Profile: Population 55,000; Officers 107

Component Two: Meaningful Training

To address and prevent racial profiling, departments must move beyond rote training and standard lectures. Training should inculcate attitudes of bias-free policing.

Departmental policies that define, prohibit, and denounce racial profiling form a critical foundation, but the existence of even the best policy is not, by itself, enough. Training officers to avoid racial profiling and to practice bias-free policing is a critical responsibility for all departments. Police executives must ensure that all training strategies are coordinated, free of internal contradictions, and clearly and consistently communicated across the command structure. To this end, police executives must be vigilant in ensuring that training about racial profiling policies in the academy is not subverted by field training officers (FTO) or front-line supervisors who tell their officers to forget what they learned in the academy. FTOs and departmental culture must not be allowed to contradict explicit department policies and clear messages communicated through training. Training at every level must send the clear message that department policies are to be taken seriously.

The scope and content of racial profiling training will necessarily depend on the specific programs in effect in a particular department. For instance, if an agency is involved in racial profiling data collection, specific instruction on data-collection protocols should be included. Racial profiling training for all departments, however, should include instruction on relevant legal and ethical standards, instruction on handling stops effectively, and instruction on diversity and cultural awareness.

As departments offer training in these critical areas, many are discovering that particular training techniques are especially effective. Many departments have found that to engage officers, the use of active, scenario-based trainings are more effective than passive, lecture-based training. Many departments have also found that to instill a commitment to bias-free policing in officers, positive, nonaccusatory trainings are more effective than those that stress compliance based on negative sanctions or fear.

Understanding the Legal and Ethical Rationale for Bias-Free Policing

Racial profiling training should stress adherence to the constitutional protections afforded every citizen as well as to the state and local laws that prohibit racial profiling. Based on clear definitions and scenario training, officers should be taught to apply these standards in real-life settings. Officers must understand that all citizens are guaranteed equal protection under the law. Officers should also understand that preventing racial profiling is an ethical as well as a legal imperative. Training should alert officers to the detrimental effects of racial profiling on effective policing and community relations.

Developing an Understanding of Cultural Diversity

To prevent racial profiling, departments commonly offer training in diversity and cultural awareness. Diversity and cultural awareness training sensitizes officers to the multicultural communities in which they work. This training often encourages officers to acknowledge and come to terms with any biases they may have as a first step in overcoming them. It also encourages officers to build respect for the diverse cultures among which they work. It accomplishes this by encouraging officers to develop a fuller understanding and appreciation of different ethnic or cultural groups within their jurisdiction. This training addresses the different value systems that may define various cultural groups. It offers officers practical instruction on interpreting such value systems and the behaviors that may result from them. Such training may focus specifically on how officers ought to treat members of major cultural groups within the jurisdiction in day-to-day encounters.

Police Chief Gary R. Coderoni of the Muscatine (Iowa) Police Department acknowledges the power of diversity and cultural awareness training to build on officers' understanding of multiple cultures to incorporate them into the community they police. In an *FBI Law Bulletin* article, "The Relationship between Multicultural Training for Police and Effective Law Enforcement," Coderoni writes:

> Cultural diversity training helps police break free from their traditional stance of being "apart from" the community to a more inclusive philosophy of being "a part of" the community. Realizing the difficulty of becoming a part of something that they do not understand causes a desperate need for an intense and ongoing educational process for developing an understanding of cultural differences and how those differences affect policing a free and culturally diverse society....With appropriate, well-developed training, law enforcement agencies can provide their officers with the tools to understand, appreciate, and deal with the cultural differences that impact their daily interactions with the citizens they are sworn to protect.[11]

Departments' ability to prevent racial profiling is enhanced through continual diversity and cultural awareness training. Changes in community demographics, such as the emergence of new immigrant groups within a department's jurisdiction, make continual training a necessity. Similarly, changes in the political climate, such as a potential backlash crimes against Arab, Muslim, and Sikh populations following September 11, 2001, also necessitate continual review and adjustments of diversity and cultural awareness training. Officers who better understand the cultures with which they are surrounded provide better services to individuals within these cultures.

The Community Relations Service (CRS) of the U.S. Department of Justice has developed training material to promote awareness of Arab, Muslim, and Sikh cultures. This outreach has resulted in various regional train-the-trainer seminars. In addition, CRS sponsored the development of *The First Three to Five Seconds*, a video on Arab and Muslim cultural awareness suitable for play at roll call.[12]

Courtesy and Respect in Stops
From a technical standpoint, racial profiling occurs when race or other group status is an inappropriate factor in an officer's decision to stop an individual or to take action (i.e., search or arrest) subsequent to that stop. Perceptions of racial profiling, however, may arise as a result of the way in which even an appropriate stop is handled. Departments that train and supervise officers in handling stops with courtesy, professionalism, and respect may diminish perceptions of racial profiling.

All departments should train officers to handle stops effectively by doing the following:

- Introducing themselves at the time of encounter
- Stating the reason for contact as soon as possible even if the civilian does not ask
- Keeping detention time as short as possible
- Answering all relevant questions posed by the civilian to the fullest extent possible
- Referring the civilian to an appropriate source within the department if unable to answer all questions
- Providing the civilian with complete name and badge number upon request
- Remaining respectful and polite
- Thanking any civilian who turns out to be cleared of any wrongdoing for his or her time and apologizing for the inconvenience.

The motorist who is approached with courtesy, professionalism, and respect; told the reason for the stop; and detained for a minimal amount of time is less likely to perceive bias—be it racial, gender, etc.—as the reason for the stop than an individual treated disrespectfully. Officers' behavior can have a beneficial effect on diminishing community perceptions of racial profiling.

Component Three: Maintaining a Culture of Accountability

To address and prevent racial profiling, departments must maintain a culture of accountability by establishing the proper accountability mechanisms and developing a culture of accountability.

Departments that have established policies against racial profiling and have instituted ongoing training should then monitor officers' responsiveness to these policies and training. Establishing and maintaining external and internal accountability mechanisms should be a critical piece of every department's efforts to address and prevent racial profiling. Externally, departments should ensure the open receipt and thorough assessment of citizen complaints regarding racial profiling. Internally, departments should ensure that early intervention systems or personnel performance systems are fully operational, used effectively by supervisors, and contain quality data that are complete and up-to-date.

As an external accountability mechanism, citizen complaints can provide valuable information regarding racial profiling for at least three reasons. First, the citizen complaints may expose isolated incidents of racial profiling that would otherwise remain hidden within aggregate statistics. For instance, racial profiling by a few officers might be masked by overall patterns of equal enforcement within a department's stop-and-search data. Second, citizen complaints will allow law enforcement officials to assess the extent to which perceptions of racial bias exist in different communities or geographic sectors. The more that officials know about where perceptions of racial bias exist, the better they can use this information to inform internal training, community outreach, and community education programs. Finally, citizen complaints can be tracked alongside stop-and-search data as a way of validating or cross-checking trends. While citizen complaint data serve this useful role, it is important to remember that merely counting complaints of racial profiling is not necessarily a statistically reliable gauge of racial profiling itself. Not all persons complain and complaint activity is affected by how open and accessible a department's complaint process is to the community.

As an internal accountability mechanism, departments operating early intervention or personnel performance systems should incorporate stop-and-search data into these systems, which will allow law enforcement supervisors to compare individual officers with their peers. If an officer exhibits inordinately high ratios of minority stops compared with peers serving in similar duties and geographic areas, intervention may be warranted. Supervisors must first review the circumstances that may have given rise to any statistical disparity based on race or ethnicity. When appropriate, supervisors should provide training and counseling to officers for whom data suggest racial profiling patterns in enforcement activity or delivery of services and for whom the behavior is determined to be unintentional. When supervisors detect a pattern of willful and blatant racial profiling, they must use appropriate disciplinary processes. The proper selection and training of supervisors clearly is key to the success of this approach.

Departmental hiring and promotion processes should be designed with these commitments to bias-free policing in mind. To the extent possible, departmental hiring processes should seek out individuals who demonstrate conscientious attitudes about equal protection and equal service. These processes should screen out persons who demonstrate racial bias or animus. Similarly, departmental processes should seek to retain and promote persons who demonstrate effective law enforcement practices while upholding the ideals of unbiased enforcement and equitable provision of services.

Component Four: Maintaining Broad-based Community Relations
To address and mitigate community groups' perceptions of racial profiling, departments must communicate regularly with the communities they serve.

Having established clear and comprehensive policies against racial profiling, training strategies, and accountability mechanisms, departments should avail themselves of every opportunity to communicate these efforts with their communities. At the level of individual street encounters, officers should demonstrate the effectiveness of departmental training by ensuring that every subject who is stopped understands the reason for the stop as well as the subject's right to complain if he or she feels that the police action was racially based or the subject feels mistreated in any way. On a departmental level, police executives should publicize departmental policies and mission statements that advocate bias-free policing through agency web sites, annual reports, and other vital forums for communicating with the public. Additionally, police executives should be willing to meet with concerned community groups and leaders to discuss racial profiling and to develop collaborative solutions to this problem. Finally, a department's commitment to equal protection and service and bias-free policing should be a central tenet of the department's community policing strategy.

Component Five: Sustaining a Systemic Approach
To address and prevent racial profiling, departments must ensure the ongoing consistency of the policies, training, accountability mechanisms, and community outreach that they establish.

Departments will succeed in addressing and preventing racial profiling to the extent that they recognize that their efforts to establish policies, offer training, maintain accountability, and communicate with their communities do not exist in isolation from each other. Each department must ensure, on a continuing basis, that these efforts are consistent with each other as well as with all departmental policies. To the extent that departments succeed in this regard, the existence of racial profiling policies, training, accountability mechanisms, and means of communicating with their communities will enable them to detect early on any trends in behavior that might result in negative perceptions among community members or in violations of the standards of bias-free and community policing.

Beyond the Basic Components: Considering Racial Profiling Data Collection and Analysis

In addition to the above-mentioned efforts to prevent racial profiling that the International Association of Chiefs of Police (IACP) recommends to all departments, there currently is a marked trend toward the collection and analysis of racial profiling data. A growing number of states are mandating collection of traffic stop data to assess patterns of potential racial bias. In addition, local agencies may be required to collect racial profiling data as a result of lawsuits, court settlements, consent decrees, and memorandums of understanding. Finally, a growing number of local agencies are collecting data voluntarily to proactively respond to public concerns.

At this point, the IACP believes that a blanket recommendation that all departments should engage in the collection and analysis of racial profiling data is premature. Although the IACP does not offer a general recommendation, it acknowledges that officers' behavior is being increasingly scrutinized and that, as increasing numbers of agencies collect stop-and-search data, pressure to collect data will increase. Against this backdrop, the issue of whether and how best to collect racial profiling data will need to be continually reassessed by law enforcement leaders. A basic understanding of data collection and analyses processes and controversies is critical, even for those executives who are not currently facing the challenges of racial profiling allegations or data collection.

Many departments have found value in partnering with universities to enhance research and evaluation across a wide spectrum of policing practices and strategies. A recent publication by the IACP, *Improving Partnerships Between Law Enforcement Leaders and University Based Researchers*, addresses these issues.[13] University researchers can also provide valuable assistance with methodology, analysis, and drawing conclusions from data collected on racial profiling, and can enhance credibility. It is also important, however, that the researchers are able to approach the problem from a practical, rather than "ivory tower" perspective. They should have an appreciation of police work as it is experienced in the streets.

Assessing the Prevalence of Racial Profiling Data Collection and Analysis

Although racial profiling data collection is becoming increasingly prevalent, there is no precise count of the number of police agencies engaged in these efforts. The fact that more agencies are collecting data as mandated or voluntarily is obvious. For instance, the collection of data on traffic stops was required for 8 of 14 law enforcement agencies that currently are, or have been, under federal agreements (consent decrees or memorandums of agreement [MOA]) with the Civil Rights Division of the Department of Justice. In other agreements, for instance with the Cincinnati Police Department, the MOA required the department to videotape traffic stops. Additionally, several recent statewide assessments of racial profiling data collection and analysis efforts recently released their findings:

- In May 2004, the Institute on Race and Justice at Northeastern University released a study of racial profiling in Massachusetts, addressing data on approximately 250 law enforcement agencies.[14]
- In February 2005, a report by the Steward Research Group and the Texas Criminal Justice Coalition analyzed data from more than 1,000 law enforcement agencies in Texas. The data on which the report was based had been mandated by Texas Senate Bill 1074, which required law enforcement agencies across the state to collect data and report detailed statistical summaries of traffic stop data. This particular report, rather than focusing on stop rates, addressed disparities in search rates and rates at which contraband was found.[15]
- On July 1, 2005, Illinois released its racial profiling report, *The Illinois Traffic Stop Study*. The analysis, conducted by the Northwestern University Center for Public Safety, addressed data from nearly 1,000 municipal, county, and state police, and special jurisdiction agencies for the calendar year 2004.[16]

As is evident from these three recent statewide efforts, data collection has become the norm in some areas of the nation. Despite this, however, it is rather difficult to assess national trends. Individual states have their own policies, data-collection protocols, and other idiosyncrasies. The same holds true for departments that have initiated data collection on their own.

The Data Collection Resource Center, part of the Institute on Race and Justice at Northeastern University, maintains a web site that assesses a complex array of information about mandatory and voluntary data-collection efforts on a state-by-state basis. Data available on this site underscores how each state's approach to racial profiling data collection (as well as requirements about policies, training, and the processing of complaints) is unique. Some states have enacted legislation requiring data collection while others have enacted legislation that encourages collection. Still, other states require data collection only from certain departments. Most states that require data collection have stipulated a limited window of time under which data collection is required. Colorado House Bill 1114 enacted in 2001, for instance, mandated data collection for all traffic stops occurring between July 1, 2001 and December 31, 2004. Other states have similar provisions. As a result, classification of states into a simple dichotomy of *requires data collection* and *does not require data collection* would be extremely difficult because the conditions vary and the time frames are dynamic.

States also vary in the type of events for which data collection is required. Some require data to be collected for all traffic stops, while others require data collection only for traffic stops resulting in defined actions (e.g., citations, arrests, or use of force). Some expressly include pedestrian stops, and others do not. In some states, mandatory data collection is required by *all* agencies, while in other states only specified agencies are mandated to collect data. Northeastern University's Data Collection Resource Center provides a valuable resource for keeping up with the status of state legislation and executive orders. It is also links to information about data collection and other efforts of state legislatures and executives to promote bias-free policing.

The Benefits and Limitations of Racial Profiling Data Collection and Analysis

In determining whether or not to collect and analyze racial profiling data, individual departments must consider the benefits and limitations of the process. Departments should weigh not only financial considerations, but also considerations of department morale, community relations, public perceptions, and the potential use—or misuse—of collected data. While departments may realize benefits in addition to those they realize as they work to prevent racial profiling through other means (policies, training, and an internal accountability mechanism), they may expose themselves to additional risks if they elect to collect data. The potential benefits and risks, presented below, underscore why individual agencies must consider this choice carefully. Decisions about data collection can have a profound effect on the department and the community it serves, particularly in those communities where perceptions of a problem exist.

Benefits

Racial profiling data collection may result in specific benefits in addition to those benefits that agencies gain through other efforts, such as clear policies and training, to promote bias-free policing. Potential benefits include the following:

- **Creating an effective management tool that is consistent with evolving data-driven management standards:** Analyses comparing racial profiling data on officers who perform similar duties in similar neighborhoods may enable agencies to identify officers who may be engaging in racial profiling and to determine in what instances intervention or discipline may be appropriate.

- **Sending a clear message to the community:** The fact that an agency collects racial profiling data may have an important symbolic value. Data collection sends the message to the community that the department is willing to assess itself. Denying that there is a problem and refusing to address the issue can result in substantial community resentment.

- **Establishing a foundation for constructive dialogue with the community:** Agencies that collect racial profiling data can use the results to establish an important foundation for constructive dialogue with the community, particularly when data collection and analysis is approached from a perspective of partnership and in the context of genuine community policing.

- **Ensuring control and flexibility to meet particular agency needs:** Agencies that take proactive steps to collect data ensure their own control and maintain more flexibility in instituting a process that meets their needs. Failure to take proactive steps can result in a mandated data collection process that may be inflexible and out of the agency's control.

Limitations and Drawbacks of Data Collection and Analysis

Although the collection of racial profiling data collection and analysis can potentially provide the benefits discussed above, specific risks are also associated. Potential risks include the following:

- **Draining agency resources:** Data collection efforts often are costly and time-consuming. They can take resources away from other areas of priority. Absent concerns articulated by citizen groups or problematic histories involving allegations of racial profiling, agencies may find little need to collect these data. Collecting data proactively when there is no pattern of past behavior that would warrant these efforts could cause undue financial burdens, particularly in times of budgetary shortfalls or when staffing levels are below target.

- **Effect on agency morale:** Data-collection requirements that appear to be imposed unilaterally by a chief, by state law, or by court mandate can cause morale problems. In particular, mandated collection may drive a wedge of distrust between first-line supervisors and front-line officers. (If the department is required to collect data or determines that data collection is warranted, efforts should be made to mediate these problems through effective leadership, communication, and supervisory practices.)

- **Inconclusive results:** Analyses of racial profiling data seldom yields unequivocal results. Although analyses may reveal disproportionalities in stop rates, data seldom definitively reveal whether or not an agency is engaged in systematic racial profiling. Given methodological challenges, such as benchmarking, alternative interpretations will exist even when racial disparities in stops appear pronounced. Even when disparities are not evident, some may feel that that racial profiling still exists and that the data either mask the problem or are misleading. While racial profiling data collection presents the hope that a complex problem can be adequately understood by being measured, some observers feel that the analysis of these data generates more confusion rather than helping resolve a problem. (Most proponents of data collection concede that data collection and analysis problems exist, but counter that the effort is a step in the right direction.)

- **Arming critics with data:** Related to the previous limitation, some observers contend that collecting racial profiling data, which is inevitably open to interpretation, arms those who may be predisposed to believe that racial profiling exists with data to challenge and critique the police. Law enforcement agencies are being asked to bear the burden and cost of collecting information that ultimately may be used against them.

- **Depolicing:** At the individual level, fear of being implicated as a racial profiler could result in officers avoiding activity that might expose them to this label. In an effort to avoid accusations of profiling, the number of traffic stops or pedestrian stops individual officers make may decline. At the department level, this depolicing may result in diminished public safety and less effective law enforcement. Again, however, if the agency deems that racial profiling data collection is necessary or is required by state mandate, these concerns should be mediated with effective leadership, supervision, and accountability mechanisms.

- **Potential of encouraging spurious stops:** Some have argued that the imposition of traffic stop data collection may result in spurious stops of nonminority drivers as officers attempt to offset statistical disparities that might otherwise exist. Again, however, these concerns can be abated by imposing proper supervisory and accountability mechanisms.

Assessing Benefits and Limitations of Data Collection and Analysis
When not required to do so by state law or agency mandates specific to the agency (e.g., consent decrees, litigation settlements, or judgments), a police executive's decision about racial profiling data collection is complex and will often be made in a politically charged environment. Decisions about data collection also entail legitimate and highly practical concerns about resource allocation and the potential complexities of data analysis and

interpretation. As a result, chief executives must consider the problem of whether or not to voluntarily collect racial profiling data in the broadest context. This process, however, must include a forthright appraisal of an agency's past history and its reputation across the entire community. Absent a specific problem, some chiefs and sheriffs may feel completely confident in their decisions not to collect data, particularly when they already benefit from widespread community support.

In short, this guide does not offer a blanket recommendation about the advisability of collecting data to assess racial profiling. Clearly, the perception or actual practice of racial profiling is an issue with which all law enforcement executives must concern themselves. Because of differences in demographics, in police functions, and historical circumstances, each executive will have to address this critical issue from his or her agency's own perspective. Whether or not a department collects racial profiling data, however, it should be prepared to confront the issue through clear and compelling policies, training, and accountability mechanisms. Departments must also demonstrate to the community, through mission statements and targeted outreach where necessary, that they are committed to bias-free policing.

Basic Questions Addressed by Racial Profiling Data Collection and Analysis

If agencies decide to collect data, racial profiling data collection and analysis can serve as an accountability mechanism to ensure that a department's policies against and training about racial profiling are effective. Departments that collect and analyze racial profiling data generally try to determine whether minority groups are stopped more often than other groups and whether they are treated differently during those stops.

To answer the first part of this question, analysis is first directed at establishing whether minorities are stopped in proportion to—or disproportionately to—their representation in the population. For instance, results from *The Illinois Traffic Stop Study* found that minority drivers accounted for 32.77 percent of traffic stops while they made up 28.48 percent of the estimated driving population. Expressed as a ratio, the minority stop ratio was 1.15 (32.77/28.48), compared against a theoretical baseline ratio of 1.0 (28.48/28.48), which would be the situation if minorities were stopped in equal proportion to their representation in the estimated driving age population. Individual department ratios varied around the statewide average. For instance, ratios in the three largest cities were 1.15 for Chicago, 2.07 for Rockford, and 1.71 for Peoria. The ratio for the Illinois State Police was determined to be 0.6, meaning that the state police stop fewer minorities than are estimated to be in the Illinois driving population.

In the Illinois study, and in nearly every study of racial profiling data, the first analytical step is to establish whether disproportionality in stops exists. It is important to note, however, that the mere existence of disproportionality does not necessarily mean that racial profiling is taking place.

The collection of stop data is also necessary to address two key questions: (1) whether minorities are searched more or less often when stopped; and (2) whether minorities are more or less often found to possess contraband as a result of those searches.

Steps in Data Collection and Analysis Process

To help illustrate the complex data collection and analysis process, the following sections break the process into a sequence of steps. These sections are not intended to provide an exhaustive discussion of the myriad issues related to data collection and analysis. Readers should also recognize that this is a rapidly evolving area of studying terms of policy, data collection, and research methodology.

Step One: Collecting Racial Profiling Data

Any agency that decides to collect and analyze racial profiling data confronts the critical decision of what data to collect. Agencies may collect information regarding drivers, legal and procedural variables, passengers, and the officers themselves. While the scope of data collection varies widely across agencies, language from federal consent decrees and MOAs helps bring clarity to this complicated issue. The consent decree of the Pittsburgh Bureau of Police (PBP), for instance, includes the following requirements:

> The City shall develop, and require all officers to complete, a written report each time a PBP officer makes a traffic stop. The record shall include the officer's name and badge number; the race and gender of the individual searched or stopped; approximate time and location; whether the stop involved a frisk or pat-down search; any weapons, evidence, contraband found during the search; whether the individual involved was arrested or cited, and if so, the charges.[17]

Differences of opinion exist about the advisability of collecting various data. For instance, controversy still exists as to whether information should be collected about officers involved in stops and how that information may be used. To varying extents, this is affected by local bargaining agreements, policies, or state law.

Drawing on data from the federal agreements, related literature, and individual agency practice, the IACP staff identified the following data elements that are often collected and analyzed. Individual consent decrees and MOAs between police agencies and the U.S. Department of Justice stipulated different data elements, depending on the particular circumstances that existed at each locale.

The list of the broad range of data elements in the subsections below does not imply that these are the scope of data that the IACP recommends to collect across all agencies engaged in data collection. Other resources, including the Department of Justice Office of Community Oriented Policing Services publication on *How to Correctly Collect* and *Analyze Racial Profiling Data: Your Reputation Depends on It!*, should also be referenced as a resource.[18] Clearly, each agency should make its own decisions based on available resources and the issues that it feels need to be analyzed. The data elements are organized under general categories and are meant to serve as reference points to aid agency personnel in assessing what data should be collected. The potential relevance and analytic function of each data element is discussed briefly.

Driver Characteristic Data

- Race/Ethnicity of Driver

The officer should record the race/ethnicity of the driver. Clearly a critical data element, this is a remarkably challenging one to collect and analyze. The officer may not know what the driver's race/ethnicity is and may not find this information on a driver's license. In such circumstances, most departments encourage officers themselves to identify, to the best of their ability, the race/ethnicity of the driver. Although this remains a contentious topic, departments offer two justifications for this approach over having officers ask the driver to identify his or her race/ethnicity. First, the officer's own perception of the driver's race/ethnicity is what really matters given that racial profiling is focused on potential police bias.[19] Second, asking individuals to identify their race/ethnicity is awkward and potentially offensive even in routine conversation. The potential for offense is heightened in a traffic stop situation.

Classifying this information to analyze it effectively presents additional challenges. Currently, there is no definitive classification scheme. Data systems vary not only in their categorization of race/ethnicity, but in their treatment of these as single or separate dimensions. Many departments, through forms and data systems, for example, require officers to determine whether a driver is White, Black, Hispanic, Asian, or Native American. In some departments, this may be sufficient. In others, it will not be sufficient. For instance, allegations of racial profiling rose sharply after September 11, 2001 in areas with high concentrations of Arabs, Muslims, and persons of Middle Eastern origin. Appropriate analysis of racial profiling data can occur only to the extent that appropriate categories of race/ethnicity are used. Similarly, departments must ensure that their categories of race/ethnicity correspond to the categories of the population groups to which they will be compared. For instance, if departments intend to use census data to measure the proportions of minority populations in their jurisdictions, they will have to convert this census data—with its more complicated race/ethnicity categories—to be consistent with their own terminology.[20]

- Gender of Driver

The officer should record the gender of the driver. Racial profiling has often been identified as particularly problematic for gender subgroups such as African-American and Hispanic males. Recording the gender of the driver allows departments to analyze these subgroups separately.

- Age of Driver

The officer should record the age of the driver. Racial profiling may be statistically confounded by issues of age. For instance, community demographics may be such that the age composition of African-Americans is substantially different from that of Whites. Because young drivers are stopped more often than older drivers, if one demographic group contains proportionally more young drivers than the other, the analysis ought to address this. Date of birth may be obtained from driver's license information. If not, an approximation of the age is usually sufficient.

Legal and Procedural Data

- Reason for Stop

The officer should record the reason for the stop, whether it is a violation of a traffic law or suspicious behavior. In the case of a traffic violation, the specific violation should be recorded. In the case of suspicious behavior, a description of the behavior—in greater detail than "appeared suspicious"—should be recorded. Standard forms that include checkboxes—equipment violation, moving violation, BOLO, etc.—should be extensive enough to cover and distinguish between high-discretion stops (e.g., minor equipment violations or driving a few miles above the speed limit) and low-discretion stops (e.g., reckless driving, DUI, or excessive speeding).

- **Methods Used in Detection**

The officer should record the method used in detecting the alleged violation or suspicion. For instance, in the case of speeding, the officer should note whether the stop was based on use of radar, by pacing, or some other method. In the case of a stop based on suspicious behavior, the officer should record the nature of the suspicion, including whether the stop was in response to a BOLO notification or specific articulable behavioral factors of the subject.

- **Disposition**

The officer should record the way in which the stop was disposed. Typical checkbox categories should include verbal warning, written warning, citation issued, custody arrest, or field interview card completed.

- **Search**

The officer should record whether a search was conducted.

- **Basis of Search/Type of Search**

The officer should record whether the search was consensual or based on other factors such as incident to arrest, probable cause, or inventory search. The officer should also record whether the search was of the driver, a passenger, and/or the vehicle.

- **Consent Search**

Some departments require officers to indicate whether the officer attempted to make a consent search and record whether on not the subject consented to be searched.

- **Contraband Found/Seized**

The officer should record whether contraband was found, of what type (e.g., drugs or weapons), and, if applicable, the amount seized.

- **Other Items Found/Seized**

The officer should record whether other items, such as instruments of crime (e.g., burglary tools) or fruits of crime were found.

- **Location of Stop**

The officer should record the location of the stop by reference to cross streets, the street address in front of which the stop occurred, or the highway milepost. In departments with appropriate technology, the data may be mapped and compared to maps of other activities such as crimes, police calls for service, etc. This may be a particularly useful data element in that it can be used to assess whether stops are geographically correlated with the location of other police events (e.g., calls for service, crime incident sites, or sites of frequent traffic accidents). It may be useful to know, for instance, how traffic stop locations relate to accident locations and how these patterns may be related to the demographics of neighborhoods.

- **Vehicle Information**

The officer should record standard information about the vehicle including make, model, year, color, license plate number, and state of issue. Officers should also report on the status of the vehicle in the event that the driver was not allowed to drive away (e.g., vehicle towed or vehicle left parked at location).

- **Duration of Stop**

The officer should record the duration of the stop, by noting either the beginning and ending times of the stop or by noting the duration of the stop in minutes.

- **Passenger Data**

  – Number of passengers in car
  – Race/ethnicity of passengers
  – Gender of passengers
  – Age of passengers.

- **Officer Data**

  – Name of officer
  – Badge/ID number of officer
  – Duty status of officer (on duty/off duty).

Many departments collect officer data to ensure that their data collection and analysis efforts will result in an understanding of racial profiling at the agency level, the unit level, and the individual level. Collecting the officer's name and/or badge/ID number is critical if the agency is attempting to identify individuals who may be engaged in racial profiling. In this event, stop data can become a critical element in early intervention efforts. If supervisors determine that profiling was unintentional or based on a misunderstanding of policies and procedures, they may attempt to work with these officers through counseling and/or retraining. If profiling is determined to be blatant and intentional, disciplinary proceedings are warranted.

In other departments, however, collective bargaining agreements discourage or prohibit the collection of officer data. A compromise position between these two options exists. Some departments allow the collection of data about officers with the assurance that the data will be used only within the department. Under such provision, the identity of individual officers is not revealed. The St. Paul (Minnesota) Police Department uses an approach similar to this.

Step Two: Posing the Questions that Racial Profiling Data Can Answer

To determine whether particular groups are stopped more often or treated differently during those stops than other groups, departments ask four fundamental questions based on the data collected.

(1) Are some groups stopped disproportionately based on race, ethnicity, or other status?

To establish whether any given group is stopped in proportion to—or disproportionately to—its population, a department must first analyze the data it collects to determine what percentage of stops involve a particular status group and then compare this number with the percentage of the population that the status group comprises. Determining that latter number is a complicated statistical problem that will be discussed at length below. In *The Illinois Traffic Stop Study*, the data on minority stops collected by departments was compared to the estimated percentage of minority drivers in the population. Based on that comparison, the study revealed that minorities were 15 percent more likely to be stopped than their proportion in the *estimated driving population* would suggest.

(2) Following stops, are different groups issued citations, written warnings, or verbal warnings at different rates?

This question of disposition seeks to understand whether different groups are treated differently once a stop has occurred. A traffic stop can involve one or more of several outcomes. Departments interested in evaluating the possible presence of racial profiling seek to determine how many citations or verbal warnings a particular status group receives when compared to other groups. Answering this question is more statistically straightforward than determining whether a group is stopped disproportionately because there is no need to establish baseline *estimated driving populations*. Departments can simply compare the outcomes for a particular group to the outcomes of other groups. For instance, *The Illinois Traffic Stop Study* determined, on the basis of statewide data, that minority drivers were issued citations in 68.00 percent of stops, written warnings in 16.50 percent of stops, and verbal warnings/stop cards in 15.48 percent of stops while the comparable rates for Caucasian drivers were 60.51 percent, 24.77 percent, and 14.71 percent, respectively.

(3) Following stops, are different groups searched at different rates?

Departments interested in evaluating the possible presence of racial profiling also seek to determine how many times a particular status group is subject to searches when compared to other groups. The central concern is whether minorities are more often subjected to searches subsequent to stops than other groups. On the basis of statewide data, the Illinois study found that 2.27 percent of stops of minorities resulted in consent searches while 0.88 percent of stops of Caucasians resulted in consent searches.

(4) Following searches, do rates of finding contraband vary across the different groups?

By asking this "hit rate" question, departments seek to determine what proportions of searches for different status groups result in contraband. *The Illinois Traffic Stop Study* did not address contraband hit rates. A 2002 Missouri study that posed this question revealed that contraband hit rates varied across drivers' race/ethnicity.[21] Based on the specific categories used in that analysis, hit rates varied from 22.60 percent for Whites to 17.47 percent for Blacks, 17.26 percent for Hispanics, 14.76 percent for Asians, and 7.90 percent for Native Americans.

Findings that show variation in contraband hit rates often spur debate among observers. Some contend that the lower contraband hit rate for minorities, such as illustrated in the Missouri study, are suggestive of the fact that minorities are more often stopped at lower levels of suspicion. Relatively high hit rates for Whites suggest that they are stopped only for higher levels of suspicion that may be more consistent with reasonable suspicion standards.

Step Three: Analyzing Racial Profiling Data
Having collected data and having posed the critical questions that these data can answer, departments face the responsibility of analyzing the data to provide those answers. As the discussion of the questions implied, answering the question of whether groups are stopped in proportion—or disproportionately—to their presence in the population requires more complicated analyses than answering the remaining questions regarding disposition, searches, and contraband hit rates.

To answer this question of proportionality, departments must compare their own stop data against the percentage of the population that the defined minority group or groups comprise. Establishing this comparison or baseline index, while complicated and methodologically challenging, is critical to analysis. For instance, the Illinois study measured its stop rate against an *estimated* minority percentage of the driving population *likely* to have driven in the jurisdiction. Clearly, this is not a straightforward and unambiguous measure.

Different studies have relied on a variety of baseline comparisons. For instance, in attempting to determine whether African-Americans are disproportionately stopped for speeding, traffic stop studies have calculated the stop rate by dividing the number of African-Americans stopped by the number of African-Americans who reside in the jurisdiction (census data), by the number of African-Americans in the driving age population (refined census data), or by the number of African-American persons with driver's licenses in the jurisdiction. The question of which comparison method will yield the most accurate assessment of profiling is present often is referred to as the benchmark issue.

A Conceptual Overview of Benchmarking
Benchmarking refers to the process of measuring data against an established standard for the purpose of evaluation or judgment. In a field such as land surveying, for example, the term benchmark connotes a precise measurement (e.g., of elevation) that is established against a fixed reference point (e.g., sea level). Ideally, a benchmark provides an objective and unambiguous standard against which to judge data.

As analysts have attempted to define these baseline populations for purpose of assessing racial profiling, however, they have inevitably fallen short of this ideal. The reasons they have fallen short, however, are not due to any limitations of the analysts. Rather, there are a host of methodological and practical challenges to benchmarking that are difficult and expensive to overcome. As a result, establishing proportionality—or disproportionality—in an effort to determine whether racial profiling occurs, often falls short of the ideal notion of benchmarking that may exist in other disciplines.

A Simplified Example of Benchmarking
To illustrate the challenges that benchmarking presents, consider a simplified municipal police department with only two groups of drivers. If the department's study finds that 25 percent of a municipal police department's traffic stops involve African-American drivers and that 75 percent involve White drivers, the department can make no inference about racial profiling unless they are able to compare these data with the percentages of African-Americans and Whites in the population. Suppose that 20 percent of the population in that municipality (based on census data) are African-American and that 80 percent are White. Clearly, African-Americans are over-represented among the traffic stop population relative to the residential

population. Expressed in the statistical terms used in *The Illinois Traffic Stop Study*, the ratio of African-American drivers stopped to their population percentage is 1.25, meaning that African-Americans are 25 percent more likely to be stopped than their representation in the population would suggest. This simplified hypothetical example raises critical questions. Does this disproportionality in and of itself indicate racial profiling? Is it based on the correct comparison population?

As the analysis of racial profiling data has progressed, more sophisticated methods of benchmarking have been developed as analysts attempt to better answer these questions. For instance, in response to early analyses of racial profiling data, many observers were quick to note that the residential population may not represent the driving age population. Now, benchmarks based on residential population are generally deemed inadequate. Alternatives have been offered, each with advantages and disadvantages of its own. To a large extent, the choice of benchmarks must be dependent on the population data available in a particular jurisdiction as well as the resources available to support racial profiling analysis. In any event, there is not yet a fixed method of benchmarking population.

Common Benchmarking Methods
Different departments and different analysts rely on different benchmarks, depending on the data available to them and on the resources they have to collect benchmark data. The text that follows below provides synopses of common benchmarking options as well as the benefits and limitations associated with each as they relate to traffic stop data.

Alternative Benchmarks for Traffic Stop Data: Pros and Cons

Alternative benchmarks, as presented below, represent a sequential progression in the sophistication of benchmarking methods. Most analysts agree that observational methods are preferable, but they are extremely resource intensive. New methods for benchmarking that use sophisticated driving population estimates (DPE) are being lauded as a major step forward to using standard census data. These methods are complex, but do not require the costs and time commitments necessary for observational approaches.

Simple Census Breakdown by Race/Ethnic Groups: The earliest and most basic method of benchmarking is to use the census data collected every 10 years. From these data, an agency can compare the racial and ethnic breakdown of persons stopped to corresponding population breakdowns based on census data. This information can be easily obtained for just about any jurisdiction whose boundaries correspond with a municipality, county, or state. If precinct or district boundaries correspond to census tracts, data can be aggregated and comparisons can be made across geographic regions within a department.

While census data are a practical and free source of information, numerous limitations have been associated with using basic census data as a benchmark.

- A law enforcement agency's categories of race and ethnicity may not match those used in the census. This may be a minor problem because census categories could potentially be converted to match the department's categories. Appendix B of the book, By the Numbers: A Guide for Analyzing Race Data from Vehicle Stops, provides a detailed explanation and examples of this process.

- In addition, census data may not be truly representative at the time of the profiling analysis. Full census data are collected every 10 years, although some population estimates can be obtained between censuses, but these are estimates based on samples and usually are not reliable for smaller jurisdictions or areas with small population bases.
- Also limiting the value of census data is the fact that minority populations in some areas tend to be undercounted in the census. This applies to areas with concentrations of immigrants, particularly areas with high numbers of illegal immigrants. Given that counts based on "official" minority populations (the denominator) will tend to be undercounted, stop rates for these groups have the potential for being inflated.
- The racial and ethnic proportion in the general population breakdowns may not mirror the respective proportions in the driving population. Differences in age distributions between the racial and ethnic groups, for instance, may contribute to differences in the real proportion of driving age persons in the different groups. In addition, economic factors may vary between groups and contribute to different rates of car ownership, in driving patterns, or time behind the wheel.
- Perhaps the most problematic limitation of using census data about residential populations, however, is that the drivers on the road at risk of being stopped in any jurisdiction include both residents and nonresidents. The real at-risk population may be quite different from the residential population counts obtained from the census. For instance, if a predominately White suburb has a shopping mall that draws many minorities from a neighboring jurisdiction, the residential population base of driving-age individuals clearly would not be representative of persons using the roads, particularly during hours when the mall is in operation.

Driving Age Population Breakdowns: A better alternative to the simple population proportion is the use of driving-age population data for respective racial and ethnic groups. This corrects for the possibility of different age distributions among these groups. Most often, this is based on counting only persons above the minimum driving age (e.g., 16 years old). This requires a bit more sophistication in extracting data from publicly available census data, but is an improvement over the simple, unadjusted breakdowns discussed above. This method, however, is still subject to many of the limitations noted above (undercounting of minorities, immigrants, and not accounting for drivers who are not residents of the jurisdiction).

Observational methods: As an alternative and an improvement over the above two benchmarks, some researchers have sought to create an estimate of the racial and ethnic composition of drivers within the jurisdiction through observational methods. In general, this method involves using independent observers to determine a racial breakdown of drivers by establishing a statistically representative comparison sample. Since observers cannot be everywhere and cannot observe at all times, analysts typically use some type of representative sampling. While this method avoids many of the limitations of the benchmarks described above, obtaining statistically representative samples of drivers tends to be costly, time-consuming, and is not without its own limitations.

One of the often-cited limitations of observational methods is that the race/ethnicity of drivers on the road is difficult to determine reliably, particularly on high-speed highways and particularly at night. Another limitation often cited is that an estimate of drivers on the road based on race and ethnicity categories may not account for differences in driving habits. In other words, this method assumes that the racial and ethnic groups are all equal in terms of the behaviors (e.g., speeding) and conditions (e.g., clearly visible equipment violations or expired vehicle tags) that might give rise to legitimate traffic stops.

Racial/ethnic breakdown of drivers on the road who are violating the traffic laws: To overcome the last limitation, some analysts have attempted to assess the racial breakdown of persons on the road who are in violation of the law. In essence, analysts assess both the race/ethnicity of the driver and the behavior of the driver. A study by John Lamberth, for instance, focused on the New Jersey Turnpike and compared the racial make-up of drivers who were observed driving at least 6 miles over the speed limit to the proportions stopped for traffic violations.[22] He found that African-Americans accounted for 14 percent of the drivers on the road and 15 percent of the drivers who were observed by researchers to be driving at least 6 miles over the speed limit. Depending on the section of highway and using only cases where police noted the race/ethnicity of the driver, at least 35 percent of those stopped were African-American.

This study is noteworthy for its attempt to control for differences in the risk of being stopped based on specific driving behavior that violates the law. It was limited, however, by the fact that it did not take into account other types of violations (e.g., equipment violations or erratic driving). Some critics also question how realistic this criterion was. Would the 6 mile-per-hour over the speed limit criteria used to define the comparison (or baseline group) actually result in many stops by the police in real-life circumstances? Critics contend that analysis based on a different threshold (i.e., a presumably more realistic 10 or 15 miles per hour over the speed limit), or analysis that included other reasons for traffic stops besides speeding might have yielded markedly different findings.

Driving Population Estimates Accounting for Resident Mobility between Jurisdictions: New methods being developed are based on sophisticated travel models that attempt to estimate the racial and ethnic breakdown of drivers. These models address the shortcomings associated with the previous methods, most notably the problem of not accounting for the presence of nonresident drivers. To date, the most ambitious of such efforts is a DPE developed at the Institute on Race and Justice at Northeastern University The model relies on census data for establishing a benchmark, but adjusts the census data to account for persons who come into or leave a particular jurisdiction.[23] This model has been called the push-pull model because it statistically attempts to account for factors that push people to drive into surrounding areas or pulls people in from outside jurisdictions. The census data used in the model are more refined than the driving-age population discussed above. The DPE model includes several relevant jurisdiction-level statistics, such as the percent of car ownership and information about the number of persons commuting to and from work.

As with any statistical model, the DPE model is a simplification of highly complex human behavior; however, it has been cited as being highly promising and is a clear improvement on other nonobservational methods. While the model was developed for analysis of data from Rhode Island and Massachusetts, it may not be as well-suited for use in areas with different population characteristics or road networks. Indeed, the developers themselves caution that the model should be further refined and would have to be adapted to suit other types of jurisdictions.[24] Readers can refer to the original study for a more detailed explanation.

Comparison to Accident Data: Some agencies and consultants have attempted to use accident data as a reasonable proxy for a benchmark for drivers on the road. In some cases, the benchmark has been set against those drivers involved in accidents who were not at fault or to those not involved in hit-and-run accidents. The presumption is that these groupings of drivers are less likely to be statistically biased in racial/ethnic composition. While this may be a convenient source of information (not as difficult to obtain as observational methods or statistically complex driving population estimates), they are problematic in several ways. Notably, they may reflect variations in accident reporting (for instance, certain population groups such as the uninsured and illegal immigrants may under-report accidents) and geographically based risk (in some areas minority populations are concentrated in areas with heavier concentrations of traffic and accidents). Some of this bias can be addressed by comparing the relevant populations (stopped persons versus not-at-fault accident drivers) within specific geographic areas such as a stretch of highway known for being dangerous and where accidents are unlikely to go unreported. Some analysts see such a geographically specific approach as a potential proxy for observational methods that can be cheaper and less time-consuming to collect. While expressing some caution, for instance, the Alpert Group believes that not-at-fault accident data holds promise as a benchmark:

> [A]ccident data will not necessarily reflect the driving population for an entire city, county, or state, but rather will reflect the driving population in those areas where accidents are most likely to occur. Nonetheless, in the context of a racial profiling study, the effect of this bias is minimized because police traffic stops tend to be concentrated on the same roadways on which accidents occur. Consequently, *if they can be validated* as an approximation of the driving population through traffic observation or other means, then not-at-fault accident data should provide an excellent benchmark against which to compare police traffic stop activity, most of which occurs conjointly with traffic accidents [emphasis added].[25]

Step Four: Drawing Inferences from Proportionality Findings

Some observers suggest that the proof of racial profiling is in the outcome and that findings of disproportionality in traffic stop data automatically imply that racial profiling exists. As the above discussion of data analysis reveals, however, the questions about how disproportionality is determined and whether disproportionality can be equated with racial profiling are subject to intense debate. Does the fact that *The Illinois Traffic Stop Study* revealed some level of disproportionality in the cities of Chicago, Rockford, and Peoria mean that racial profiling is necessarily taking place in those cities? In addition to the difficulties of establishing an objective and unambiguous population benchmark, alternative explanations may exist for disproportionalities. Such explanations may include the following:

- The differences in stop rates may reflect differences in behavior. Minorities might be stopped more because they more often engage in traffic violations or drive older vehicles more likely to have visually apparent equipment violations.
- The differences in stop rates may reflect differences in police deployment. Minorities, particularly African-Americans and Hispanics, are more apt to be poor and live in areas

where crime is high and police presence is greater. Their higher stop rates might be attributable to a greater police presence in their neighborhoods.
- With respect to search rates, differences between groups might be attributable to variations in educational levels and in knowledge that consent search requests can be denied.

Pedestrian Stops: The Unique Challenges of Street Encounters

Much discussion and debate surrounding racial profiling focuses on traffic stops. In many urban areas where car ownership rates are low and where reliance on public transportation is high, the issue of racial profiling frequently arises in the context of pedestrian stops. Indeed, the Los Angeles Police Department Consent Decree requires the collection of data on pedestrian stops that parallels data collected on traffic stops. Pedestrian stops raise concerns about racial profiling that are similar to traffic stops. Data collection and analysis for pedestrian stops is probably even more challenging, controversial, and convoluted than for traffic stop data.

Pedestrian stops present at least two unique challenges for departments determined to collect and analyze racial profiling data. First, police officers stop pedestrians for reasons that may not appear as straightforward as their reasons for traffic stops. The Austin (Texas) Police Department presents both traffic and pedestrian stop data on its web site. As the selected portions of text below indicate, differences in the factors that affect the traffic stop and pedestrian stop rates are clearly noted.[26]

Traffic and Pedestrian Stops, 2003

	Traffic		Pedestrian		Total Stops		Austin Demographics
White	91,663	52%	9,108	46%	100,771	51%	53%
Hispanic	56,025	32%	5,254	26%	61.279	31%	31%
Black	23,069	13%	5,477	27%	28,546	14%	10%
Asian	4,062	2%	107	1%	4,169	2%	5%
Other	2,375	1%	67	0%	2,442	1%	1%
Grand Total	177,194	100%	20,013	100%	197,207	100%	100%

"Traffic stops make up 90 percent of all stops and the background of the drivers closely mirrors the demographics of Austin. The primary reason for making a traffic stop is a violation of the transportation code (speeding, illegal turn, etc.) Pedestrian stops make up 10 percent of all stops and reflect the neighborhoods where walking beat officers patrol: downtown and east 11th and 12th Streets. The primary reason for a pedestrian stop is when someone is acting suspicious."

Source: Austin (Texas) Police Department
Population 623,327; Officers 1,189

Where the primary reason for most traffic stops is relatively concrete—a perceived violation—the primary reason for pedestrian stops is more subjective—generalized suspicion. This challenge, noted by the Austin Police Department, is likely to apply to other urban departments as well.

A second challenge is that traffic stops are easy to identify and count, whereas perceptions of what constitutes a pedestrian stop can be more ambiguous. Police encounters with pedestrians include a wide range of interactions that police might call "consensual contacts," "walk and talks," "field interviews," and "stop and frisks." Although civilians may not always be cognizant of the legal distinctions among these types of encounters, police officers are. From the police officer's perspective, the critical and operative distinction among these interactions is the occurrence or absence of detention. For instance, Texas Senate Bill 1074 stipulates the following definition for use throughout the state.

> "Pedestrian stop" means an interaction between a peace officer and an individual who is being detained for the purpose of a criminal investigation in which the individual is not under arrest.

Similarly, beginning in 2003, the Chicago Police Department started encouraging the collection of "Contact Cards" containing demographic data about persons whom officers encounter and who are not necessarily considered suspicious persons.[27] These stops are discretionary, but detailed information about the stopped person's address, aliases, and gang affiliations may be noted. Persons who are subjected to these discretionary contacts may feel they are being singled out or even racially profiled and may never be cognizant of whether the encounter was a street detention or not. The question about disproportionality in nondetention stops has received scant attention relative to questions about traffic stops and street encounters that are considered detentions.

Thus, potential problems exist to the extent that the police officers' and civilians' perceptions of their street interactions differ. While it is relatively easy to ensure that all traffic stops are recorded, this might not be the case with pedestrian stops. Officers may fail to perceive or record instances of detention, or some officers may wittingly decide that they can get away with not recording them. Courts have generally defined the difference between a detention and other types of contact as lying within the reasonable civilian's perception. If a "reasonable person" would feel free to leave after such an encounter, even if the civilian in the encounter claims to have felt differently, then the encounter is considered consensual. If a "reasonable person" would not feel free to leave, then the civilian is, by definition, detained. A detention need not be explicitly stated. Rather, it can be implicit in the officer's words and deeds. As a result, pedestrian stop data may be incomplete.[28]

One solution to such a problem is to treat pedestrian stops as equivalent to traffic stops. Rather than leaving the distinction between a street detention and other street encounters unarticulated—and therefore within the perception of a "reasonable person" whose perspectives may differ—department policy and training should require that the officer articulate when a detention stop is being made. This requirement could help ensure that data collection related to pedestrian stops would be completed.

Recommendations

On the basis of its assessment of federal consent decrees and memorandums of agreement as well as the preceding discussion, the IACP offers the following recommendations. These recommendations correspond to the imperatives of creating clear departmental policies prohibiting racial profiling, implementing sound training, and sustaining accountability mechanisms. Specific recommendations are also offered to agencies engaged in racial profiling data collection and analysis.

1. Develop a clear and unequivocal departmental policy prohibiting racial profiling.

This policy directive should include a clear and unambiguous departmental definition of racial profiling and related terminology. The policy should clearly convey that behavior and evidentiary standards—not race or ethnicity—should guide police stop-and-search decisions. In writing policies, departments should be aware of the potential message conveyed by clauses such as "solely on the bases of race, ethnicity....." The consensus opinion of advisors to this project is that such language is to be avoided. The policy should specify that the only circumstances where the consideration of race (or other group status) is permissible is in "be on the look-out" (BOLO) situations.

2. Ensure that the departmental policy is, at the very least, consistent with all laws and professional standards applicable to its jurisdiction.

Many states have specific legislation or Police Officer Standards Training (POST) standards that prohibit racial profiling. Any local departmental policy should be consistent with these standards or more exacting than these standards.

3. Ensure that departmental policies and practices designed to promote bias-free policing are designed to protect all relevant groups within the jurisdiction.

Departments vary in the extent to which they specify which groups should be protected from profiling and are entitled to equal service. Department policies should be written to be as inclusive as possible. If the department makes reference to a specific list of group statuses, it would be advisable to include a "but not limited to" clause to assure that other groups are not by implication excluded from these protections. For the purposes of training and outreach, an agency must make efforts to remain aware of the relevant demographic groups within its jurisdiction. Given expanded concerns about racial profiling in the post-September 11 world, agencies should make certain that their policies and training address fair and equal treatment of persons of Middle Eastern, Arab, Muslim, and Sikh backgrounds.

4. Develop comprehensive and effective training programs to reduce racial biases among all personnel engaged in stop-and-search activity.

The departmental commitment to preventing racial profiling must be reinforced with officer training that focuses on legal and ethical standards, handling stops, and cultural awareness.

5. Ensure that training is ongoing, comprehensive, relevant, and compelling.

Training on issues of racial profiling should include all relevant topics including operational definitions, legal considerations, accountability mechanisms, and (if applicable) data-collection requirements. This training should be ongoing and addressed in all instructional settings, i.e., in the academy, during field training, and as part of in-service training. Training should address the complexities of racial profiling in a forthright manner. The best way to achieve meaningful and memorable training is by incorporating realistic examples, scenario-based training, and active discussion among participants.

6. Reinforce bias-free policing throughout agency culture.

While racial profiling training should begin in the academy, as part of field training, and be regularly updated through in-service training, the message should be routinely reinforced in a variety of settings. Any changes in policies or procedures should be routinely addressed in roll calls and any apparent problems identified through early intervention systems or citizen complaints should be clearly communicated. Executives must periodically reinforce this message as part of comprehensive and coordinated community outreach strategies.

7. Embed the ideals of bias-free policing within the department's mission statement.

The department's commitment to bias-free policing should be reinforced in the agency's mission statement. Often appearing on agency web sites or in annual reports, the mission statement provides the department with a critical medium for communicating its commitment to bias-free policing to the public as part of the agency's core values.

8. Ensure that the departmental commitment to bias-free policing is part of an ongoing community outreach program.

In addition to setting the tone with a clear policy directive against racial profiling and a mission statement advocating bias-free policing, departments should avail themselves of every opportunity to reinforce this message with community groups and through public service announcements.

9. Incorporate stop-and-search data as performance indicators in early intervention systems.

Early intervention systems that incorporate stop-and-search data will enable departments to identify and intervene on behalf of officers who seem to unwittingly demonstrate biased behaviors.

10. Use appropriate disciplinary mechanisms for officers who show a pattern of willful racial profiling.

Willful and blatant racial profiling is unethical and unlawful. Appropriate disciplinary processes should be use in response to any officer displaying such behavior.

11. Continually and systematically maintain organizational personnel practices that reinforce bias-free policing and a commitment to equal protection and service.

To the extent possible, department hiring and promotion processes should assess candidates and officers on their commitments to maintain bias-free policing and a service-oriented approach. Performance assessments should include measures addressing and rewarding these attributes.

12. Promote a diverse police force that is reflective of the community that the police department serves.

Racial profiling may arise out of misperceptions about other groups. Departments can help limit misperceptions by encouraging a diverse police force that reflects the demographics of the community. All personnel will be better informed about and more sensitive to issues of racial bias to the extent that they learn directly from their peers. A diverse and representative police force will also help bridge gaps between the police and the community and may help diminish perceptions of racial bias.

13. Rely on citizen complaints as a gauge of perceptions of racial profiling.

Departments that pay careful attention to, and that systematically assess, citizen complaints will better understand the perceptions of racial bias that exist in the community. Such an understanding will enable departments to refine racial profiling training and enhance related community outreach and public education efforts.

Recommendations to Agencies Engaged in Racial Profiling Data Collection and Analysis

14. Ensure the quality and accuracy of stop-and-search data.

Whether racial profiling data is collected voluntarily or by mandate, departments should ensure that the data are complete and accurate. Data auditing procedures should be conducted routinely to ensure that all stops and all searches are recorded. Officers who fail to complete stop-and-search data forms as stipulated in department policy should be held accountable through retraining or discipline. Auditing procedures also should ensure that the information officers record is accurate, recognizing that there may be some reasonable differences when officers are asked to determine race through their own observations.

15. Set the foundation for discussions with the community before the release of racial profiling data.

Once data are released, individuals and groups within the community inevitably will make their own assessments about the meaning of stop data. Law enforcement leaders will be in a better position to influence a productive discussion, however, if they have established cooperative and trustful relationships prior to the release of data. Toward that end, a police agency should make certain that the community is aware of the policies, training, and accountability mechanisms that the agency uses to prevent racial profiling. Ideally, the community should be aware that disproportionality does not necessarily mean that profiling has occurred. Departments that already are thoroughly engaged in community policing efforts have a head start in these discussions and in maintaining a favorable image with the community.

16. Use racial profiling data-collection efforts and findings as a basis of dialogue with the community.

Police leaders should be prepared for a variety of opinions and viewpoints in response to release of data, including some respondents who automatically equate disparity with bias. Many members of the community, however, will realize that variations in the manner in which police are deployed across the community and variations in concentration of police may contribute to the disparity. Police leaders may find it useful to reenforce the message that stop data often relates to other indices such as calls for service and crime incidents. It so doing law enforcement executives must be careful not to be defensive or dismissive of community concerns. The inclusion of academics or outside experts in data analysis and presentation may prove helpful and can add credibility. These experts should be independent of the department so that they are perceived as credible.

Conclusion

This chapter has attempted to address the highly complex topic of racial profiling. It should be clear to police leaders that they must develop policies, training, and accountability practices to address the issue of racial profiling, both being attentive to community perceptions and committed to preventing its occurrence.

As to the formidable challenges of data collection, the foregoing discussion may have raised more new questions than it has answered. Some law enforcement agencies are required to collect data, and in many of those circumstances the methods of data collection are prescribed. Other law enforcement leaders need to be as aware of the complex issues as possible and assess voluntary data collection from a cost-benefit perspective. Major considerations in that analysis are the type and the extent of data to be collected as well as the sophistication of the benchmarking method to be used. Each of these considerations has implications affecting cost, data analysis, and conclusions that will be drawn from data. When presenting racial profiling data to the community, law enforcement leaders need to be aware of the limitations of analysis and the existence of various plausible explanations for disparities the data may reveal. In addition, they need to work carefully with the community to foster an understanding of the findings in the proper context.

Suggestions for Further Reading

For more information about some of the complex questions and issues raised in this chapter, the reader may want to refer to the following publications.

Blank, Rebecca M,, Marilyn Dabady, and Constance F. Citro, Editors. *Measuring Racial Discrimination*. National Research Council. Racial Discrimination, Division of Behavioral and Social Sciences and Education. The National Academy Press, Washington, DC; 2004.

Fridell, Lorie A. *By the Numbers: A Guide for Analyzing Race Data from Vehicle Stops*. U.S. Department of Justice Office of Community Oriented Policing Services, Washington, DC; 2004. www.cops.usdoj.gov/Default.asp?Item=1476

Fridell, Lorie, Robert Lunney, Drew Diamond ,and Bruce Kubu. *Racially Biased Policing: A Principled Response, Report/Evaluation*. U.S. Department of Justice Office of Community Oriented Policing Services, Washington, DC; 2005. www.cops.usdoj.gov/mime/open.pdf?Item=1598

Fridell, Lorie A. *Understanding Race Data from Vehicle Stops: A Stakeholder's Guide*. U.S. Department of Justice Office of Community Oriented Policing Services, Washington, DC; 2005. www.cops.usdoj.gov/mime/open.pdf?Item=1577

Fridell, Lorie A. *Racially Biased Policing: Guidance for Analyzing Race Data from Vehicle Stops*. U.S. Department of Justice Office of Community Oriented Policing Services, Washington, DC; 2005. www.cops.usdoj.gov/mime/open.pdf?Item=1578

McMahon, Joyce and Amanda Kraus. *A Suggested Approach to Analyzing Racial Profiling: Sample Templates for Analyzing Car-Stop Data*. Police Executive Research Forum, Washington, DC; 2005. www.ncjrs.gov/App/Topics/Topic.aspx?topicid=177

McMahon, Joyce, Joel Garner, Ronald Davis, and Amanda Kraus. *How to Correctly Collect and Analyze Racial Profiling Data: Your Reputation Depends On It!* U.S. Department of Justice Office of Community Oriented Policing Services, Washington, DC: 2002. www.cops.usdoj.gov/mime/open.pdf?Item=770

Endnotes

[1] Leach, Russ. "Racial Profiling: A Police Manager's Perspective." *Risk Management Issues in Law Enforcement – A Public Entity Risk Institute Symposium*. Retrieved December 18, 2005 from www.riskinstitute.org/symposiumdocs/RacialProfiling-PERISymposiumPaper.pdf.

[2] Bush, George W. *Address Before a Joint Session of the Congress on Administration Goals*. Washington, DC. February 27, 2001.

[3] Ludwig, Jack. *Americans See Racial Profiling as Widespread*. May 13, 2003. The Gallup Poll. Retrieved on November 8, 2005 from www.poll.gallup.com.

[4] American Civil Liberties Union and Texas Criminal Justice Coalition. *Prohibiting Racial Profiling: An Analysis of Local Implementation*. January 2002. Retrieved October 31, 2005 from www.criminaljusticecoalition.org/files/userfiles/racial_profiling/prohibiting_rp.pdf.

[5] *Bias-Based Profiling*. Fairborn, Ohio. Retrieved November 1, 2005 from www.ci.fairborn.oh.us/dept/pd/pd_bbp.htm.

[6] *Michael Ledford, Jr., Karen Ledford v. City of Highland Park*, U.S. District Court for the Northern District of Illinois Eastern Division, August 2, 2000.

[7] Ramirez, Deborah, Jack McDevitt, and Amy Farrell. *A Resource Guide on Racial Profiling Data Collection Systems Promising Practices and Lessons Learned*. U.S. Department of Justice, Washington, D.C.: 2000.

[8] *Whren v. U.S.*, 16 U.S. 95-5841 (1996).

[9] Fridell, Lorie A. *By the Numbers: A Guide for Analyzing Race Data from Vehicle Stops*. U.S. Department of Justice Office of Community Oriented Policing Services, Washington, DC: 2004.

[10] 2002. www.hamden.com/content/219/228/283/default.aspx.

[11] Coderoni, Gary. "The Relationship between Multicultural Training for Police and Effective Law Enforcement." *FBI Law Enforcement Bulletin*. November 2002. www.fbi.gov/publications/leb/2002/nov2002/nov02leb.htm.

[12] More information about the training and the video can be obtained on the CRS web site: www.usdoj.gov/crs.

[13] *Unresolved Problems & Powerful Potentials: Improving Partnerships Between Law Enforcement Agencies and University Based Researchers*. International Association of Chiefs of Police, Washington, D.C.: 2004.

[14] Ramirez, Deborah, Jack McDevitt, and Amy Farrell. *Massachusetts Racial and Gender Profiling Final Report: Executive Summary*. Northeastern University Institute on Race and Justice, Boston: 2004.

[15] Stewart, Dwight, and Molly Totman. *Racial Profiling: Don't Mind If I Do Ya? An Examination of Consent Searches and Contraband Hit Rate at Texas Traffic Stops*. Stewart Research Group and Texas Criminal Justice Coalition, Austin (Texas): 2005.

[16] Weiss, Alexander, and Aviva Grumet-Morris. Illinois Traffic Stop Statistics Act: Report for the Year 2004. Springfield: Illinois Department of Transportation, 2001.

[17] U.S. Department of Justice and City of Pittsburgh, Pittsburgh Bureau of Police, and Department of Public Safety Consent Decree, April 1997. www.usdoj.gov/crt/split/documents/pittssa.htm.

[18] McMahon, Joyce, Joel Gardner, Ronald Davis, and Amanda Kraus. *How to Correctly Collect and Analyze Racial Profiling Data: Your Reputation Depends on It!* U.S. Department of Justice Office of Community Oriented Policing Services, Washington, DC: 2002. www.cops.usdoj.gov/default.asp?Open=True&Item=770.

[19] Davis, Ronald. *Racial Profiling: What Does the Data Mean?* December 2001. Americans for Effective Law Enforcement. www.aele.org/data.html.

[20] See for example Appendices A and B in Fridell, Lorie A. *By the Numbers: A Guide for Analyzing Race Data from Vehicle Stops*. U.S. Department of Justice Office of Community Oriented Policing Services, Washington, D.C.: 2004.

[21] *2000 Annual Report on Missouri Traffic Stops*, Office of the Attorney General. Retrieved November 1, 2005 from www.ago.mo.gov/racialprofiling/2000/racialprofiling2000.htm.

[22] Lamberth, John. "Revised Statistical Analysis of the Incidence of Police Stops and Arrests of Black Drivers/Travelers on the New Jersey Turnpike Between Exits or Interchanges 1 and 3 from the Years 1988 through 1991" (1996)

[23] Farrell, Amy, Jack McDevitt, Shea Cronin, and Erica Pierce. *Rhode Island Traffic Stop Statistics Act: Final Report*. Northeastern University Institute on Race and Justice, Boston: 2003.

[24] Farrell, Amy. Remarks made at "Integrating Transportation Flow and Police Stop Data for Analysis of Racial Profiling with Spatial Data Analysis Symposium." Mayflower Hotel, Washington, DC. July 29, 2005.

[25] *Miami-Dade Police Department Racial Profiling Study*. The Alpert Group, November 2004. www.miamidade.gov/irp.

[26] *2003 Racial Profiling Report*. March 1, 2004. Austin Police Department. Retrieved November 30, 2005 from www.ci.austin.tx.us/action/2003_profiling.htm.

[27] Rosenbaum, Dennis, and Cody Stephens. *Reducing Public Violence and Homicide in Chicago: Strategies and Tactics of the Chicago Police Department*. Center for Research in Law and Justice University of Illinois at Chicago, 2005.

[28] *United States v. Mendenhall*, 446 U.S. 544, 554 (1980).

VII. Personnel Management Issues in the Context of Protecting Civil Rights and Serving the Community

Personnel Management Issues in the Context of Protecting Civil Rights and Serving the Community

> The hiring of a law enforcement officer is the single most important function of any law enforcement agency. It is the officers whom we hire who provide service to our community members. The quality of all law enforcement service is reduced to the officers our community members are dealing with. No amount of organization or equipment will replace the human relation skill of the individual officer. Selecting the best candidates in the marketplace is paramount.[1]
>
> **Chief Patrick Oliver (retired), Fairborn (Ohio) Police Department**

Introduction

Among the most important steps that law enforcement leaders can take to ensure ethical policing and respect for civil rights is to maintain, protect, and preserve their agencies' most valued resource—their employees. Law enforcement leaders must develop targeted recruitment strategies, maintain careful selection processes, and retain experienced, high-quality officers. They must make their agencies places where officers want to establish and pursue long-term careers. Law enforcement leaders also must inspire their command staff and human resources personnel to be motivated by the goals of identifying, hiring, and keeping the best candidates. These candidates are those who possess not only the aptitudes and attributes to engage in traditional, action-oriented policing, but also those who will perform in increasingly multifaceted policing environments. Law enforcement leaders must establish and then sustain a cadre of officers who are dedicated to ethical service-oriented policing that is respectful of the civil rights of all community members while maintaining safety and public order.

Law enforcement leaders today face many challenges in recruiting, hiring, and retaining high-quality officers. With many departments facing a shortage of police applicants,[2] law enforcement leaders struggle to maintain targeted staffing levels while trying to attract the best candidates. Many factors have converged to contribute to the recruitment shortfalls that plague many departments. Low unemployment and a strong job market in the late 1990s meant that prospective candidates could approach agencies selectively or opt for higher paying jobs in the private sector. And, more recently, the military call-up in response to September 11 terrorist attacks has reduced the pool of potential candidates as well as the ranks of sworn officers who have been called to fulfill their commitments as military reservists.[3] Together, these factors have contributed to record lows in the number of police applicants.

Personnel Management Issues

Law enforcement leaders also confront the challenge of retaining the officers they had successfully recruited, particularly young, college-educated recruits. These individuals are too often lured into private industry or other agencies. One study estimated that 14 percent of state and county officers in Florida and 20 percent of local police officers terminate within 18 months of their hire date.[4] A recent study of North Carolina agencies found a 14.2 percent attrition rate overall, with smaller agencies experiencing a higher average attrition rate (18.2 percent) than larger agencies (10.2 percent). Officers leave the law enforcement profession entirely or seek employment in other agencies for many reasons including varied opportunities, better pay, and less stressful environments.

Regrettably, high turnover is costly and presents a significant challenge to law enforcement leaders. Training and recruiting are considerable expenses. This investment is lost when officers leave to join a neighboring jurisdiction or a different industry with better pay or better working conditions. Besides the recruitment and training costs, agencies confront an even higher cost when their experienced officers leave the force. Research in several departments has demonstrated that officers with more tenure are more judicious in their use of force[6] and less likely to have complaints lodged against them.[7] The benefits of having a good balance of experienced officers to complement and mentor new recruits cannot be underestimated. The retention of highly experienced, high-caliber officers committed to protecting the civil rights of the community they serve is critical for agency stability. Failure to select and retain exemplary officers can have devastating negative effects in the long run, including poor community relations and cooperation and increased fiscal liability through lawsuits and high turnover.

Chapter Overview and Objectives

This chapter offers a series of recommendations on how to handle the challenges that law enforcement leaders and personnel managers confront as they work to recruit, hire, and retain high-quality officers. The recommendations in this chapter are offered with the recognition that law enforcement agencies are continually being asked to do more with less and while many face shortages in applicants. This chapter urges law enforcement leaders and personnel managers to act with diligence and innovation. It also advocates that law enforcement leaders and personnel managers remain steadfast in their commitment to attracting and retaining qualified officers. The need to uphold the core values of community oriented policing, customer-service approaches, and civil rights protections—even in the face of significant recruitment and retention challenges—remains vitally important.

Recommendations

Recommendations for recruitment, selection, and hiring are provided under separate headings. Throughout this guide, community policing and protection of civil rights have been stressed as complementary themes. These recommendations are offered with this focus in mind and are not meant to be an exhaustive list of considerations for recruitment, selection, and hiring.

Personnel Management Issues

Recommendations for Recruitment and Hiring

In their efforts to recruit, select, and hire qualified officers committed to effective law enforcement while protecting the civil rights of all in the community, law enforcement agencies should do the following:

1. Undertake an agencywide self-assessment to determine the attractiveness of the agency as a workplace.

To meet current recruiting and hiring challenges, law enforcement leaders and their managers should undertake a serious assessment of their agencies then take the necessary steps to improve the attractiveness of their agencies as a workplace. Current officers are a vital source of information on workplace quality and satisfaction. Police management should rely on formal (e.g., focus groups or anonymous surveys) and informal methods to elicit officers' opinions on agency strengths and weaknesses.

First-line supervisors or designated personnel managers should also perform routine exit interviews with employees leaving the department to identify both the attributes that make the agency a good place to work and those that contribute to job dissatisfaction. In particular, exit interviews with officers leaving after a short tenure or through lateral transfers should focus on what specific benefits and changes in the organizational culture, if any, might have persuaded them to remain with the department.

Although police management may not be able to address all perceived agency workplace weaknesses—law enforcement leaders, for instance, have little influence over base salaries or standard benefits—they will enhance their ability to recruit and hire high-quality officers as they address deficiencies within their control.

Large agencies with sufficient financial resources may wish to hire outside consultants to perform management studies focused on recruitment, hiring, and retention issues. All agencies should continually strive to make themselves aware of the strengths and weaknesses of their departments as a place to work. This must remain a critical focus of law enforcement leaders and their personnel managers.

2. Build on the results of agency assessment to develop a recruiting and hiring strategy.

Given current shortages of potential police applicants, law enforcement leaders can no longer passively wait for applicants to come to them. To attract high-quality applicants, law enforcement leaders must develop proactive recruiting and hiring strategies that emphasize the strengths of their agencies when considered in contrast to private sector workplaces or other law enforcement agencies.

3. Capitalize on agency personnel for recruitment efforts.

Law enforcement leaders should use agency officers to recruit others. No one is better able to represent the strengths of a law enforcement agency than the officers who work within that agency. Two strategies are common.

The first is to offer incentives to existing personnel who refer successful candidates. Incentives can be monetary or something else of value such as days off. To ensure that staff are referring appropriate clients, the incentive should be tied to some achievement milestone for the referred recruit, such as qualifying for the academy or successfully completing academy training.

A second strategy is to identify particular officers who can be used specifically for recruitment and outreach, typically on a part-time basis. These officers will staff booths at job fairs or community functions and who can be identified as points of contact for interested persons.

Selecting which agency officers to use in recruiting efforts should be purposeful and result in putting forward those officers who most favorably represent the department, exhibit enthusiasm for the job, and are good ambassadors of the department. Leaders must carefully choose officers who represent the highest qualities of the agency and who will convey the agency's mission effectively and accurately. Police executives and senior officers should make certain that these recruitment positions are held in high esteem in the agency and are perceived as positions of status by those who fill them. Quality recruiting officers who exhibit the attributes most valued by the department are the most likely to draw recruits with similar characteristics.

4. Recognize police explorer troops, police athletic leagues, and other youth organizations as promising forums for future recruits.

Police agencies can succeed in attracting more recruits by beginning the recruiting process early. They can attract recruits of high quality and motivation by focusing on persons who are already predisposed to law enforcement careers. Hundreds of youth gain familiarity with agencies through explorer troops and police athletic leagues. Many law enforcement agencies recognize the potential of such programs to serve as pools of potential recruits. Agencies that currently do not support these programs should consider creating them. Developing these youth programs and actively encouraging program participation throughout the community can pay dividends once participants reach the age of eligibility.

Besides their recruitment benefit, these programs also provide the advantage of improving community outreach with youth. Involving youth from at-risk neighborhoods, may benefit the youth, the community, and the law enforcement agency. The structure and direction offered by these programs can steer individuals along the right path, while helping to draw recruits from the neighborhoods that are often under-represented within the ranks of policing.

5. Recognize civilians involved in community policing efforts as promising recruits.

Besides focusing on youth, law enforcement leaders and personnel managers also should recruit among the graduates of citizen police academies and persons involved in community policing efforts such as neighborhood watch groups or attendance at agency-community meetings. Among the individuals brought together by these activities are those already familiar with law enforcement work and generally possess a strong commitment to law enforcement agencies and their missions. Appropriate individuals within these programs might be convinced to make law enforcement a second career. Agencies not currently engaged in these programs should consider creating them for recruitment and other benefits.

6. Consider changing maximum age restrictions.

Law enforcement leaders and personnel managers are increasingly looking to experienced adults as promising recruits. Many departments have increased the maximum age restrictions for recruits, while some departments have even done away with these restrictions altogether. Law enforcement agencies, such as the Hillsborough County Sheriff's Office discussed below, are realizing the benefits of hiring mature individuals with significant life experiences. Older recruits may handle stress more effectively and may be less prone to impulsive action than their younger counterparts with less life experience. Mature candidates with previous life experiences may be more attracted to community policing and the customer service facets of policing, on average, than young recruits who may be drawn by action-oriented facets.

Departments that have increased or done away with maximum age restrictions can expand their pool of potential recruits. Clearly, other considerations such as physical fitness and mental health must continue to be considered.

7. Develop recruitment strategies tailored to ethnic and minority communities.

Law enforcement leaders have long recognized the benefits of having agency personnel who mirror the communities they serve. While most agencies are dealing with overall recruiting and hiring challenges, many are experiencing even more acute challenges in recruiting and hiring minority and female candidates. The limited availability or hesitancy of minority group members to seek out careers in law enforcement is a reality in many jurisdictions. Research has consistently found that African-Americans and Hispanic-Americans have less favorable opinions of the police on average than do nonminorities. In addition, recruitment of candidates from within immigrant communities often is forestalled by requirements for U.S. citizenship. Recruitment remains difficult even among naturalized citizens or children of immigrants. Many children of immigrants may not perceive policing as a viable career, often because the police from their home parent's native countries are perceived as corrupt and as instruments of government repression. A text box on page 41 of Chapter 2, for instance, discusses how police in St. Paul, Minnesota, developed a citizens' academy specifically for the sizable Hmong population residing there. Similar outreach programs, geared toward educating immigrant populations about local policing practice and building trust, are becoming more commonplace in other jurisdictions.

The quality of relationships between individual departments and local minority communities varies widely. Some agencies still find themselves in the position of needing to overcome high levels of distrust within minority communities, yet many are making strides in minority recruitment. Certainly, the agency's wider approach to community outreach and record of accomplishment in civil rights are important factors in building trust. The specific strategies discussed below should be considered when seeking to recruit more minority candidates. They are also consistent with the key tenets of community policing.

- **When recruiting within ethnic and minority communities, work through existing community organizations, social and faith institutions, and media outlets particular to those communities.** Particular attention should be focused on those organizations that have both stature in the relevant communities and a positive working relationship with the police.

- **To enhance recruiting within ethnic and minority communities, develop and maintain good relations with key stakeholders including clergy, educators, business owners, and representatives of community organizations.** A general commitment to reaching out to a wide cross-section of stakeholders across all communities in the jurisdiction creates a sense of equity and inclusion that can pay dividends in recruitment. Law enforcement leaders need to remain keenly aware of demographic changes and dynamics within all neighborhoods within their jurisdiction to identify new organizations and new leaders.

- **When recruiting within ethnic and minority communities, select recruiters from within the department who have connections to these communities.** Ultimately, the goal is to use high-caliber officers who can personally attest to the qualities of the department. Persons with a similar background as the potential recruits are able to relate more directly to the candidate.

The Farmington (Connecticut) Police Department applies several of these strategies in its efforts to attract minority and female recruits. A description of its recruiting efforts is posted on the department web site.

> The department will work in conjunction with the Town Manager's office in establishing the recruitment efforts for the police department. Female and minority employees will participate in job fairs and other functions in area high schools to demonstrate a commitment to equal employment. Job fairs and similar community events will be a primary focus of the Town's effort to attract more minority candidates…The Department will send notification to community organizations with information for our website link to gather information on job openings. In addition, the consultant hired to do the testing process [will place] announcements in [multiple newspapers]. The department will update the website in conjunction with recruitment processes. The recruitment plan will be evaluated annually in October by the police department and Town Manager's Office.[8]
>
> Source: Town of Farmington (Connecticut) and Police Department
> Agency Profile: Population 23,641; Officers 411

11. Develop recruitment materials that accurately reflect agency interests in balancing traditional policing and community policing.

Departments that have adopted community policing approaches still retain traditional law enforcement functions. In an era of budget constraints, demands resulting from confronting the challenges of terrorism, and diminished federal funding for personnel, law enforcement agencies are required to do more with less. Consequently, today's officers are expected to be more well-rounded than ever before. Today's recruits need to meet the physical, cognitive, and moral standards that have long been the foundation of policing. They must possess the ability to cope with stressful situations. They must also possess other attributes that suit them to the unique demands of community policing and to work ethically, professionally, and effectively with culturally diverse communities. As one author states," the model community policing officer must have the traits of kindness—not to be mistaken for weakness—and desire to serve as a potential mentor for young adults."[9] While the need for officers with a wide array of attributes presents recruiting challenges, the call to hire officers on the basis of their commitment to service and their ability to interact with youth can actually expand the pool of potential recruits if police executives and their managers think outside of traditional policing.

When it comes to recruitment, many agencies still present themselves as largely paramilitary organizations with an emphasis on the action-oriented rather than service-oriented elements of the job. Some do this despite their concerted efforts to incorporate community policing alongside traditional policing in day-to-day operations. Recruitment materials should present an accurate and balanced image of all of the attributes expected of police officers. While agencies should continue to express the need for candidates who are physically fit and capable of reacting quickly to crisis situations, they must also communicate the need for candidates who possess considerable analytic ability, strong communication skills, a sense of diplomacy, and a commitment to community service. Agencies should make their allegiance to community policing evident in all recruitment materials. As they do so, they are more likely to target the right recruits. Edward J. Tully, a former FBI special agent and former director of the Major City Chiefs Association, summarized this approach well:

> Do not use your limited resources pursuing individuals looking for the excitement in policing, as they will join anyway! Rather, look for those that believe and support the values of your organization. It is the part-time waiters or waitresses at your local restaurants, the tellers at your community financial institutions, the substitute teachers at your children's schools, or the salespersons at your favorite stores that can be the future of your agency.[10]

Personnel Management Issues

The textbox describing a program used by Hillsborough County Sheriff's Office in Florida outlines a comprehensive hiring strategy—including many of the elements contained in the recommendations above—that is grounded in a customer-service model of policing.

Hillsborough County Sheriff's Office: Hiring in the Spirit of Service

Building on their implementation of a community policing strategy that originated in the late 1980s, the Hillsborough (Florida) County Sheriff's Office developed a *Hiring in the Spirit of Service* program in August 2004. The comprehensive strategy addresses marketing, community involvement, job analysis, and candidate screening. The program integrates two mutually re-enforcing objectives; allowing the community to provide input on personality attributes that the sheriff's office should use in selecting recruits and hiring deputies who are devoted to community service. As a result of these efforts, the sheriff's office has devised a highly targeted marketing strategy to attract the officers who are committed to the agencies' mission and who strive to reflect the attributes that the community most desires.

After a series of meetings with community groups, the sheriff's office identified a set of desired traits for deputies: leadership, integrity, flexibility, interpersonal communication, and community service. This information obtained from the meetings led to the development of a questionnaire that was distributed to a cross-section of community group members. That questionnaire indicated that the top five skills desired were communications, admission of shortcomings, lack of procrastination, work patterns, and frustration tolerance.

As part of their recruitment strategy, the sheriff's office uses a cadre of deputies who convey to potential candidates their personal experiences and the reasons why they personally find their jobs rewarding. Printed testimonials from these deputies are used as part of the process and a high-quality printed recruitment packet, *"Courage, Integrity, Compassion: Could You Answer the Call?,"* is widely distributed. The packet includes series of testimonials and basic information about the department, including agency mission, candidate requirements, and job benefits. The overall recruitment and outreach strategy is designed to achieve diversity within the department, not only demographically but also in terms of life experiences. The sheriff's office does not have a maximum age limit (but does require physical agility), which allows them to appeal to persons who may be looking for second careers.

Instead of just focusing on the paramilitary skills traditionally emphasized in law enforcement recruiting, the broad goal of recruitment is to attract persons with sound managerial, organizational, communication, and people skills. Recruitment strategies integrate the qualities of deputies valued by the community and incorporate them into the sheriff's office's pre-employment screening and testing processes.

The press release announcing the program is available at www.hcso.tampa.fl.us/Press_Releases/2004/August/04-326.htm.

Brochures and videos of "Hiring in the Spirit of Service" can be obtained from program manager, Lorelei Bowden, Hillsborough County Sheriffs Office (lbowden@acso.tampa.fl.us)

Source: Hillsborough County (Florida) Sheriff's Office
Agency Profile: Population 1,055,000; Officers 1,125

12. If necessary, recruit broadly beyond the jurisdictional boundaries.

Unfortunately, law enforcement agencies find themselves competing for scarce candidates. The New York City Police Department, the Los Angeles Police Department, and other large departments are engaged in ambitious national recruiting campaigns. As a result, small agencies and agencies whose salaries are below the regional norm face stiff competition. This not only affects their risk of losing qualified candidates but also puts them in the position of losing trained rookies and experienced officers through lateral transfers to other departments.

To remain competitive with agencies that recruit ambitiously at the national level, agencies must broaden their recruitment efforts while continuing to stress the benefits associated with working in their particular jurisdiction. Recruitment need not—and, indeed, should not—be limited to jurisdictional boundaries.

While potential recruits from smaller municipalities may be drawn to the big cities, the same big cities may contain potential recruits who may be lured by the benefits associated with smaller jurisdictions. Realistically, smaller departments may not have the power to draw candidates to the same degree that larger departments do, but they still should strive to recruit regionally. In addition, these departments could benefit by devoting some effort to assessing where current members of the force had been living when they applied and by comparing notes and strategies with nearby departments, particularly those of similar size.

Personnel Management Issues

13. Consider the benefit of using the Internet for recruiting and processing applicants.

Many departments are leveraging the Internet to inform the public about their agency and specifically to broaden their reach in recruiting candidates. While web sites can be an added resource for recruitment, they are not a panacea and may give rise to more work. For instance, a poorly designed web site may draw candidates who are not well suited for the agency's policing mission. This creates more candidates to process, many of which will be screened out. It is paramount for agencies to design their web sites so that they are consistent with their agency's mission and provide details about specific qualifications.

The following excerpts from San Antonio (Texas) Police Department, the Littleton (Colorado) Police Department, and the Phoenix (Arizona) Police Department demonstrate the ways in which web sites can become effective recruitment tools for hiring candidates committed to community service.

> Our department is seeking men and women from all backgrounds who welcome a challenge, and share our philosophy of community service. To those who accept the challenge, we offer not only excellent training, great pay and benefits, and ample opportunities for advancement, but also the opportunity to provide a service to the community as San Antonio Police Officers.[11]
>
> Source: San Antonio (Texas) Police Department
> Agency Profile: Population 1,144,646; Officers 2,054
>
> The mission of the Littleton Police Department, in partnership with our community, is to protect life and property, safeguard constitutional rights, enhance the quality of life, and reduce fear through professionalism, problem solving, and personal commitment.[12]
>
> Source: Littleton (Colorado) Police Department
> Agency Profile: Population 43,000; Officers 72
>
> "A great force in a great city"—The slogan used on recruiting billboards around Phoenix in 1955 really is as true today as it was back then. The main difference is that we don't refer to our department as a "police force", because we go beyond just being a "force" in the community. The Phoenix Police Department is a professional organization dedicated to providing unparalleled service to the community we represent. As such, one thing certain to never change is the fact that being a police officer is "A Job You Can Be Proud Of". This section of our web site is devoted to providing you with everything you need to know about becoming a police officer for our agency.[13]
>
> Source: Phoenix (Arizona) Police Department
> Agency Profile: Population 1,300,000; Officers 2,800

Using the Internet can reach a wider audience and, when carefully designed, can provide an opportunity to streamline a paperwork process. More departments are allowing applicants to provide basic information on line, which saves resources because department personnel do not have to enter information from pen-and-paper forms. In addition, more departments are following a strategy that now is widespread in the United Kingdom, using a "Do you have what it takes?" approach. These web pages can be effective ways to market the department, while providing an opportunity for prospective recruits to prescreen themselves.

Examples of interactive online application forms:
- Pennsylvania State Police (www.psp.state.pa.us)
- Philadelphia Police Department (www.ppdonline.org/career/career_apply.php).

The British approach to the online recruitment and applications can be found at the following sites:
- www.policecouldyou.co.uk/home
- www.policecouldyou.co.uk/apply.

As discussed above, these Internet approaches must meet "truth in advertising" standards. An attempt to lure persons with action-oriented narrative and graphics may attract the wrong balance of candidates. It will result in the need to screen out a significant number of applicants and may result in attrition when the action-oriented recruits find out what the job really entails.

Recommendations for Retention

Having worked hard to recruit and hire qualified officers committed to public safety and the protection of community members' civil rights, law enforcement leaders and personnel managers must continue to work to retain them. In their efforts to retain qualified officers, law enforcement agencies should do the following:

14. Provide opportunities for diverse and challenging work that is tailored to the specific interests of individual officers.

On a national level, the traditional commitment to establishing a career within a single organization is being replaced by a notion of serial employment. Law enforcement employment, however, continues to be presented as a career, with good reason. Law enforcement agencies can counteract the tendency of favoring serial employment by offering careers in which officers continually feel productive, valued, and challenged.

Law enforcement leaders and personnel managers should ensure that individual officers who exhibit aptitudes for particular types of work are recognized for special skill sets and are given opportunities to have exposure to or specialize in these areas. Agencies should offer training and educational opportunities to hone individual officers' skills and interests. For instance, individual officers could be encouraged to act as liaisons with particular communities, to perform outreach to schools, to engage in language immersion programs, or to become field training officers.

Law enforcement leaders should work particularly hard to establish recognition and esteem for all department positions. For instance, law enforcement leaders and personnel managers must recognize the critical role of patrol officers. In the event that opportunities for advancement within such roles are limited, they should create specialized positions, such as master patrol officers, to sustain the interest of their officers and create value and esteem for all positions.

15. Create an environment in which officers feel genuine ownership in the agency.

One of the most promising ways to retain high-quality officers is to ensure that they share in the agency's mission and act as vital contributors to that mission. Law enforcement leaders and personnel managers must empower their officers to become stakeholders in the organization. In many ways, community policing strategies are well designed to achieve this objective. Although community policing is implemented in a variety of ways in different jurisdictions, there is some evidence to suggest the community poling is associated with higher levels of job satisfaction.[14] A genuine sense of joint ownership in the agency and the community is a promising strategy for retention.

16. Offer competitive compensation and benefits.

To the extent possible, law enforcement leaders and personnel managers should ensure that their officers are competitively paid and supported through job benefits. The level of pay itself is not the sole factor in retaining quality police officers. The total package of benefits as well as the quality and reputation of the department can be important considerations in drawing recruits.

The impact that law enforcement leaders can have on salary and benefit packages may be limited. At the very least, however, police executives should remain up to date about how surrounding jurisdictions compare in pay and benefits. They should also be prepared to make the case to potential recruits that some benefits may compensate for lower pay. Better health benefits or more opportunities for advancement and educational opportunities, for instance, may compensate for lower starting salaries.

17. Ensure that officers are given the support they need to handle the stresses of their occupation.

Law enforcement will always be a stressful occupation, but the varied expectations placed on today's officers heighten that stress. Today's officers are both crime fighters and engaged community problem-solvers. An officer may deal with a traumatic accident, put himself or herself in danger, handle a routine traffic stop, and respond empathically to a lost Alzheimer sufferer during the course of a single shift. The resulting stress manifests itself in higher-than-average rates of suicide, substance abuse, domestic violence, and symptoms such as post-traumatic stress disorder. Stress can reduce officer effectiveness as well as heighten the risk for verbal mistreatment of civilians and use of excessive force. Too many officers leave law enforcement prematurely because of stress. Stress can contribute to the need for disciplinary action and, ultimately, dismissal. Stress may shorten careers when officers feel compelled to leave because health concerns or concerns about relationships at home.

Law enforcement leaders and personnel managers must ensure that officers are given the support they need to deal with a stressful and demanding job. Law enforcement leaders may offer this support, in part, through the development of genuine early intervention systems and associated supervisory practices explored extensively in Chapter 3 of this guide. Early intervention strategies allow supervisors to identify problematic behavior and provide nondisciplinary intervention to help officers get back on track. In this sense, these systems aid law enforcement leaders in retaining officers by providing them with the support they need to deal with a stressful environment. Apart from or in conjunction with early intervention systems, many agencies also rely on employee assistance programs to provide support to personnel and their families in times of need. Law enforcement leaders and personnel managers must be steadfast in ensuring that these programs are perceived as aids to individual officers and not as parts of a punitive disciplinary system.

Conclusion

Recruiting, hiring, and retaining good officers who can simultaneously respond to the physical demands and stress of policing while maintaining a commitment to community service and respect for civil rights is a daunting task. This work is time-consuming and can be expensive. Careful recruitment and selection procedures should be thought of as a long-time investment. In responding to shortages, quick fixes such as lowering standards or hiring officers who have left other departments under questionable circumstances can have negative and costly repercussions, both in the short term and the long term. Lowering standards may result in higher rates of dismissal. Attempting to lure officers with flashy action-oriented recruitment drives with an emphasis on weaponry and high technology could result in attrition by officers once they discover that the job is not what was promised. Recruitment should not be treated as a process isolated from overall management. The image that the department projects to recruits must be consistent with the department's mission statement and reflective of its culture. Truth in advertising is critical for maintaining a department's credibility with the recruits, with existing staff, and with the community.

Suggestions for Further Reading

Police personnel issues evolve as the police profession evolves and society changes. Addressing current shortages in candidates for policing, while maintaining commitment to integrity, high standards, and sustaining a service-oriented mission, presents a formidable challenge to today's law enforcement executive. The two recent publications listed below speak to current challenges and efforts to overcome those challenges.

Scrivner, Ellen. Innovations in Police Recruitment and Hiring: Hiring in the Spirit of Service. U.S. Department of Justice Office of Community Oriented Policing Services, Washington, DC; 2006. www.cops.usdoj.gov/mime/open.pdf?Item=1655

Taylor, Bruce, Bruce Kubu, Lorie Fridell, Carter Rees, Tom Jordan, and Jason Cheney. The Cop Crunch: Recruiting and the Hiring Crisis in Law Enforcement (presented in a three-part series) The Police Foundation, Washington, DC; May, 2006. www.policeforum.org

Endnotes

[1] Henson, Henry P., and Kevin L. Livingston. "Law Enforcement Officers Wanted: Good People for a Thankless Job." *FBI Law Enforcement Bulletin*. April 2003. www.fbi.gov/publications/leb/2003/apr2003/april03leb.htm.

[2] Hall, Mimi. "Police, Fire Departments See Shortages Across USA." USA Today, November, 28, 2004:3. www.usatoday.com/news/nation/2004-11-28-police-shortages-cover_x.htm.

[3] Tita, Bob, Paul Merrion, and Greg Hinz. "Tallying the Cost of War." Crain's Chicago Business, November 14, 2003 (Internet).

[4] "Criminal Justice Attrition Study." Tallahassee: Florida Department of Law Enforcement. (Not Dated). Retrieved October 12, 2005 from www.fdle.state.fl.us/cjst/Publications/Attrition Study.

[5] Yearwood, Douglas, and Stephanie Freeman. "Analyzing Concerns among Police Administrators: Recruitment and Retention of Police Officers." The Police Chief, March 2004:3. www.policechiefmagazine.org/magazine select "Archives."

[6] Terrill, William. Use of Force Analysis, July 1, 2001 - December 31, 2002: Final Report. City of San Antonio Texas Police Department, 2003. www.sanantonio.gov/sapd/pdf/UOFcomplete.pdf.

[7] Cao, Liqun and Bu Huang Bu. "Determinants of Citizen Complaints Against Police Abuse of Power." Journal of Criminal Justice 28.3 (May/June 2000): 203-213.

[8] "Recruiting Information." Respecting History Planning the Future. Town of Farmington Connecticut. Retrieved November 10, 2005 from www.farmington-ct.org/TownServices/PoliceDepartment/Recruiting.aspx.

[9] Kocher, Charles J. "Screening for Success in Community. Community Policing Exchange. (March/April 1999) Retrieved on November 1, 2005 from www.communitypolicing.org/publications/exchange/e25_99/e25koche.htm.

[10] Tully, Edward. "Filling Vacancies, Effective Recruiting Strategies." March 15, 2005. Retrieved October 30, 2005 through www.IACPNet.com.

[11] "San Antonio Police Department Recruiting Detail: Career Opportunities with SAPD. "Official Website of the City of San Antonio Police." Retrieved October 30, 2005 from www.ci.sat.tx.us/sapd/Recruiting.asp.

[12] "Littleton Police Department: Mission Statement." Littleton Police Department web page. Retrieved October 28, 2005 from www.littletongov.org/police/default.asp.

[13] "Police Officer Recruitment." Phoenix Police Department Website. Retrieved on October 28, 2005 www.fromphoenix.gov/POLICE/pdjob1.html.

[14] Brody, David, Christianne DeMarco, and Nicholas Lovrich. "Community Policing and Job Satisfaction: Suggestive Evidence of Positive Workforce Effects From a Multijurisdictional Comparison in Washington State." Police Quarterly, Fall 2002: 181-205.

VIII. Data-Management Issues in the Context of Protecting Civil Rights and Serving the Community

Data-Management Issues in the Context of Protecting Civil Rights and Serving the Community

> To work effectively with the community law enforcement must be willing to share information. We must first have the ability to collect and manage information before we develop strategies to disseminate the information in ways that will inform and benefit the community. This openness will build trust.[1]
>
> **Chief James Hussey, Cohasset (Massachusetts) Police Department**

Introduction

To what extent can data-management strategies—particularly those that have been credited with helping police agencies improve efficiency in personnel management and public safety—be of help to police executives pursuing commitments to protecting civil rights and to policing from a customer-service perspective? Despite the fact that law enforcement agencies have made great strides in data management over the last decade, the answer to this question is still unfolding.

During the last decade, more agency leaders have asserted that data-driven strategies have played a major role improving the management of police agencies, perhaps even a direct role in crime reduction. Data-driven management is considered a cornerstone of the highly popular CompStat approach, which originated in the New York City Police Department (NYPD) and now is being emulated in scores of law enforcement agencies throughout the United States and the world.[2] According to Jack Maple, a former NYPD transit officer who later became a deputy superintendent, the success of CompStat relies on "accurate, timely intelligence clearly communicated to all."[3]

The overall value of data for improving the functioning of law enforcement agencies has never been more clearly recognized and valued than in the present. Leaders have witnessed increases in the volume of data collected and the proliferation of CompStat-like data-driven strategies. The Chicago Police Department's CLEAR (Citizen Law Enforcement Analysis and Reporting)[4] program and the Tucson Police Department's TOP (Targeted Operational Planning)[5] program are two recent examples of ambitious data-driven management systems that are receiving acclaim for their comprehensiveness and sophistication.

Despite these broad and far-reaching advances, the new era of data-driven management still remains largely focused on *traditional* police data and missions. This traditional focus persists even though the mission of law enforcement agencies has expanded greatly over the same decade in which technological advances have taken place. With proper organization and sound data-management policies, this chapter asserts that agency leaders can take action to ensure that data management strategies are used to enhance more contemporary (less traditional) agency missions, including the protection of civil rights, improving community outreach, and enhancing residents' engagement in the civil process.

Chapter Overview and Objectives

This chapter underscores the lessons addressed in previous chapters about the effective use and dissemination of data and highlights promising practices. This chapter stresses that the same benefits that have been derived from management and analysis of traditional police data can be achieved by using less-traditional data to improve contemporary police missions.

As policing has evolved from a reactive model to one that stresses proactive and preventive approaches, data collection has also evolved. As part of this process, some agencies are focusing more attention on indicators of police performance relevant to civil rights and community policing models that stress partnership, service orientations, and problem solving.

Prudent leaders are proactive in their use of both traditional and non-traditional data. Rather than waiting for crises to occur and potentially having their own data used against them, law enforcement leaders are taking proactive steps to use data to manage their performance and hone their public image. They are embracing data-driven management strategies not only to limit liability, but also to improve agency performance in the areas of civil rights and community policing. They are collecting data about issues such as use of force and citizen complaints to clarify their missions, enhance responsiveness to the community, measure progress, improve transparency, and to showcase their successes.

This chapter begins by briefly reviewing data-management issues raised in preceding chapters and then presents four core reasons why law enforcement executives should consider augmenting their collection of traditional data with nontraditional data. In addition, this chapter offers a series of recommendations consistent with this approach.

This chapter's recommendations regarding data collection, analysis, and dissemination focus specifically on nontraditional data. In many ways, however, these data create the same types of methodological questions and challenges raised by traditional measurements of police performance, data such as Uniform Crime Reports (UCR), calls for service, citations issued, arrests, and clearance rates.

Whether tracking crime or assessing officers' performance in respecting civil rights, law enforcement leaders must take the necessary steps to ensure optimal quality data and fully acknowledge the capacities and limitations of their data. Administrative data, no matter how carefully collected, will always carry inherent limitations. An intimate understanding of an agency's data-collection processes and data quality is critical. This is true whether conducting analysis solely for internal use or when sharing information with the public.

Data-Management Issues Raised in Preceding Chapters

The importance of data collection and analysis in the protection of civil rights is interwoven throughout the preceding chapters of this guide. As was discussed in Chapter 2, law enforcement agencies committed to community policing and community outreach often depend on data-driven management for problem-solving strategies and often rely on surveys of residents to assess performance from a customer service perspective. In departments of all sizes, successful early intervention strategies (Chapter 3) depend on systematically collected information that helps supervisors make informed decisions regarding interventions designed to address problematic behavior in officers before they escalate to misconduct that require disciplinary means. Early intervention strategies in a growing number of large departments are built around computerized data-management systems, some of which rely on very ambitious and comprehensive data-collection efforts. Data on civilian and internal complaints (Chapter 4) and on use of force (Chapter 5) are among the indicators most commonly used to assess officer performance in these early intervention systems. Through web sites and annual reports, more agencies are making aggregate-level data about the quality of police performance, in particular use of force and civilian complaint data, available to the public. Rather than treating civilian complaints and allegations of excessive force as isolated cases that need to be administratively adjudicated, departments are now recognizing they can treat these data as a barometer of citizen satisfaction and then analyze the data to spot patterns and craft solutions. The shift from adjudication of individual cases to a more comprehensive management perspective is consistent with the tenets of problem-solving approaches.

Law enforcement leaders are also facing pressing demands in response to allegations of racial profiling and are confronting decisions about whether or not to collect data on traffic and pedestrian stops (Chapter 6). Police leaders whose agencies have chosen to—or are being required to—collect racial profiling data remain in dire need of assistance in addressing complex issues of data collection, analysis, and interpretation. They confront significant challenges regarding how to best interpret and use findings to engage in constructive dialogue with their communities.

Finally, police leaders are facing challenges in recruiting, hiring, and retaining qualified personnel to meet the new challenges of law enforcement (Chapter 7). These challenges include additional responsibilities brought about by post-September 11 demands while striving to maintain commitments to community policing. Even as they try to do more with less, many leaders continue their efforts to make their agencies mirror the communities they serve. Given these realities, it would be difficult to overstate the importance of data collection, management, and analysis in assessing and managing civil rights protections and sustaining a commitment to community policing.

Rationales for Expanding Data Collection and Analysis by Including Nontraditional Data

Law enforcement leaders have heard the common adage that to manage effectively they must measure. Data collection and analysis are critical to effective policing, but these efforts can be daunting, time-consuming, and costly. The costs, however, of not adequately supporting data collection, maintenance, and analysis may be far greater. Quality data collection and analysis can improve law enforcement management and operational efficiency. Not having relevant data, or not having the ability to access and properly analyze the data, can increase an agency's liability risk and undermine its credibility.

In contrast, when a law enforcement agency engages in comprehensive data collection and analysis and shares that information with the public, it exhibits its ability to serve the community with fairness and transparency. Data collection and analysis can validate police performance and enhance public relations. Moreover, data can be most beneficial if managers treat data as a feedback mechanism and use it to retool policies, procedures, and practices for both traditional law-and-order missions and those defined from a customer-service perspective. As law enforcement leaders broaden their missions under the banners of community policing or improving quality of life, they must make every effort to spotlight their successes in these areas by using concrete measurement, systemic analysis, and public dissemination of findings in formats that the public can readily understand.

Police agencies benefit when they collect and analyze traditional crime data such as calls for service, traffic citations issues, crime incidents, arrests, and response times. Many of these are traditional measures that police executives use to focus on internal agency functions. Increasingly, police managers are recognizing the benefit of collecting and analyzing less traditional data, including indices such as community meeting attendance, citizen complaints, and satisfaction surveys, all of which help police gauge how well they are serving the community and protecting the rights of citizens.

Collecting and sharing nontraditional data relating to civil rights protections and community outreach can benefit law enforcement in at least four ways.

Benefit One: Data collection and analysis promote effective management and accountability

The first rationale for collecting and analyzing nontraditional data is the same as for collecting traditional data: data are critical to effective management. Even if law enforcement agencies collect these data only for internal uses (for some reason opting not to share data and analysis with the public), effective managers can capitalize on this information to assess officer performance, modify policies and training, fine-tune practices, develop new strategies, and hold individuals responsible. As has been discussed in the preceding chapters, leaders can readily track and analyze indices such as civilian complaints, civilian commendations, and use-of-force deployments with these objectives in mind. Fundamentally, this requires a commitment to collect and analyze these nontraditional indices with the same vigor and diligence that agencies routinely commit to collecting traditional police data.

Under CompStat-style management strategies, commanders may be held liable for spikes in crime or rewarded for crime reductions. They are reprimanded or rewarded based on their unit's ability to meet performance measures such as crime rates, activity levels, clearance rates, or reductions of overtime hours. If nontraditional data are collected, analyzed carefully, and understood in context, commanders can also be held responsible for upswings in civilian complaints or spikes in use-of-force incidents. At the same time, they could be rewarded when civilian complaint data show decreases or when citizen commendations attributed to unit personnel increase.

The Importance of Context in Analyzing Data Trends

As discussed with respect to early intervention systems in Chapter 3, contextual factors are always a critical consideration in the analysis of data. Increases in deployment of reportable use of force, for instance, may not necessarily be indicative of lapses in restraint among a department's officers. If analysis indicates that this trend corresponds to increases in subject resistance, the focus of attention could be directed to problematic groups or areas within the community rather than to officers. In a similar vein, use-of-force deployments and levels of civilian complaints will track statistically to some extent with levels of crime and arrest. Taken together, different work shifts and geographic assignments often correspond to different levels of risk exposure and different types of police-civilian encounters. Neighborhoods with higher densities of late-night liquor license establishments, for instance, may give rise to higher incidences of reportable use-of-force deployments and civilian complaints stemming from altercations with police. Managers and analysts always must gauge their interpretations of trends with these contextual factors in mind.

While it would be unwise to hold qualitatively different precincts or divisions to the same expectations, comparisons within units can be made over time. Each subdivision/shift can be assessed over time to determine whether it is moving in the right direction and in a manner that is consistent with the department's overall trends. A prototype for this type of analysis was illustrated clearly in the study "Can Effective Policing Also Be Respectful? Two Examples in the South Bronx."[6] In that study, researchers found that while crime was dropping in New York City during a period in the 1990s, there was a corresponding citywide increase in civilian complaints. Although some observers would speculate that this indicated that increases in citizen complaints were an inevitable outcome of crime-control efforts, the researchers found evidence to refute that generalization. Specifically, they identified two precincts in the Bronx where both crime and citizen complaints dropped during the study period. On closer examination, the researchers were able to identify how the commanders in these precincts were able to oversee drops in both indices. Common contributing factors in both precincts were the strong leadership qualities of the commanders and their ability to identify and hold accountable those officers responsible for a disproportionate share of complaints. Although outside researchers conducted the analysis, similar analyses could be conducted by department analysts to assess internal trends and identify promising practices within a department that are worthy of emulation throughout the department.

Benefit Two: Data collection and sharing help enhance the credibility of the agency and contribute to building trust with the community.

A second rationale for law enforcement to engage in collection and analysis of nontraditional data is that these efforts can help engage the community and other important constituencies as allies, rather than as mere consumers of police services. Data presented in clear and compelling formats can go a long way toward informing the public, managing public relations, and actively engaging residents in community policing strategies. Agency leaders who strive to be proactive and deliberate in sharing data are in a better position to ensure that information is understood in context and will be better positioned to demonstrate their successes. In addition, law enforcement leaders can help cultivate common understandings of civil rights issues and remedies by routinely sharing outcome measures with the public. These proactive approaches clearly are better than those that are apt to be seen as reactive or defensive, such as responding *only* when critical incidents spark outside requests for data.

Sharing information with the public can facilitate two-way communication. Objective and clear data routinely made available to the public can help communities develop a fairer and more balanced perspective of the police and the actions that they take. At the same time, police will be in a better position to access accurately and realistically the public's reaction to the data and their general perception of the agency.

Benefit Three: Data collection and analysis support broadly defined problem-solving strategies and partnership building.

A third rationale for collecting and analyzing nontraditional data is closely related to the second. Collection of these types of data can expand police-community problem-solving efforts. While community members expect departments to keep them safe, they also expect departments to be responsive to their needs and treat them respectfully and fairly. In some jurisdictions, residents have come to rely on the police to help them become more engaged in civic processes. The same problem-solving strategies that have won favor in addressing crime and public disorder can be used to assess civil rights and community outreach problems and to craft joint solutions.

Analysts may uncover, for instance, that the police are responding to a flood of calls from an immigrant community but are not getting members of that community to attend local precinct meetings. When a police leader takes proactive measures to reach out to leaders within this community, the department can begin to develop broader community networks.

Discussions about the data and continued analysis of information with leaders from the immigrant community can be useful for developing collaborative approaches and building partnerships. Having cemented relationships with key community stakeholders, police can work collectively with leaders to help foster new relationships with the wider immigrant community and to cultivate long-term relationships. Several examples of just this approach were provided in the Chapter 2 on community policing. Data help the police and community to understand and define issues from a similar perspective; data form a foundation for constructive partnerships; and data provide the ability to measure progress. These are key components of the problem-solving process.

Benefit Four: Data collection and analysis efforts can be used to establish new allies and bring more resources to the table.

A fourth reason for expanding data collection and analysis efforts is that relevant outcomes, particularly successful ones, can be widely shared. When police inform journalists, legislators, and other government officials about what they do they take a proactive role managing their public image. Officials from other government agencies, such as the mayor's or governor's office, will want to associate themselves with successful practices and positive outcomes. This can result in positive exposure and the funding necessary to maintain effective practices.

Risks of Not Sharing Data with the Public

If the benefits of sharing data are not enough to convince leaders, considering what happens when agencies do not share data may be compelling. In the absence of adequate data sharing, the public, the media, and oversight agencies may be prone to draw their own conclusions. Without the proper context, they may be more apt to engage in knee-jerk responses to exceptional events like a highly publicized use of lethal force, or fall back into the politically expedient response of blaming the police.

Collecting and sharing relevant data can be invaluable to law enforcement leaders by helping put isolated incidents in a broader and more definitive context. A chief with reliable and compelling data about an overall downward trend in use-of-force deployments or civilian complaints, for instance, will be in a better position to quell public outcries when controversial incidents occur. Similarly, a sheriff who can readily demonstrate that his or her deputies' lethal-force deployment rates compare favorably to similar jurisdictions will be in a better position to manage public relations when isolated use-of-force deployments raise public concern.

Recommendations

Recognizing the benefits discussed above, this chapter's recommendations are focused on basic data-management issues that will promote data sharing and will optimize the value of the data shared, particularly data that relate to civil rights and community outreach.

These recommendations are not intended to be an all-inclusive treatise on data management. Presented in this manner, law enforcement executives need not be experts in data management or statistical analysis to find the recommendations useful. Recommendations appear under three categories: data collection, data analysis, and data dissemination.

Data Collection Recommendations

In their data collection efforts, all law enforcement agencies should do the following:

1. Capitalize on sources of data that already exist within the department.

To assess and manage their performance in protecting civil rights and promoting community policing, law enforcement agencies should make full use of data that they already routinely collect. As police agencies have expanded their mission beyond traditional policing, data other than those associated with reactive responses to crime have become increasingly relevant. As a result, a fair amount of data relevant to civil rights protection and community policing is already collected for routine administrative purposes.

Although these data are collected with increasing frequency, the data are not always fully used for purposes of management and evaluation. For instance, data on citizen complaints or reportable uses of force may be tracked to assess individual officers through an early intervention system. Partially as a result of alleged civil rights violations and the imposition of several consent decrees and memorandums of agreement, for example, more departments are tracking their deployment of canines as a force-control option. Departments and units are being held accountable for reducing the overall deployment of canines in this manner and for keeping their bite-to-release ratios to a minimum.

These types of data are being used in departments to assess the overall direction of the department or to compare whether all units are moving in the right direction. Prudent police executives and managers should make the best use of the following types of information and use it to assess and refine their protections of civil rights.

- Use-of-force incidents, ideally broken down by types of deployment/equipment use, by geographic unit, and by subject demographics
- Citizen complaint data, ideally broken down in the manner mentioned above
- Traffic stop and pedestrian stop data with sufficient detail to assess racial profiling
- A broad range of data used within early intervention or personnel performance management systems.

The public expects both equal protection and equal service from the police. Police also have at their disposal administrative data that can be used to assess whether they are serving the needs of the public and whether they are serving all constituent groups within their community effectively and equitably. Administrative data used to assess and refine community policing could include the following:

- Community participation at police-sponsored meetings (e.g., monthly precinct or beat meetings), for comparison purposes ideally broken down by the participants' gender, age, race/ethnicity, and area of residence
- Police attendance and involvement in community-sponsored meetings and activities, including those sponsored by churches, civic organization, or tenant associations
- Community participation in police-sponsored activities such as police athletic leagues, police explorer programs, or citizen academies, ideally broken down by the demographic categories listed above
- Community volunteer participation in the agency.

Police agencies should use such information to identify particular groups or neighborhoods for which additional outreach efforts may be warranted as well as to document agency successes such as improvement in minority participation.

2. Agencies should continually seek to expand nontraditional data-collection efforts

To assess and manage their performance in protecting civil rights and promoting community policing, law enforcement agencies should review and expand their data-collection efforts on a continuous basis. As police agencies have adopted community policing and customer-oriented approaches, many have successfully expanded their use of surveys and customer feedback. This enables agencies to compensate for limitations associated with administrative data. For instance, little research exists to shed light on the extent to which the volume of citizen complaints that an agency receives is a reflection of the behavior of its officers or its openness and willingness to receive and investigate complaints.[7] Collecting data on citizens' opinions of police performance through systematic surveys is one way to offset some of the limitations associated with administrative data. Survey data can also serve as a method of cross-validating administrative data. If survey data indicate that satisfaction is increasing and that misconduct complaints against officers are also increasing, this may actually indicate that efforts to make the citizen complaint process more open have been effective.

Using citizen complaints to assess police performance is critical, for instance, but it must be recognized that not all persons who have experienced negative encounters with the police will report them. Indeed, the willingness to complain (or to compliment) the police may vary considerably across the jurisdiction or by demographic groups. Surveys, whether sophisticated and scientific or more modest in design, can be of great benefit, as discussed below.

Agencies should consider two basic types of surveys and recognize the relative benefits and limitations of each.

Data-Management Issues

- Use community surveys that strive to be representative of the jurisdiction at large and that can represent the view of distinct communities within the jurisdiction

Law enforcement agencies that embrace community policing often consider community surveys a core component of their data-collection strategy. Community surveys are very flexible. Questions on community surveys can be tailored to address issues that are of concern to police managers or issues that are of concern to community members. Questions also can be designed to identify and compare issues confronting different communities served by the police department. The communities may be defined geographically or by demographic traits.

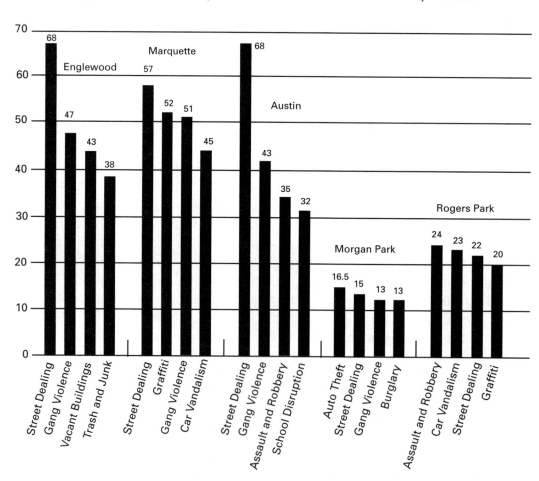

Biggest Problems in Experimental Districts: Wave 1 Survey Results

The graph displayed here, for example, illustrates the responses elicited through a community survey conducted in five police districts in Chicago at a time when the police department was piloting its community policing program.[8] These responses demonstrate quite clearly the types of problems that are shared across these communities as well as those that are unique to particular communities. Such data can be valuable to district commanders when planning their community policing strategies and working with the community to establish neighborhood-specific problem-solving priorities.

While similar types of conclusions could possibly be gleaned from existing data sources, such calls to station houses or crime reports, these would be subject to a reporting bias because different communities may be more or less willing to call the police. A random scientific survey can compensate for some of these statistical biases and can help to validate inference drawn from administrative data.

Community surveys, in particular, can be crafted to assess whether citizens are satisfied with different facets of police service. The graph titled "2004: Citizen Satisfaction with Police Responsiveness" illustrates how residents in Shoreline, Washington who reported having direct interactions with officers from the King County Sheriff's Office—the agency with which the city contracts to provide police services—rated officer responsiveness in 2004.[9]

Citizen Survey Results Re: Officer Responsiveness

The City of Shoreline via Northwest Research Group administered the Police Satisfaction Survey in 2004. Shoreline anticipates surveys again in the fall of 2007.

Citizens of Shoreline *who interacted with the police* gave the following responses to survey questions about police officer responsiveness.

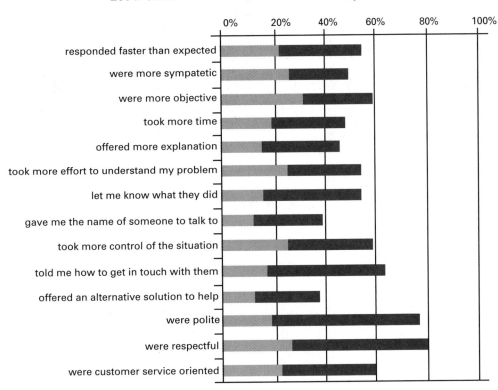

Data-Management Issues

Community satisfaction surveys can also assess whether levels of satisfaction vary across communities. Groups within a jurisdiction may vary in their satisfaction with police services. In larger jurisdictions, agencies may wish to collect survey data in sufficient sample sizes and with full demographic information about the respondents to make comparisons across different geographic areas and across different groups defined by variables such as race/ethnicity, age, gender, and home ownership status. A wide variety of studies and national opinion polls demonstrate that levels of citizen satisfaction are statistically related to these demographic factors.[10] For assistance in conducting community surveys see the publication *Conducting Community Surveys: A Practical Guide for Law Enforcement Agencies*.[11]

- **Use opportunistic (nonscientific) surveys.**

Police departments need not limit themselves to scientific surveys. Surveys that are designed to be scientifically representative can be expensive and time-consuming, in large part because of the rigorous procedures and standards required for obtaining random samples. Other options, such as short questionnaires distributed in neighborhoods, distributed on car windshields, or made available on an agency's web site, can be collected more easily and cheaply. They can still be very useful, but must be interpreted with more caution than representative scientific surveys.

Increasingly, police departments are collecting data using consumer-based feedback approaches through the Internet. While similar in format to those discussed earlier, these surveys are considered *opportunistic* rather than *scientific* because participation is voluntary. The graphic represents a portion of an opportunistic survey form made available on the web from the Kent Police in England.[12]

Q4) In your opinion what priority should Kent Police give to each of the following? (Please tick the appropriate answers)	High Priority	Medium Priority	Low Priority	No Priority
Reducing serious crimes i.e. murder, rape	○	○	○	○
Protecting children from abuse	○	○	○	○
Fighting Drugs	○	○	○	○
Reducing burglaries for peoples homes	○	○	○	○
Providing information and advice to the public	○	○	○	○
Answering 999 telephone calls	○	○	○	○
Providing a visible Police presence	○	○	○	○
Reassuring victims and witnesses of crime	○	○	○	○
Reducing vehicle crime	○	○	○	○
Responding to 999 calls for assistance	○	○	○	○
Reducing public disturbances i.e. fights	○	○	○	○
Protecting people from domestic violence	○	○	○	○
Answering non-999 telephone calls	○	○	○	○
Reducing crime against minority groups	○	○	○	○

While such data collection can be of real benefit to police departments, it is important to sound a clear note of caution regarding opportunistic sampling. The voluntary nature of these types of surveys makes them prone to statistical bias. Responses are likely skewed by the fact they are available only to persons with web access. Also, people with the strongest opinions—either for or against a given policy or practice—are most likely to respond to surveys such as these. No generalizations can be made about the wider community because the findings based on opportunity samples reflect only those opinions of persons responding to the survey or data-collection instrument. If data from opportunistic surveys are shared with the public, the information must include a disclaimer to the effect that the data reflect the results of a nonscientific survey.

Another example of an opportunistic data-collection effort is the Maryland State Police's use of traffic stops as an occasion to get feedback from motorists. The form below provides a systematic way to collect both commendations and complaints of citizen-trooper interaction in traffic stops.

COMMENDATION/COMPLAINT FORM

Please provide the following information if you wish to commend or express your concerns about the actions of a Maryland state trooper.

YOUR NAME _____ or call 1-800-525-5555 **In Maryland**
YOUR ADDRESS _____ 1-800-333-9890 **Outside Maryland**
DATE/TIME/LOCATION OF ENCOUNTER _____ TDD 1-410-486-0677
TROOPER'S NAME & ID _____
DESCRIBE ENCOUNTER _____
_____
_____
_____
_____
_____

MSP 225(8-03) DETACH THIS CARD, PLACE IN ENVELOPE, APPLY POSTAGE AND MAIL TO ADDRESS ON REVERSE SIDE.

In this particular example, the respondents are allowed to describe the nature of the contact in their own words. This narrative information is systematically reviewed by supervisors to assess the performance of individual officers and to assess aggregate patterns in the agency and across geographically defined troops.

This type of free-field response format does not limit the type of information a person may submit. Since the response is open-ended, the type of information submitted may be rich in content but may be more difficult to analyze statistically. Supervisors or analysts at the Maryland State Police first would have to code information from the text to tabulate how many complaints alleged rudeness, excessive force, or racial profiling.

Data-Management Issues

Agencies are increasingly relying on their web sites to collect both complaint and commendation information. The Fairfax County (Virginia) Police Department[13] (www.fairfaxva.gov/Police/inform.asp) and the Phoenix (Arizona) Police Department[14] (www.phoenix.gov/EMAIL/emcommend.html) are two of many examples by which feedback can be submitted online.

3. Agencies must pay close attention to data quality and completeness.

All organizations collecting data confront data quality and completeness issues. Given the scope of administrative data collection occurring in law enforcement agencies, these concerns range from mundane issues such as mis-keyed data to major issues such as misclassifications of crimes.

In law enforcement agencies, data analysts and data consumers must also recognize that data frequently tell only a partial story. For instance, law enforcement leaders recognize that UCR data reflect only those crimes known to the police rather than all crimes occurring within a jurisdiction. In addressing data relevant to civil rights protection and the promotion of community policing, data quality concerns are critically important.

The following recommendations specify further law enforcement agencies' obligations to control the quality of the data they collect.

- **Collect data in a standardized and uniform manner.**

Law enforcement agencies must make every effort to ensure that data are collected in a standardized and uniform manner. This is true whether the agencies rely on existing administrative data, community surveys, or customer feedback forms. Even in the case of administrative data, the importance of quality assurance and consistency of data collection cannot be overstated. The collection of racial-profiling data, for instance, illustrates the complications that can arise in the process of standardization. The collection of racial-profiling data is an inherently subjective determination—officers must ascertain the race or ethnicity of a motorist based on their perceptions—and yet every effort must be made, through training and data instrument design, to assure as much consistency as possible. Agencies must train officers specifically on how to fill out traffic stop forms. If, for instance, a traffic stop form contains the options "Black," "White," and "Hispanic," the agency must prepare an officer to record information about an individual he perceives to be Black and Hispanic. Perhaps the agency will change its form to include categories such as "White-Hispanic," "White-non-Hispanic," "Black-Hispanic," "Black-non-Hispanic," etc., or perhaps the agency will direct officers to record Hispanic ethnicity in a field separate from race. In any event, standardization is critical.

- **Offer clear operational policies on data collection.**

Just as agencies must ensure that officers collect data in a standardized and uniform manner, they must ensure that officers know when such data must be collected. Agencies must offer clear operational policies on data collection. For instance, an agency must specify whether or not it requires officers to collect racial profiling data for all traffic stops or only for those stops that result in a formal action. Alternatively, in the case of pedestrian stops, agencies must draw clear distinctions between a street detention that requires the completion of a form from any other type of pedestrian-officer interaction that does not require data collection. Departmental policies and training must be consistent and clear. If they are not, officers will not complete data forms consistently and, as a result, missing observations will become a threat to the integrity of the agency's data collection and analysis efforts. Inconsistencies in data collection can skew results. Agencies must not collect incomplete or inconsistent data only to have analysis of these data result in misinformation.

- ***Engage in routine data auditing and validation.***

To maximize the collection of complete, consistent, and accurate administrative data, agencies should engage in routine data auditing and validation. Law enforcement supervisors routinely and rigorously review and approve traditional data-collection forms such as incident and arrest reports, as well as nontraditional data-collection forms, including use-of-force report forms and citizen complaint forms, which are used to assess civil rights protections and to promote community policing. In the case of racial profiling data forms, for instance, agency supervisors may check officers' designations of driver race/ethnicity against department of motor vehicle data to ensure accuracy. Routine data auditing may reveal whether particular individuals or units exhibit a greater-than-normal tendency to fall back on "unknown" or "not applicable" as a response. The same review and quality assurance measures that are undertaken for the purpose of assessing individual officers and to make sure that the forms are in compliance with policy also will enhance the reliability of aggregate statistical analyses.

To ensure compliance with operational policies governing data collection, agencies have been known to use sting audits. For instance, in its consent decree with the Los Angeles Police Department, the Department of Justice calls for sting audits to identify officers "who discourage the filing of a complaint or fail to report misconduct or complaints."[15] While the main purpose of these audits is to ensure compliance with policies, procedures, and ethical requirements, such audits also help to enhance the reliability of the data collected and analyzed.

Data Analysis Recommendations

Once data have been collected, the data must be analyzed. Data analysis generally requires specialized skills, including a familiarity with statistics and research methodology. To respond productively to the results of data analysis, police executives, managers, and, when appropriate, the public, must understand the information. Law enforcement data analysts, therefore, must ensure that the results of their analyses are accessible, are presented in a straightforward manner, and are comprehensible. The following recommendations address such steps.

4. Acknowledge the limitations inherent in data.

An accurate understanding of data analysis and results depends on a keen awareness of the limitations often inherent in administrative data. Data analysts must make such limitations clear to their chief, supervisory personnel, and the public. In the analysis of traditional

crime data, for instance, when presenting a department's annual UCR crime counts or rates, analysts routinely make clear that they have analyzed "reported" crime or "incidents known to the police." It is important to distinguish between these known data and the total number of crimes (which includes an unknown number of unreported crimes).

The same caveats routinely applied to traditional data should be applied to nontraditional data. Analysts should make clear that indices such citizen complaints, for example, are prone to similar underreporting. Not every citizen who has a grievance against an officer will file a formal complaint.

Analysts should also make clear that the implications of such underreporting could be affected by a host of factors. In the case of citizen complaints, for instance, it is important for analysts to communicate the fact that the number of citizen complaints filed can be affected by factors such as the openness of the complaint process and that, for this reason, making comparisons of the number of complaints filed across different law enforcement agencies is inadvisable.

5. Analyze and interpret data in context.

Analysts should make clear that the results of their data analysis must be placed in context to be understood correctly. The public—and sometimes even police executives and managers—may see rising and falling trends in crime incidents, use-of-force incidents, or citizen complaints and feel inclined to make inferences about these trends without considering context. For instance, community members may be alarmed to learn that the number of crimes in a jurisdiction rose 30 percent in a given year until they understand that the jurisdiction's population increased by 40 percent in the same year.

Similarly, community members may be concerned about a rising trend in citizen complaints. If this increase, however, is the result of policy changes dictated by a federal consent decree that required the agency to make its citizen complaint process more accessible and less burdensome, an apparently alarming spike in citizen complaints should be presented and interpreted in the proper context. Analysts, whether they are sworn officers or civilian employees, must be trained and proficient in data analysis and familiar with the capacities and limitations of agency data so that the information can be presented in the proper context.

The general term for putting one data measure in the context of another data measure—such as understanding the number of crimes in the context of a population shift—is called normalizing the data. Following the logic of data normalization, analysts should assess trends in citizen complaints or use-of-force incidents within the context of those police activities most likely to generate complaints or necessitate the use of force. For instance, if the number of traffic citations and arrests rise, a commensurate increase in the number of use-of-force incidents may not be alarming.

Analysts should regularly normalize data. In general, the number of citizen complaints should be presented in the context of the number of police-citizen contacts. Similarly, the number of use-of-force incidents should be presented in the context of the number of arrests. Analysts who establish ratios of such as these, allow police executives, managers, and, when appropriate, the public to understand trends in their proper context.

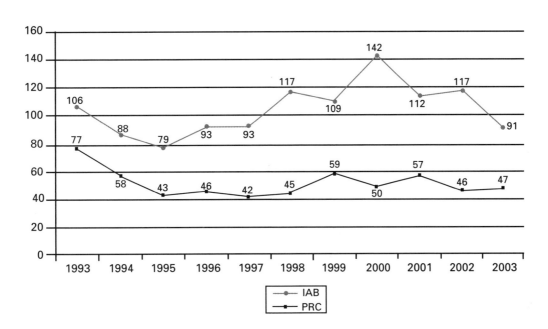

Analysts also facilitate understanding of data by establishing comparisons between data. Graphics should provide viewers with the opportunity to compare and contrast related indices. The graph included here illustrates trends of citizen complaints for the Berkley (California) Police Department by comparing those processed through the independent Police Review Commission (PRC) to those processed by the department's Internal Affairs Bureau.[16]

6. Analyze data over sufficient periods of time.

Of course, trends in data emerge over time. Analysts must assume responsibility for ensuring that law enforcement executives, managers, and, when appropriate, the public, understand trends accurately by presenting them over a sufficiently long period of observation.

Truncated periods of observation may yield inaccurate or misleading results. For instance, in the following hypothetical example, the first graph would seem to suggest that a department's verbal judo training had no clear impact in the 6-month period following implementation. If the period of observation is extended to include a longer period both before and after the training, however, the implications about the effectiveness of the training are altogether different.

The second graph allows the viewer to recognize that use-of-force incidents are seasonal and that use-of-force deployments generally increase in the summer months. As a result, the viewer presented with the first graph may inaccurately conclude that the department's verbal judo training failed while the viewer presented with the second graph is likely to attribute the increase in use-of-force incidents immediately following the verbal judo training to the arrival of summer. As a result, while the viewer of the first graph may advocate discontinuing verbal judo training, the viewer of the second graph would recognize—accurately—that the number of monthly use-of-force incidents from January to May 2004 is substantially lower than that for January to May 2005 and recommend that the training be continued.

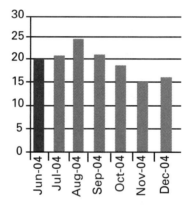

Use-of-Force Incidents: 6 Months Following Verbal Judo Training in June 2004

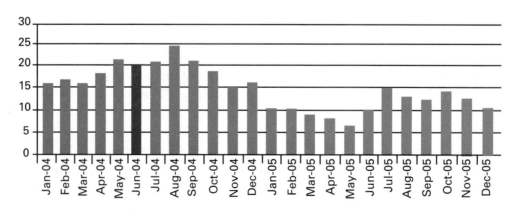

Use-of-Force Incidents: Before and After Verbal Judo Training in June 2004

This hypothetical example illustrates a general truth: it is vitally important to assess trends over a sufficiently long period of observation. This is true when police executives are assessing the impact of a programmatic change, a change in policy, or assessing the impact of the introducing new equipment. Ensuring that a sufficiently long period of observation is established may be particularly critical following the introduction of practices or equipment that may be viewed as controversial. For instance, analyses regarding the introduction of conducted energy devices (CEDs or Tasers™) should track data for months before and after their introduction to provide an accurate appreciation for the effects of this new technology. Examining trends over the long term results in more meaningful, reliable analyses.

7. Break data down into meaningful categories (disaggregation).

Whenever possible, data should be broken down into discrete categories to make the analysis more meaningful. While it is useful to know, for instance, whether citizen complaints are rising or falling, it is even more meaningful to know more specifically whether citizen complaints regarding rudeness, racial profiling, and excessive force in particular are rising or falling.

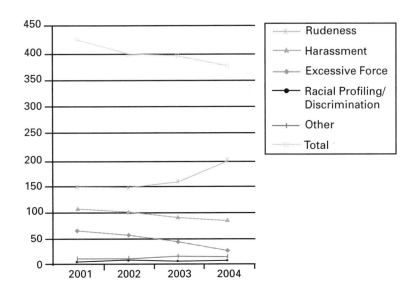

The hypothetical graph presented here demonstrates the usefulness of dividing total citizen complaints into discrete categories. Police executives and managers responsible for designing training initiatives would surely want to note that while the number of total complaints has fallen during 4 years, the number of complaints regarding officer rudeness has actually increased.

Data should also be presented with relevant contextual factors. Indicating the rate of complaint per officer would be particularly important, for instance, if the size of the department changes appreciably over time.

8. Map data and results when possible.

During the last decade, law enforcement analysts have embraced mapping as an effective way to understand the distribution of crime within their jurisdictions and to respond more effectively to public safety problems through tactical and strategic analysis. Agencies are now beginning to realize these same benefits as they work to protect civil rights and promote community policing. Analysts within the police and from community-based organizations now are beginning to map use-of-force incidents and citizen complaints to understand their geographic distribution, interpret the patterns, and to plan accordingly.

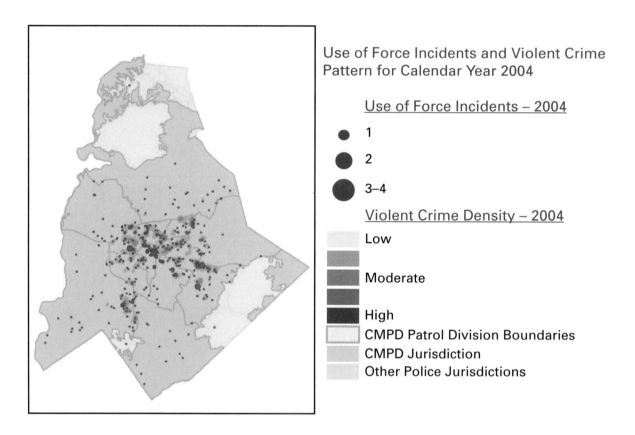

Analysts should be sure, when mapping nontraditional data such as use-of-force deployments or citizen complaints, to normalize the data or put it into its proper context. The graphic included here, from the Charlotte-Mecklenburg (North Carolina) Police Department's 2004 Internal Affairs Annual Report, illustrates the utility of such data normalization in mapping.[17]

The map clearly shows that the geographic concentrations of use-of-force incidents correspond to the concentrations of arrests. The department uses similar maps to illustrate that use-of-force incidents also geographically corresponded to other police activities such as violent crime incidents, citizen calls for service, and officer-initiated computer-aided dispatch calls. Such maps can be effective tools for guiding discussions with community leaders about the factors associated with the use of force.

9. If necessary, hire staff with data analysis skills and/or use consultants, including university based researchers.

Data analysis ranges from the basic, such as tracking crime levels or community meeting attendance over time, to the highly complex. Collecting, analyzing, and drawing inferences from racial profiling data or engaging in scientifically defensible evaluations of innovative agency programs, for instance, require expertise in statistics and research methodology. Executives in larger agencies sometimes have the luxury of hiring skilled analysts and researchers that smaller departments cannot afford. Leaders of agencies of any size occasionally may need to hire research experts.

A recent IACP publication on improving partnerships between police leaders and university based researchers provides practical solutions for making the most of these partnerships.[18] Independent and objective assessment of agency performance is among the benefits of these partnerships. Openness to sharing data and being evaluated by outside experts also helps build community trust. Use of university based researchers can be more cost-effective then hiring private consultants, particularly when the data analysis meets the needs of both the police agency and the university researcher. The work of independent university researchers may be supported by grant funds and a department's willingness to engage outside researchers and evaluators can increase its opportunity to obtain grant funds. Under fiscal constraints and general tenets of accountability, federal and state funding agencies are being more selective in the programs they support. Increasingly, funding decisions are being made on an empirically based "what works" standard.

Data Dissemination Recommendations

In addition to the basic rules of data collection and data analysis, there are useful guidelines to follow when sharing data with the public. The following recommendations can help to ensure that law enforcement agency data will not be misinterpreted.

10. Assess carefully and continually what—and in what format—information should be shared with the public.

While most of the graphs and maps illustrating this chapter were drawn from publicly available annual reports or web sites, law enforcement leaders and their data management staff must carefully and continually assess what information to share with the public and in what format that information should appear. Although sharing data with the public can be a double-edged sword, law enforcement leaders should recognize the net benefits of data sharing. It is true that when trends are not favorable, data sharing creates the potential for public relations challenges. It is also true, however, that when trends are favorable, data may serve to enhance the image of the department.

Sharing both favorable and unfavorable data sends the message that the department is committed to transparency and has nothing to hide. When such transparency is coupled with sustained outreach to all communities within the jurisdiction, police executives will be well positioned to address any negative trends and work cooperatively with a community from a problem-solving perspective to address any concerns raised by the data.

With any commitment to data sharing, certain safeguards must be in place. Foremost among these is that all legal and administrative requirements regarding the privacy and confidentiality of the subject and of police officers must be upheld. Just as important, no data should be released if release would constitute a breach of public safety. Departments must also be sensitive to the restrictions on sharing certain types of data that may exist as a result of collective bargaining agreements.

11. Revisit data presentation strategies and formats to ensure optimal effectiveness in public information.

Consistency in reporting data is a hallmark of good analysis because it permits analysts and consumers of that data to compare performance over time. Departments, however, should not let commitments to consistency inhibit them from changing or enhancing formats when necessary. Clearly, if data report formats result in confusion or are not understood by the intended audiences, then alternative forms of presentation should be considered. Actively sharing data and seeking feedback from the public on a continuous basis, through public meetings or in the course of problem-solving, will help ensure that data are being presented meaningfully and clearly, in ways that both the police and the public can understand.

Changes in policies, procedures, or the addition of new units may affect reporting formats and trends. For instance, if a department switches from internal review of citizen complaints to the use of a citizen review board, new report data and outcome formats will be required. Likewise, if a department changes the level of force for which reports are required, adjustments should be made and noted in standardized reports. Similar modifications should be made if changes are made to geographic boundaries (e.g., new alignments or an existing unit being split in two).

Conclusion

This chapter addressed how law enforcement agencies can collect, analyze, and share data related to their missions to protect civil rights and to reach out to their constituents and partners in the community. Overall, this chapter stressed that law enforcement leaders should incorporate these outcomes, alongside traditional law enforcement measures, in their efforts to capitalize most effectively on data-management strategies. Several illustrative examples were provided. Examples, however, are becoming more prevalent and novel approaches, such as mapping civilian complaint and police use-of-force locations, continue to emerge. Data management should be considered a core component of any community outreach plan and as a tool to assess an agency's effectiveness in protecting and promoting the civil rights of all persons within the community it serves.

Suggestions for Further Reading

Data management and analysis affect all facets of law enforcement. Publications that address data collection from the perspective of protecting civil rights and promoting community partnerships and trust include the following.

Carter, David L. *Law Enforcement Intelligence: A Guide for State, Local, and Tribal Law Enforcement Agencies*. U.S. Department of Justice Office of Community Oriented Policing Services, Washington, D.C.: 2004. www.cops.usdoj.gov/Default.asp?Item=1439.

Skogan, Wesley G., Susan M. Hartnett, Jill DuBois, and Jason Bennis. *Policing Smarter Through IT: Lessons in Enterprise Implementation*. U.S. Department of Justice Office of Community Oriented Policing Services, Washington, D.C.: 2004. www.cops.usdoj.gov/Default.asp?Item=1331.

Fridell, Lorie A. *Understanding Race Data from Vehicle Stops: A Stakeholder's Guide*. U.S. Department of Justice Office of Community Oriented Policing Services, Washington, D.C.: 2005. www.cops.usdoj.gov/mime/open/pdf?Item=1577.

Weisel, Deborah. *Conducting Community Surveys: A Practical Guide for Law Enforcement Agencies*. U.S. Department of Justice Office of Justice Programs, Washington D.C.: 2003l. www.ojp.usdoj.gov/bjs/pub/pdf/ccspglea.pdf.

Endnotes

[1] Hussey, James, Chief of Cohasset (Massachusetts) Police Department. Personal Correspondence. December 1, 2005.

[2] Weisburd, David, Stephen D. Mastrofski, Rosann Greenspan, and James J. Willis. *The Growth of Compstat in American Policing*. Washington, DC: Police Foundation, 2004.

[3] Dussault, Raymond. "Jack Maple: Betting on Intelligence." *Government Technology*. April 1999. www.govtech.net/magazine/story.php?id=94865&issue=4:1999.

[4] Skogan, Wesley G., Susan M. Hartnett, Jill DuBois, Jason Bennis, So Young Kim, Dennis Rosenbaum, Lisa Graziano, and Cody Stephens. *Policing Smarter Through IT: Learning from Chicago's Citizen and Law Enforcement Analysis and Reporting (CLEAR) System*. U.S. Department of Justice Office of Community Oriented Policing Service, Washington, DC: 2003. www.cops.usdoj.gov/mime/open.pdf?Item=1264.

[5] See reference to the program in *Strategic Visions: Our Blueprint for the Future* (Tucson [Arizona] Police Department 2002 Annual Report). Tucson Police Department, 2002.

[6] Davis, Robert C., Pedro Mateu-Gelabert, and Joel Miller. "Can Effective Policing Also Be Respectful? Two Examples in the South Bronx." *Police Quarterly*, 2005: pp. 229-247.

[7] Skogan, Wesley, and Kathleen Frydl, eds. *Fairness and Effectiveness in Policing: The Evidence*. The National Academy Press (National Research Council of the National Academies), Washington, D.C.: 2004. (See page 161).

[8] Reproduced from: Skogan, Wesley G. "Measuring What Matters: Crime, Disorder, and Fear." *Measuring What Matters: Proceedings from the Policing Research Institute Meetings*. U.S. Department of Justice: National Institute of Justice and the Office of Community Oriented Policing Services, July 1999, pp 37-54. www.ncjrs.org/pdffiles1/170610-2.pdf.

[9] *Service Efforts and Accomplishments 2004: Fifth Annual Report of Police Performance*. King County Sheriff's Department for the City of Shoreline, Washington: 2004. www.metrokc.gov/sheriff/downloads/partners/seasho04.pdf.

[10] See for instance: *Satisfaction with Police—What Matters?* U.S. Department of Justice Office of Justice Programs, National Institute of Justice, Washington, D.C.: 2002. www.ncjrs.gov/pdffiles1/nij/194077.pdf.

[11] Weisel, Deborah. *Conducting Community Surveys: A Practical Guide for Law Enforcement Agencies*. U.S. Department of Justice Office of Justice Programs; Washington D.C.: 2003l. www.ojp.usdoj.gov/bjs/pub/pdf/ccspglea.pdf.

[12] *Your Police Service Survey*. Kent Police, United Kingdom. Retrieved on October 10, 2005 from www.kent.police.uk/sites/internetsurvey/questionnaire.php.

[13] www.fairfaxva.gov/Police/inform.asp.

[14] www.phoenix.gov/EMAIL/emcommend.html.

[15] *United States* v. *City of Los Angeles* Consent Decree (June 15, 2001). www.usdoj.gov/crt/split/documents/laconsent.htm.

[16] *City of Berkley Police Review Commission: 2003 Statistical Report*. www.ci.berkeley.ca.us/prc.

[17] Internal Affairs 2004 Annual Report. Charlotte-Mecklenburg Police Department. www.charmeck.org/Departments/Police/Home.htm.

[18] *Unresolved Problems & Powerful Potentials: Improving Partnerships Between Law Enforcement Agencies and University Based Researchers*. International Association of Chiefs of Police, Washington, D.C.: 2004.

Appendixes A–E

Appendix A

IACP Civil Rights Committee

The following people either are current members of the IACP Civil Rights Committee or were members during the time that the *Protecting Civil Rights* project was in progress.

Chairs

John J. Finnegan
Chief of Police
Barnstable (Massachusetts) Police Department

Barbara S. Wallace
(previous chair)
Chief (retired)
Community Relations Unit
Federal Bureau of Investigation
Washington, D.C.

IACP Board Members with Committee Oversight

Joseph C. Carter
Chief of Police
Massachusetts Bay Transportation Authority Police Department
Boston, Massachusetts

Mary Ann Viverette
(previous oversight /current member)
Chief of Police
Gaithersburg (Maryland) Police Department

Committee Members

Francis Amoroso
Regional Director
New England Regional Office
Community Relations Service
U.S. Department of Justice
Boston, Massachusetts

John J. Bennett
Chief of Police
Caln Township (Pennsylvania) Police Department

Erik G. Blake
Chief of Police
Oak Bluffs (Massachusetts) Police Department

Lawrence C. Burnson
Chief of Police
Homewood (Illinois) Police Department

Melvin J. Carraway
Federal Security Director (retired)
U.S. Department of Homeland Security
Washington, D.C.

Michael J. Carroll
Chief of Police
West Goshen Township (Pennsylvania) Police Department

John P. Chase
Chief of Staff, Preparedness
U.S. Department of Homeland Security
Washington, D.C.

Leonard G. Cooke
Director
Virginia Department of Criminal Justice Services
Richmond, Virginia

Appendix A

Janet A. Crumley
Captain
Carter County (Tennessee) Sheriff's Department

Shanetta Y. Cutlar
Chief
Special Litigation Section
Civil Rights Divisions
U.S. Department of Justice
Washington, D.C.

Edward J. Delaney (retired)
Chief of Police
Orange (Connecticut) Police Department

Dean M. Esserman
(past member)
Chief of Police
Providence (Rhode Island) Police Department

Preston L. Felton
First Deputy Superintendent
New York State Police

Sharee Freeman
Director
Community Relations Service
U.S. Department of Justice
Washington, D.C.

Rafael P. Hernandez, Jr.
Deputy Chief
Tallahassee (Florida) Police Department

James M. Hussey
Chief of Police
Cohasset (Massachusetts) Police Department

Scott M. Jordan
Chief of Police
Tustin (California) Police Department

Charles R. McDonald
Chief Investigator
Illinois Law Enforcement Training and Standards Board
Edwardsville, Illinois

William McManus
Chief of Police
Minneapolis (Minnesota) Police Department
(formerly with Dayton, Ohio Police Department)

Bobby D. Moody
Chief of Police
Marietta (Georgia) Police Department

Jerry Oliver
(past member)
Chief of Police (retired)
Detroit (Michigan) Police Department

Patrick Oliver
Chief of Police (retired)
Fairborn (Ohio) Police Department

Sonya T. Proctor
Chief of Police and Security
Amtrak
Washington, D.C.

Louis F. Quijas
Assistant Director
Law Enforcement Coordination
Federal Bureau of Investigation
Washington, D.C.

Richard J. Rappoport
Chief of Police
Fairfax City (Virginia) Police Department

Charles D. Reynolds
Chief of Police (retired)
Dover (New Hampshire) Police Department

Susan Riseling
Chief of Police
University of Wisconsin-Madison Police
  Department

Marcia Thompson
Mediator
Resolving Conflict Institute, LLC
Alexandria, Virginia

Paul Vorvis
(past member)
Inspector
Toronto (Canada) Police Service

Appendix B

IACP Professional Standards Committee

The following people either are current members of the IACP Professional Standards Committee or were members when the *Protecting Civil Rights* project was in progress.

Chair

Charles A. Gruber
Chief of Police
South Barrington (Illinois) Police Department

IACP Board Members with Committee Oversight

Mary Ann Viverette
Chief of Police
Gaithersburg (Maryland) Police Department

Joseph Estey
(previous oversight)
Chief of Police
Hartford (Vermont) Police Department

Joseph Polisar
(previous oversight)
Chief of Police
Garden Grove (California) Police Department

Committee Members

Elena Danishevskaya
Chief of Police
Memphis (Tennessee) Police Department

James W. McMahon
Director
New York State Office of Homeland Security
New York, New York

Ronald Miller
Chief of Police
Kansas City (Kansas) Police Department

Mark O'Toole
Captain
Lynn (Massachusetts) Police Department

Dennis E. Nowicki
Chief of Police (retired)
Charlotte-Mecklenburg (North Carolina) Police Department

Steven J. Sarver
Chief of Police
Colerain Township (Ohio) Police Department

Appendix C

Project Advisory Group

The following people participated in the Project Advisory Group meeting in Memphis, Tennessee in April 2004 to help launch the *Protecting Civil Rights* project. They provided feedback on the substantive outline of the project and helped define the scope of the *Leadership Guide*.

James H. Bolden
Director of Police (retired)
Memphis (Tennessee) Police Department

Pamela Cammarata
Deputy Director
Office of Community Oriented Policing Services
U.S. Department of Justice
Washington, D.C.

Allyson Collins
Deputy Director
Police Assessment Resource Center
Los Angeles, California

Steve Conrad
Chief
Glendale (Kentucky) Police Department
(formerly assistant chief, Louisville Metro Police Department)

Edward T. Crawford
Chief of Police (retired)
Kent (Washington) Police Department

Shanetta Y. Cutlar
Chief
Special Litigation Section
Civil Rights Division
U.S. Department of Justice
Washington, D.C.

Ronald Davis
Chief of Police
East Palo Alto (California) Police Department
(formerly with the Oakland Police Department)

Joseph R. Fuentes
Superintendent
New Jersey State Police
West Trenton, New Jersey

Jim Ginger
Chief Executive Officer
Public Management Resources, Inc.
Willis, Virginia

Charles A. Gruber
Chief of Police
South Barrington Police (Illinois) Department

Bobbie J. Johnson
Superintendent
Boston (Massachusetts) Police Department

Russ Leach
Chief of Police
Riverside (California) Police Department

Robert McNeilly
Chief of Police (retired)
Pittsburgh (Pennsylvania) Bureau of Police

Appendix C

Dennis E. Nowicki
Chief of Police (retired)
Charlotte-Mecklenburg (North Carolina)
   Police Department

Carl Peed
Director
Office of Community Oriented Policing
   Services
U.S. Department of Justice
Washington, D.C.

Richard J. Pennington
Chief of Police
City of Atlanta (Georgia) Police Department

Timothy Ross
Research Director
Vera Institute of Justice
New York, New York

Jeffrey Schlanger
President
Kroll Government Services
Washington, D.C.

George Selim
Special Assistant to the Director
U.S. Department of Justice
Community Relations Service
Washington, D.C.
(formerly with the Arab American Institute)

Ronal W. Serpas
Chief of Police
Metropolitan Nashville (Tennessee) Police
   Department

Barbara S. Wallace
Chief (retired)
Community Relations Unit
Federal Bureau of Investigation
Washington, D.C.

Appendix D
Project Focus Group

The following people participated in the Project Focus Group in Pittsburgh in April 2005. They provided feedback on chapter content and helped hone recommendations for policies and practices that were included in the *Leadership Guide*.

Orlando Barnes
Lieutenant Colonel
Prince George's County (Maryland) Police

Michael J. Carroll
Chief of Police
West Goshen Township (Pennsylvania)
  Police Department

Richard Eddington
Chief of Police
Mount Prospect (Illinois) Police Department

Joseph R. Fuentes
Superintendent
New Jersey State Police
West Trenton, New Jersey

Brenda Bernot
Lieutenant
Pennsylvania State Police
Harrisburg, Pennsylvania

Shanetta Y. Cutlar
Chief
Special Litigation Section
Civil Rights Division
U.S. Department of Justice
Washington, D.C.

Charles A. Gruber
Chief
South Barrington (Illinois) Police
  Department

Sandra (Sam) Pailca
Director
Office of Professional Accountability
Seattle (Washington) Police Department

Lloyd Perkins
Chief of Police
Village of Skaneateles (New York) Police
  Department
(formerly with Camillus [New York] Police
  Department)

Michael Semkiu
Deputy Chief
Mount Prospect (Illinois) Police Department

William Valenta
Commander (retired)
Pittsburgh (Pennsylvania) Bureau of Police

Earl Woodyard
Assistant Chief
Pittsburgh (Pennsylvania) Bureau of Police

Appendix E

Community Relations Service U.S. Department of Justice

National Headquarters
Community Relations Service
U.S. Department of Justice
600 E Street, N.W., Suite 6000
Washington, DC 20530
Voice: 202.305.2935
Fax: 202.305.3009
Web: www.usdoj.gov/crs

Region I – New England Region
(Serving: CT, MA, ME, NH, RI, VT)
Community Relations Service
U.S. Department of Justice
408 Atlantic Avenue, Suite 222
Boston, MA 02110
Voice: 617.424.5715
Fax: 617.424.5727

Region II – Northeast Region
(Serving: NJ, NY, Puerto Rico, U.S. Virgin Islands)
Community Relations Service
U.S. Department of Justice
26 Federal Plaza, Suite 36-118
New York, NY 10278
Voice: 212.264.0700
Fax: 212.264.2143

Region III – Mid-Atlantic Region
(Serving: DC, DE, MD, PA, VA, WV)
Community Relations Service
U.S. Department of Justice
2nd and Chestnut Streets, Suite 208
Philadelphia, PA 19106
Voice: 215.597.2344
Fax: 215.597.9148

Region IV – Southeast Region
(Serving: AL, FL, GA, KY, MS, NC, SC, TN)
Community Relations Service
U.S. Department of Justice
75 Piedmont Avenue, N.E. Suite 900
Atlanta, GA 30303
Voice: 404.331.6883
Fax: 404.331.4471

Region 4 Field Office
Community Relations Service
U.S. Department of Justice
51 S.W. First Avenue, Suite 624
Miami, FL 33130
Voice: 305.536.5206
Fax: 305.536.6778

Region V – Midwest Region
(Serving: IL, IN, MI, MN, OH, WI)
Community Relations Service
U.S. Department of Justice
55 West Monroe Street, Suite 420
Chicago, IL 60603
Voice: 312.353.4391
Fax: 312.353.4390

Region V Field Office
Community Relations Service
U.S. Department of Justice
211 West Fort Street, Suite 1404
Detroit, MI 48226
Voice: 313.226.4010
Fax: 313.226.2568

Region VI – Southwest Region
(Serving: AR, LA, NM, OK, TX)
Community Relations Service
U.S. Department of Justice
1420 West Mockingbird Lane, Suite 250
Dallas, TX 75247
Voice: 214.655.8175
Fax: 214.655.8184

Region VI Field Office
Community Relations Service
U.S. Department of Justice
515 Rusk Avenue, Suite 12605
Houston, TX 77002
Voice: 713.718.4861
Fax: 713.718.4862

Region VII – Central Region
(Serving: IA, KS, MO, NE)
Community Relations Service
U.S. Department of Justice
1100 Main Street, Suite 1320
Kansas City, MO 64105
Voice: 816.426.7434
Fax: 816.426.7441

Region VIII – Rocky Mountain Region
(Serving: CO, MT, ND, SD, UT, WY)
Community Relations Service
U.S. Department of Justice
1244 Speer Blvd., Suite 650
Denver, CO 80204
Voice: 303.844.2973
Fax: 303.844.2907

Region IX – Western Region
(Serving: AZ, CA, GU, HI, NV)
Community Relations Service
U.S. Department of Justice
888 South Figueroa Street, Suite 1880
Los Angeles, CA 90017
Voice: 213.894.2941
Fax: 213.894.2880

Region IX Field Office
Community Relations Service
U.S. Department of Justice
120 Howard Street, Suite 790
San Francisco, CA 94105
Voice: 415.744.6565
Fax: 415.744.6590

Region X – Northwest Region
(Serving: AK, ID, OR, WA)
Community Relations Service
U.S. Department of Justice
915 Second Avenue, Suite 1808
Seattle, WA 98174
Voice: 206.220.6700
Fax: 206.220.6706